THAT PLACE ON ILKLEY MOOR:
THE HISTORY OF WHITE WELLS

THAT PLACE ON ILKLEY MOOR:

❧

THE HISTORY OF WHITE WELLS

❧

MARK HUNNEBELL

CROFT
PUBLICATIONS

First published in 2010 by
Croft Publications
on behalf of
Mark Hunnebell FRGS
White Wells Spa Cottage Tea Rooms
Ilkley Moor, Wells Road,
Ilkley, West Yorkshire LS29 9RF

© Mark Hunnebell FRGS 2010

ISBN 978 0 9555126 2 9

Designed and typeset by
CROFT PUBLICATIONS
The Croft
8 St James Meadow
Boroughbridge YO51 9NW

Printed and bound by
SMITH SETTLE
Gateway Drive, Yeadon
West Yorkshire LS19 7XY

CONTENTS

	List of Illustrations	VI
	Introduction	XI
	Acknowledgements	XIV
CHAPTER ONE	Humble Beginnings	1
CHAPTER TWO	Into the Nineteenth Century	10
CHAPTER THREE	Taking the Plunge With Mr Butterfield	12
CHAPTER FOUR	The development of 'Hydropathy'	20
CHAPTER FIVE	The establishment of the 'Hydros' and the development of Ilkley	32
CHAPTER SIX	Out of the Nineteenth and Into the Twentieth Century	56
CHAPTER SEVEN	Between the Wars	82
CHAPTER EIGHT	The Second World War & The Post War Years	101
CHAPTER NINE	Out with the old, in with the New. Decline & Dereliction	126
CHAPTER TEN	Eric Busby & The Renovation of White Wells	135
CHAPTER ELEVEN	The Modern Era	143
CHAPTER TWELVE	Into The Twenty First Century	160
CHAPTER THRTEEN	Epilogue White Wells Today	170
	White Wells Timeline	172
	Index	195

LIST OF ILLUSTRATIONS:

Chapter One: Humble Beginnings
Large stone block outside White Wells *(authors photograph)* — 4
The drinking fountain to the rear of White Wells *(authors photograph)* — 6
A tragic event. Anne Harper's plaque *(authors photograph)* — 8

Chapter Two: Into the Nineteenth Century
Impression of White Wells before roofs were added to the bathhouses
(authors sketch) — 10

Chapter Three: Taking the Plunge With Mr Butterfield
Mr Butterfield next to the drinking fountain
(photograph: Courtesy of Sally Gunton) — 13
Mr Butterfield next to the plunge bath
(photograph: Courtesy of Sally Gunton) — 15
Last in the family line *(photograph: Courtesy of Sally Gunton)* — 17

Chapter Four: The development of 'Hydropathy'
The 'Charity Bath' building, 2009 *(authors photograph)* — 25
Mounting block outside White Wells, 2009 *(authors photograph)* — 29
Mounting block on Wells Road, 2009 *(authors photograph)* — 30
John 'Donkey' Jackson *(photograph: Courtesy of Sally Gunton)* — 31

Chapter Five:
The establishment of the 'Hydros' and the development of Ilkley
Ben Rhydding Hydropathic Establishment
(photograph: Courtesy of Sally Gunton) — 33
Ben Rhydding golf course, 2009 *(authors photograph)* — 34
Wells House Hydropathic Establishment
(photograph: Courtesy of Sally Gunton) — 37
Leeds Town Hall *(authors photograph)* — 38
Corn Exchange, Leeds *(authors photograph)* — 39
Grand Hotel, Scarborough *(authors photograph)* — 40

LIST OF ILLUSTRATAIONS VII

'Hillside Court', 2009 *(authors photograph)* 42
'Grove House', 2009 *(authors photograph)* 44
Stone markers outside White Wells *(authors photograph)* 50
The lower tarn *(photograph: Courtesy of Sally Gunton)* 53

Chapter Six: Out of the Nineteenth and Into the Twentieth Century
Skating on the lower tarn *(photograph: Courtesy of Sally Gunton)* 57
The Tarn in summer *(photograph: Courtesy of Sally Gunton)* 58
The Tarn today *(authors photograph)* 59
The bandstand in West View Park *(photograph: Courtesy of Sally Gunton)* 60
Mr Cooper's Pierrots' buildings at the Tarn
(photograph: Courtesy of Sally Gunton) 61
White Wells, circa 1897 *(photograph: Courtesy of Sally Gunton)* 62
White Wells in the 1900's *(photograph: Courtesy of Sally Gunton)* 63
Rear of White Wells prior to improvements
(photograph: Courtesy of Sally Gunton) 66
Ventillation pipe and west gable of White Wells
(photograph: Courtesy of Sally Gunton) 68
Rear of White Wells following improvements to back door
(photograph: Courtesy of Sally Gunton) 69
Photograph taken after the previous two showing improvements
(photograph: Courtesy of Sally Gunton) 70
The Charity Bath building prior to conversion into public toilets
(photograph: Courtesy of Sally Gunton) 74
The Charity Bath building following conversion into public toilets
(photograph: Courtesy of Sally Gunton) 76
Tree growth screening public toilets *(photograph: Courtesy of Sally Gunton)* 77
West plunge bath showing inflow pipe *(photograph: Courtesy of Sally Gunton)* 78
Ilkley silver spoon advertisement
(photograph: Courtesy of Wharfedale Newspapers)* 79
White Wells Whisky advertisement
(photograph: Courtesy of Wharfedale Newspapers)* 80

Chapter Seven: Between the Wars
Looking down into the plunge bath *(photograph: Courtesy of Sally Gunton)* 83
Moorland Tea Pavilion *(photograph: Courtesy of Sally Gunton)* 85
Interior of Moorland Tea Pavilion *(photograph: Courtesy of Sally Gunton)* 86
The paddling pool, 2009 *(authors photograph)* 89

VIII LIST OF ILLUSTRATAIONS

Advertisement for train travel to the total eclipse viewing sites, 1927
(image: Courtesy of National Railway Museum/SSPL) 91
Excavations of the original bathhouse
(photograph: Courtesy of Wharfedale Newspapers) 92
West plunge bath showing stone face spout inflow feature
(photograph: Courtesy of Sally Gunton) 93
White Wells by floodlight
(photograph: Courtesy of Wharfedale Newspapers) 95
Signpost damaged by storm:
(photograph: Courtesy of Wharfedale Newspapers) 96
Direction marker outside White Wells.
(photograph: Courtesy of Sally Gunton) 97
"Catch Me If You Can." Busby's Christmas advertisement.
(photograph: Courtesy of Wharfedale Newspapers) 99

Chapter Eight: The Second World War & The Post War Years
Bullet holes in the rocks at the former Hangingstone quarry
(authors Photograph) 102
'War Weapons Week' advertisement
(photograph: Courtesy of Wharfedale Newspapers) 104
War Weapons Week Committee
(photograph: Courtesy of Wharfedale Newspapers) 105
Wartime at the Tea Pavilion (photograph: Courtesy of Mr Chris Youhill) 106
War Memorial Appeal advertisement
(photograph: Courtesy of Wharfedale Newspapers) 107
Front cover, Ilkley Town Guide, 1948
(photograph: Courtesy of Wharfedale Newspapers) 108
The removal of the bandstand
(photograph: Courtesy of Wharfedale Newspapers) 110
The Paddling Pool overflowing
(photograph: Courtesy of Wharfedale Newspapers) 111
Repairing moor shelter
(photograph: Courtesy of Wharfedale Newspapers) 113
Demolition of Ben Rhydding Hydro begins
(photograph: Courtesy of Wharfedale Newspapers) 114
The last of Ben Rhydding Hydro
(photograph: Courtesy of Wharfedale Newspapers) 115
Repairs at Willy Hall's Spout
(photograph: Courtesy of Wharfedale Newspapers) 116

LIST OF ILLUSTRATAIONS IX

The paddling pool in summer
(photograph: Courtesy of Wharfedale Newspapers)   117
Railway advertising poster depicting Ilkley (1957)
(photograph: Courtesy of National Railway Museum/SSPL)   118

Chapter Nine: Out with the old, in with the New. Decline & Dereliction
Paddling pool repairs *(photograph: Courtesy of Wharfedale Newspapers)*★   127
Council plans for White Wells restoration
(photograph: Courtesy of Wharfedale Newspapers)★   129
Repair of White Wells Begin
(photograph: Courtesy of Wharfedale Newspapers)★   130
Hooliganism at White Wells
(photograph: Courtesy of Wharfedale Newspapers)★   131
The moorland tea pavilion near White Wells
(photograph: Courtesy of Sally Gunton)   132
The foundations of the tea pavilion, 2009 *(authors photograph)*   133

Chapter Ten: Eric Busby & The Renovation of White Wells
Eric Busby *(Photograph: Courtesy of Mrs Pat Laycock)*   135
Mr Jack Spencer, Ilkley Urban District Council Chairman, 1973
(photograph: Courtesy of Wharfedale Newspapers)   137
Interior of White Wells during restoration #1
*(photograph: Courtesy of Gavin Edwards Ilkley Manor House Museum/
Bradford Museums & Archaeological Service)*   139
Interior of White Wells during restoration #2
*(photograph: Courtesy of Gavin Edwards, Ilkley Manor House Museum/
Bradford Museums & Archaeological Service)*   140
White Wells during renovation
(photograph: Courtesy of Wharfedale Newspapers)★   141
White Wells bathhouse 1974
(photograph: Courtesy of Wharfedale Newspapers)★   142
Memorial stone in bathhouse porch *(authors photograph)*   142

Chapter Eleven: The Modern Era
White Wells opening ceremony
(photograph: Courtesy of Mrs Pat Laycock)   144
Pamela Brittain and Martin Allsop
(photograph: Courtesy of Wharfedale Newspapers)★   150

Ilkley merchandise on Sale in 1990
(photograph: Courtesy of Wharfedale Newspapers)*   155
Cobbles outside White Wells (authors photograph)   157

Chapter Twelve: Into The Twenty First Century
Totem poles at White Wells (authors photograph)   163
New Year's Day Plunge, 2008 (authors photograph)   164
Queue for the bathhouse, New Year's Day 2008 (authors photograph)   166
The installation of new water filters at White Wells (September 2009)
(authors photograph)   167
Work being done on the westernmost chimney of White Wells
(October 2009) (authors photograph)   168

Chapter Thirteen: Epilogue White Wells Today
Flags flying at White Wells (authors photograph)   171

(* Images marked with an asterisk are relatively poor quality. Unfortunately the *'Ilkley Gazette'* records from 1958 to the present day are held on microfilm in Ilkley Library, and the images have to be photocopied from the microfilm. This inevitably means that the picture quality is compromised. However every effort has been made to obtain the best results available from the images held in the public records.)

I thank Sheena Stavert for the various images and captions courtesy of *'Wharfedale Newspapers'*, reproduced and quoted from copies of the *'Ilkley Gazette'* that have been used in this book.

INTRODUCTION

WHITE WELLS holds a special place in the affections of many local people. Especially those who have grown up in the Ilkley area and remember the moors from childhood familiarity.

My own memories of White Wells date to when I was around six or seven years old. Particularly during Sunday afternoon walks on the moors with my parents, Edwin and Margaret Hunnebell. The tea pavilion was open for pop, sweets and lollies; and tea and toasted teacakes for the grown ups.

White Wells was always locked. At the back door, and in the bathhouse porch which didn't have an outer door then, but was overgrown with nettles, I would stand and listen intently with my Dad, to the enigmatic sound of running water echoing inside. My Dad told me, erroneously, that there were two deep 'Roman' baths inside. (Although there are indeed two baths inside they are not Roman, as will be explained.) I was fascinated, and I thought of the mysterious White Wells baths each time I heard the bath at home being filled.

The tea pavilion closed, which was very sad. It was demolished in a controlled burning after becoming badly vandalised. White Wells too became vandalised. However on a positive note, for me at least, the fact that the back door had been kicked in meant that the great mystery of the 'Roman' baths could now be solved. I'd be around eight years old at the time.

One Sunday afternoon my Dad and I clambered past the broken back door and inside the building. We found ourselves in a dusty derelict room with parts of the roof missing. Slowly and carefully we picked our way through the debris and across the rickety floor to the steps leading down into the bathhouse. The sight of one of the baths greeted me at last. It met my expectations. The bath was somewhat overgrown with moss and ferns; it was almost empty, a deep and mysterious hole in the ground. There were no railings around it then. These were installed later during the renovation phase. There was water flowing into the bath through the ferns near the top, while some of the water had accumulated in the bottom prior to its departure through the drain hole. We carefully made our way down the crumbling stairs, and cautiously continued on our way past the bath. As we headed through to the other side of the building to where the other bath is, we entered the central section. This central area is now the kitchen and café entrance. Two sets of stairs at the rear of the building led to the upper level. The steps were in very bad condition. Far worse than the ones we had descended from the back door. So my Dad said that perhaps it would have been too dangerous to venture up there. Some of the steps were missing anyway, and parts of the floor above had joists in a dubious condition. Even though we had crossed a similar floor when we came in through the back door, it was perhaps best not to push our luck.

I wasn't too disappointed by not venturing upstairs. My main interest was in the baths themselves.

We entered the second bathhouse at the far end of the building from where we had come in. The bath inside appeared to be more or less the same as the first bath, only rotated through 180 degrees. It was difficult to tell how deep the bath was. Not because it was full of water though. It was full of old wooden chairs piled up one on top of the other. These had obviously come from the old tea pavilion and had been dumped in the bath. There were no windows in the walls then. These too were installed during the renovation. Instead light was provided from broken skylight windows in the roof, and a triangular hole at the apex of the wall and roof in the gable wall. After our look around we carefully retraced our footsteps and made our way back outside.

I was amazed at the sight which had greeted us inside White Wells, and pleased that at last I had been privileged to see what was in there and the mystery had been solved.

At that point it seemed highly likely that White Wells would be demolished, so my Dad was pleased too that he had been able to take me inside and see the baths, albeit thanks to vandals who had broken the back door which had made this possible.

I thought that White Wells would make a perfect house, and that I would like to live and use the baths there. At that time it seemed very unlikely that this would ever happen.

Shortly afterwards it was decided that White Wells would indeed be saved after all. However it would be a further twenty eight years before my childhood desire to live at White Wells would be realised. It was worth the wait!

It is now great to be providing pop sweets and lollies – and tea and toasted teacakes to the grown ups. But best of all it's great to live at White Wells. (And to be able to use the plunge bath if I want!) We clean the plunge bath out regularly and we have removed all the moss and ferns that were allowed to grow around it even after restoration. We have also installed a longer drainage pipe so the bath can be filled to its maximum capacity in order that it can be used as originally intended when it was built in 1791. – And to complement this, for the benefit of other visitors wishing to use the facilities, two changing cubicles have been added in the adjoining room at the top of the steps, where there is also a gas fire. The same room that was once so badly vandalised when I had first entered White Wells with my Dad all those years before.

My Dad still often asks "Do you remember the time when we came in here and it was all derelict, son?" My answer: "Yes Dad, I'll never forget." Which is why I feel so passionate about the place and never want to see it return to such a sorry state.

A number of books by various authors, as well as local newspaper articles, census returns Parish records and the minutes of meetings over the years by the Ilkley Local Board, the Ilkley Urban District Council and the Ilkley Parish Council, have proven to be valuable sources of reference in confirming some names and dates in this publication. A list of these is contained in the 'Acknowledgements' Chapter, along with my gratitude to all those who have helped in any way, shape or form in gathering together all the required facts and figures for the project. Although much of the information has been accumulated from a variety of sources, it is perhaps by virtue of the fact that I was born and have grown up in Ilkley that I've always seemed to know some of the details, without knowing where they came from.

The concept of this book has evolved as information has been sought and come to light. Originally it was intended that a short summary of facts and dates would be contained in an information leaflet. We are often asked the history of White Wells, and the publication of such a leaflet would provide a useful guide to the general visitor to the property. This quickly evolved into the idea of providing an information booklet instead, containing more information than just a simple overview. As work on this progressed, the idea of a complete volume about White Wells evolved, and this publication is the net result of that. — Following three years of research and the collating of all the necessary information.

There is a lot of information, and misinformation, about White Wells in the public domain. Hopefully now, some of the myths about White Wells can be laid to rest with the facts recorded in one single volume.

While every effort has been made to ensure that all names dates and details contained within this book are correct, errors and typing mistakes do sometimes occur.

If any evidence comes to light that any information in this book is incorrect or significantly flawed, any future editions will be amended accordingly.

I recognise that I am not infallible, and I am prepared to accept the facts in the light of greater evidence than that presented here.

ACKNOWLEDGEMENTS

There are a number of people and organisations that I wish to thank for their help, both directly and indirectly, in the research and in the gathering of information for this book.

I am grateful to: All the staff in the Ilkley Public Library, particularly Maggie Horsman and John Giles, for unfettered access to the Local History Archives, the scanning and reproduction of old photographs and arranging extra time on the computers at quiet times.

My thanks also go to Bradford Central Library, Leeds Central Library and to the Bradford Museums and Archaeological Service. Especially to Gavin Edwards of the Ilkley Manor House for supplying information and photographs from the renovation of White Wells, and Mrs Pat Laycock, Eric Busby's daughter, who also supplied useful information about the renovation and photographs of her father.

I am particularly indebted to Sally Gunton and her extensive collection of old photographs, a number of which appear in this book, and which proved extremely useful in identifying the order of various improvements and additions to White Wells at the end of the nineteenth and the beginning of the twentieth centuries.

I also thank Sheena Stavert and *'Wharfedale Newspapers'* for the use of various articles, correspondence, advertisements and photographs from *'Ilkley Gazette'* that are quoted and reproduced throughout this book.

The *'Yorkshire Post'* and the *'Leeds Intellegencer'* newspapers of the eighteenth and nineteenth centuries whose records are kept in the Leeds Central Library; the Ilkley Parish Register, the minutes of meetings of the Ilkley Local Board and the Ilkley Urban District Council and the various census returns from the nineteenth and early twentieth centuries. Although everyone connected with these records cannot all be thanked in person, I am grateful that records were kept and to the generations who recorded them.

I am also grateful to Mrs Marjorie Hill, former resident of Ilkley, now living in the of Bay of Plenty, New Zealand, for her wartime recollection of William 'Lord Haw Haw' Joyce's broadcast about White Wells being painted black.

Additionally I am grateful to Mr C. Youhill of Leeds for the photograph of Mrs Williamson, and his memories of wartime visits to the moorland tea pavilion.

Additional thanks to Bradford Council's Countryside and Rights of Way Service; Will Cartwright of Bradford Council's Department of Regeneration, Plans and Performance for information regarding White Wells being a 'Grade II Listed Building'; Ilkley Parish Council; Ilkley Civic Society; David Carpenter, author of *Ilkley: The Victorian Era* and *The Lords of Ilkley Manor: The Road to Ruin*. Mike Dixon, author of a number of books detailing local history, Frazer Irwin, 'Snappy Snaps' in Leeds, Mike Stayman at 'Custom Computer Designs' in Otley for his twenty-first century wizardry in creating the front cover photograph, Terry Nicholson of 'Croft Publications', the printers 'Smith Settle' and my long suffering partner Joanne Everall, who perhaps at times thought that I'd moved in at Ilkley Library (and maybe the Ilkley Library staff did too!) – And last but not least my parents Edwin and Margaret Hunnebell. Thanks for taking me on the moor as a child and showing me White Wells. It's all your fault!

CHAPTER ONE:
HUMBLE BEGINNINGS

A LOCAL STORY tells of a shepherd who discovered the 'healing waters' of Ilkley Moor. He had hurt one of his legs and bathed his wounds in a cold spring he found close to where White Wells would later be built. He was amazed at how quickly his wounds healed and attributed this to the water he had bathed in on the moor. No one knows who the shepherd was or even if there is any factual basis to the story. Though it is believed to date from the seventeenth century.

At the beginning of the eighteenth century White Wells was built on the moors to the south of Ilkley to exploit the developing trend for water treatments. More than a century after the concept of medicinal waters had found favour in the nearby town of Harrogate 21km/14miles away to the northeast of Ilkley.

William Slingsby had discovered the 'chalybeate water' spring and built the Tewit Well in Harrogate in 1570. Other springs were subsequently developed and in 1626 Dr Edmund Deane published his *"Spadacrene Anglica"* and described the strongest sulphur spring in Great Britain, which was to be found in Harrogate. By the nineteenth century eighty seven different springs had been identified in the Harrogate area which had differing properties. Betty Lupton, a well known local figure described as the 'Queen of the Wells', dispensed water from the sulphur well at what is now the 'Royal Pump Rooms' until her death in 1843.

However although bathing was (and still is) undertaken in Harrogate the waters there, from William Slingsby's time, were predominantly ingested as a 'medicine'. This being considered the best method to derive the most benefit from the water.

When White Wells was built Ilkley was a small village consisting of a few houses a church and the open moors to the north and south. The moors were crossed with routes to Ripon over the northern moors, following the line of an ancient Roman road, to the Aire valley over the moors to the south and along the Wharfe valley, the villages of Wheatley and Burley-in-Wharfedale downstream to the east and Addingham upstream to the west.

It is believed the central house section of White Wells dates to circa 1700; (which was around the end of the reign of King William III and the start of the reign of Queen Anne [1702]) and quite possibly the building was in use as a farm too. Whether or not it was ever tenanted by the shepherd who had discovered the 'healing waters' attributed to the spring is open to conjecture. The original bath was to the rear of the building, close to the spring at the top of the tumulus hill by the trees and close to the current collection tank. There is no trace of this bath to be seen here today. Its remains are about 1.5m/5ft beneath the surface level.

In an old description of the 'Great stone bath', it is mentioned that there was an inscription on the wall above it: *"This holds 1150 gallons and fills in 13 minutes."*

The bath would have been enclosed with a wall, but open to the air above. The construction of the bath was under the auspices of Squire Peter Middelton (c1655-1714), the local landowner.

In 1709 a gentleman called Dr Richardson described Ilkley in a letter:

> *"Ilkley is now a very mean place, and is equally dirty and insignificant and chiefly famous for a cold well, which has done very remarkable cases by bathing and in drinking of it."*

Despite Ilkley being thus described, it was nevertheless considered that the water available from the cold well was useful in the treatment of the 'King's Evil'.

In 1734 Thomas Short, a physician, made these observations about the water:

> *"The water is very clear, brisk and sparkling, has no taste colour nor smell different from the common water."* He goes on to state: *"Tho' this water is of the greatest esteem and repute of any in the North of England, in the King's Evil and other old ulcers, yet it derives these effects neither from its fixt nor volatile parts, but wholly from the coldness and purity of the elements, its drying nature from the lime-stone it washes tho' a great part of it comes from blue clay."*

('King's Evil' was a type of scrofula, a form of tuberculosis affecting the lymphatic system, which many believed could also be cured if the victim were to be touched by the King.)

Thomas Short conducted a number of experiments on the water and these observations were some of the conclusions he drew. However his knowledge of water observation was perhaps better than his knowledge of geology! The rocks on Ilkley Moor are gritstone, not the limestone he described. He would have needed to travel further up Wharfedale beyond Burnsall to observe limestone in its natural setting. Though there were small amounts of limestone moraine left over from the glacial deposits at the end of the last ice age circa

10,000 years ago, particularly in the Backstone Beck area. Very little evidence of this remains now, as it was mostly all exploited during the eighteenth and nineteenth centuries. Similarly with limestone deposits found in the river Wharfe.

Nevertheless Thomas Short was correct in so far as his conclusions on the coldness and purity of the water. Modern analysis confirms that there is no significant mineral content in the water at White Wells. The early analysis of the water could have given rise to the name White Wells. One experiment concerning the evaporation of the water resulted in a white residue. It is certainly possible that the name arose from this, and the building was consequently painted white. Though white painted buildings of a similar age, and earlier, can of course be found in other parts of Wharfedale and elsewhere too. The name itself isn't particularly unusual. There is an 'Upper White Well' farm and a 'Low White Well' farm to the west of Addingham, and an earlier corruption of it in the name of the village 'Whitwell-on-the-Hill' near Malton in North Yorkshire.

There are no records of who lived at White Wells or who operated the bath during most of the remainder of the eighteenth century.

In 1782 a writer called Maude described Ilkley and the waters:

"*Verbia, or Wharfedale, a poem, descriptive and didactic, with Historical remarks.*"
"*Must Ilkley then in slighted silence pass,*
Nor once reflect her features in the glass;
Where Roman polish, Roman arms subdu'd,
The fierce ferocity of Britain's brood?
Nor less Hygeia shall thy spring impart
The balmy succours of the medic art.
Flow on, kind stream, proceed in fame to heal,
And may each pallid nymph thy influence feel;
The swain enjoy those calm delights of health,
Superior to the guilded joys of wealth,
Then shall the rural bard thy altar raise,
And grateful waft thee thro' a world of praise.

In an accompanying note he added: "*The village is frequented in the summer season, on account of its spring, issuing from the side of a mountain near the town. Whether there are any virtues in the water, more than its purity, and the tenuity of its component parts for internal use, by which it may sooner pass the uttermost meanders of circulation, and which gives it a consequent coldness in the use of bathing, is a point which the inquisitive must determine. Certain it is, that the waters have no gustable properties, by which their quality or operation may be ascertained. It has acquired a reputation, and moreover, been long established."*

While Ilkley Moor cannot qualify for the description of a 'mountain', Maude does give us a clue to the seasonal nature of bathing at White Wells by referring to the 'summer season'. Bathing open air in winter is certainly less appealing than in summer, leading to the conclusion that the bath probably only opened during the warmer months, at least until the improvements of the 1850's.

Toward the end of the eighteenth century the bath to the rear of White Wells was replaced with two baths, thus increasing capacity and expanding the

Large stone block outside White Wells. — The original bathhouse was replaced in 1791 by Robert Dale, who built the two baths inside White Wells instead. The large stone block outside the front of the building presents something of an enigma, though it is possible that it was brought down to its present location when the original bathhouse was being demolished and some of the stone from it was perhaps being 'recycled'. The shape of it is similar to that of the 'roof' of the drinking fountain to the rear of White Wells, though what it was originally used for or intended to be used for in the improvements of 1791 remains unknown. A local story holds that the names of the Yorkshire cricket team of the 1890's are carved around its base. Whether there is any factual basis to this, or whether it is another myth associated with White Wells is also unknown. –Without actually digging the whole thing up, which would be an enormous (and potentially fruitless) task!

potential as a spa. These baths adjoined the central house section, one to the east gable and one to the west. The baths were built by Robert Dale, under the auspices of the local landowner Squire William Constable Middelton who held the estates between 1781 (when he attained the age of twenty one) and 1847.

A newspaper advertisement was placed in the *'Leeds Intelligencer'* of Tuesday, 26th April 1791 announcing the forthcoming opening of the new bathing facilities at White Wells:

> *"Robert Dale of Ilkley takes this opportunity to inform the public that he is now fitting up two commodious new baths, with sitting rooms adjoining thereto, for the accommodation of such persons as may wish to visit this Spaw for the benefit of their health. The medicinal qualities of the above spaw have long rendered it famous for the cure of tumours and sores, proceeding from scrophula and other disorders, as well as recommended it as particularly serviceable for bad eyes, and in all cases where the spine is affected or the constitution enervated.*
>
> *The alteration and improvements will be completed by the middle of May, for the reception of patients and the company that choose to frequent this spaw. Lodging and board may also be had by applying to the said Robert Dale."*

As a further point of fact King George III was on the throne of England in 1791 so, contrary to popular belief, the baths at White Wells are neither 'Roman' nor 'Victorian'.

In 1791 the two baths at White Wells, just like the original one from the beginning of the eighteenth century had been, were open air. Bathers were protected from the wind by a high wall around three sides. The wall is slightly higher to the rear of the building. The fourth side of the enclosure for the baths being the house section which contained the changing areas for the clientele.

The original height of the enclosing walls can still be seen on the outside of the building, particularly on the western gable. The baths were not roofed over until about sixty five years later. (Which is possibly where the idea of 'Victorian' baths originates. This improvement would also have enabled visitors to use the baths year round, increasing the income of the leaseholders, and justifying the cost of adding the roofs.)

The two baths are of similar sizes. The bath that can be seen today is an oval of approximately 2.5m/8ft in length, 2m/6ft 6in wide and 1.3m/4ft 6in deep, with four steps leading down into it at one end. It contains approximately 5000 litres/1160 gallons of cold water at a temperature of approximately 6 to 8 degrees centigrade/45 to 47 degrees Fahrenheit. The volume of this bath is similar to that described for the original bath behind White Wells prior to 1791.

The drinking fountain to the rear of White Wells. — The fountain is undated, but it is possible that it pre-dates the baths inside White Wells, and existed when the original 'well house' was in use on the hill above from about 1700 to 1791.

The other bath in the western side of the building, under the floor of the café, is the same length and width as the display bath, but 30cm/1ft shallower. This bath is now redundant and empty. It was disconnected from the water supply when the building was renovated in the 1970's.

To the rear of White Wells there is a drinking fountain. Contrary to a popular belief held by some visitors, the filtered water available from the drinking fountain is perfectly safe to drink. The water is frequently tested and has no significant mineral content. Another popular myth is that the drinking fountain used to dispense chalybeate or 'iron water'. This is simply a matter of confusion between this fountain and another, called the 'canker well', on the Grove by the junction with Cunliffe Road in Ilkley. The 'canker well' still exists but is disconnected. (Although the dried up 'canker well' fountain bears the date of 1923, the spring there was in use long before this date, and a fountain was previously installed there during the 1880's.) In 1883 another chalybeate spring was discovered at the top of Heber's Ghyll and a drinking fountain was created there too.

However the drinking fountain at White Wells has **never** dispensed chalybeate water.

The spring that supplies White Wells and the drinking fountain also supplies the modern toilet block. Although the water used in that building is not filtered, and therefore cannot be described as 'drinking water' under modern health and safety regulations. Of course the water at White Wells used to be consumed without any filtration systems in the past and there are no records of anyone suffering from ill effects by doing so. Indeed, that would be contrary to the very purpose of 'taking the waters' in the first place!

A Tragedy at White Wells

However it wasn't anything untoward in the content of the water that was responsible for a tragedy only two years after the new baths had been built at White Wells, rather the water itself.

The Ilkley Parish register records the event:

"Anne daughter of William Harper of Ilkley, butcher, drowned in attempting to bathe herself in one of the baths at the Spaw-well August 15th, buried the 18th in the Ch. Yd. Aged 9."

It is also mentioned on page three of the *'Leeds Intelligencer'* newspaper, of Monday, 19th August 1793:

"On Thursday in the afternoon, a girl about 9 years of age, the grand daughter of the old man who takes care of the cold bath at Ilkley, went to fetch some water therefrom, and taking the opportunity of bathing herself at the same time was unfortunately drowned, – she was found in the bath some time after, when the means recommended by the humane society were used, but without having the desired effect."

It is apparent from this description that White Wells was not being used on the day of the tragedy. – Despite it being the middle of summer. Anne's grandfather was obviously not around, and having left her horse or donkey transport outside, she must have let herself into the property in order to carry out her task of fetching water.

I have used the spelling of Anne Harper's name with an 'e' on the end when relating this information about her. Interestingly, in the parish records her birth is recorded under the spelling Ann, while her death is recorded as 15th August 1793, under the spelling Anne. Additionally the family surname is variously given the spellings 'Harper' and 'Harpur' in different sections of the Parish register.

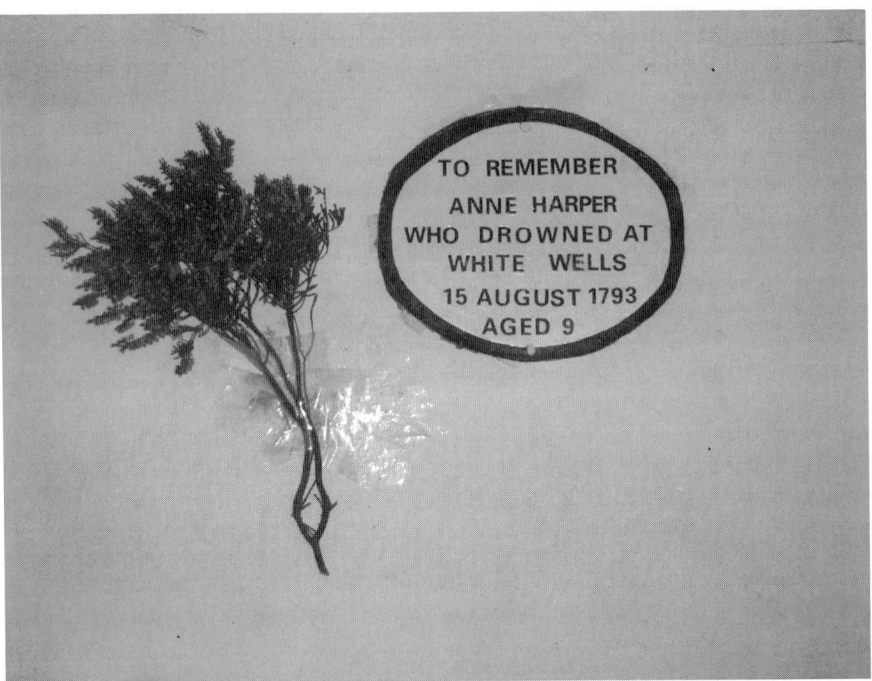

A tragic event. — The memorial plaque on the wall of the café inside White Wells. The sprig of heather is replaced on the 15th August each year. There is no evidence as to which of the two baths at White Wells Anne drowned in or, crucially, what circumstances occurred that gave rise to the event, other than she was on an errand to collect water and obviously decided to bathe at the same time.

It would appear from research into the Parish records that Anne came from a tragic family. Her parents, William Harper and Hannah Bell, were married on 29th September 1783. Anne was born on 18th May 1784. In 1785 Anne's mother gave birth to a son, called John, but he died at birth on the 15th July, and was buried the next day. The following year, Anne's mother died at the age of just twenty four, when Anne herself was only two years old. Her father remarried, and with his second wife Mercy, had further children. A daughter named Sarah died at the age of two in February 1790, and then Anne herself drowned in 1793. In 1796 another daughter was born on 9th February, and Baptised with the name of Ann, on 27th March. Sadly she died on 26th February 1810, and was buried on 2nd March. The cause of her death is unrecorded.

The newspaper reference to Anne Harper being the granddaughter of the *'old man who takes care of the cold bath'* presents something more of a mystery. In 1791 when the two baths were built, it is reported that a gentleman by the name of Robert Dale was in charge. (Though the construction of the baths had been sanctioned by the local landowner Squire William Middelton.) A few years later, in 1801, a gentleman by the name of Thomas Beanlands held the property, and remained so during the early years of the nineteenth century, until his son Joseph took it on.

The Parish records do not suggest that either Robert Dale or Thomas Beanlands were related to Anne Harper. The gentleman in question being referred to as her 'grandfather' one would have expected to be called Harper or Bell. William Harper's second marriage, to Mercy, is not recorded in the Ilkley Parish Register, but must have taken place sometime between 1786 and 1788. The name Mercy Smith is recorded in the Baptism register of 1760, and again in the marriage register of 1783, when she married a tailor named Thomas Winn of Ilkley. Whether this Mercy is one and the same woman who a few years later for whatever reason became William Harper's second wife is unclear. But even if this was the case, the surnames do not correspond, from Mercy's first husband's family. William Harper could also have remarried outside the Ilkley Parish, explaining why there is no record of the event in the register.

The other possibility of course is that Anne Harper's grandfather could have been *employed* by Robert Dale to attend to the day to day running of White Wells, when and if anyone wished to use the baths there. Which clearly they didn't on the day Anne drowned.

There is a plaque on the wall of the café in memory of Anne Harper, and a sprig of heather alongside, which is replaced on the 15th August each year.

There are no records of any other deaths by drowning at White Wells since.

CHAPTER TWO:
INTO THE NINETEENTH CENTURY

In 1801 Mr Thomas Beanlands held the 'Well house and farm' for the sum of £75 per annum. Though how extensive the 'farm' was is something of a mystery. Certainly as the century progressed and water treatments became more popular any connection with farming seems to have been severed.

Thomas Beanlands died in 1817, (there is a memorial stone on the south wall inside Ilkley Parish Church commemorating the Beanlands family, who were well respected in the area.) Thomas Beanlands son Joseph held White Wells and appointed William Butterfield as bathman in 1820. Following concerns that the building required improvements and repair, largely due to it being unoccupied. Though the Butterfield family did not live on the premises either. Their family association with White Wells was to last almost a century, until 1918.

Impression of how White Wells probably would have looked at the beginning of the nineteenth century. — This image depicts the property more than twenty years before the 'charity bath' to the west and the extension to the east, comprising of a stable with a sitting room above for clientele waiting to use the baths, were built around 1830. The roofs were not installed above the baths until the 1850's, when the 'Wells House Hydropathic Company' held the lease (between 1856 and 1872.) It is therefore most likely that bathing at White Wells, at least until the middle of the nineteenth century, was a seasonal activity taking place during the warmer months of the year.

The Butterfield family connection to White Wells is examined further in the next chapter: Taking the plunge with Mr Butterfield.

Also around 1820 Dr Adam Hunter, a physician, wrote about the water at White Wells, considering it to be the "most valuable spring he had found anywhere".

He also postulated a theory that the waters at White Wells could have been exploited by the Romans, which could well have contributed to the unfounded myth that the baths are 'Roman'. This common misconception probably originates from the fact that there was a series of Roman forts in Ilkley between the first and fifth centuries A.D. The forts all occupied the site where All Saints Parish Church and the Manor House now stand. Originally built with wood, the later forts evolved and were stone built structures.

However Dr Hunter's theory does not seem very likely upon closer examination. The Roman fort(s) was abundantly served by the two streams that now run down through culverts below modern street level. One stream runs to the east of the fort site, and one to the west. While the river Wharfe into which the streams drain flows close to the north of the site. The fort was called 'Olicana' which, according to local historian Elsie Fletcher (writing in the 1950's and influenced by the writings of the great Dr Robert Collyer from seventy years earlier) was itself a corruption of 'Llecan'. This was the name of the area under the rule of Queen Cartimandua, prior to the invasion of Britain by Claudius between 41-54 A.D. The name later became corrupted into 'Ilkley', which is familiar to us today. (For an altogether more jocular theory of the origins of 'Olicana', see the Busby's Christmas advert for a visit to the moors by Santa in 1935, in Chapter Seven: Between the Wars.) The soldiers garrisoned at the fort during some of the Roman occupation, according to archaeological evidence, were the 'II Cohort Lingonum' from the Langres region of eastern France. Coming from a warmer climate, it is highly unlikely that they would have fancied the idea of hiking halfway up the moor for a cold bath, when the water from the nearby streams or even the river could have been warmed up in the relative shelter of their fort. Furthermore, they would not have wished to compromise their security by venturing too far outside their fort only to undress and bathe on the moor.

There is simply no evidence of a Roman presence at White Wells.

CHAPTER THREE:

TAKING THE PLUNGE WITH MR BUTTERFIELD

THE BUTTERFIELD FAMILY became involved with White Wells between 1820 and 1918. The first Mr Butterfield, called William was aged about forty-four when he took up employment in the position of bathman. He was affectionately known as 'Old Billy', and along with his wife Betty, also operated a donkey transportation service in Ilkley. The forerunner of today's taxis. In the writings of A.B. Granville in 1841, Mrs Butterfield is described as *"An old primitive dame"* who brought people up to the baths using her own donkey transport and then attending to the supervision of female bathers in her capacity as bathwoman. (There will be more from A.B. Granville in the next chapter.)

The role of bathman (and bathwoman) at White Wells would have involved the assisting of bathers, attending to the changing areas and the fireplaces therein, emptying and refilling the baths where required, the selling of information leaflets about the area, maintaining White Wells in good order and promoting the appeal of the baths generally.

A description of the water at White Wells states that the softness and purity *"makes it more efficacious by passing sooner to the utmost finest limits of circulation than any water known."* Which has been compared to the *"Refreshes the parts…"* advertising slogan of the late twentieth century!

The waters were also described as beneficial: *"For scrofulous cases, long confinement in populous towns, effects arising from late hours, the abuse of liquors, &c it is certainly excellent."*

Mr Butterfield's son, also called William was born in 1818, and he became employed as the bathman at White Wells later in the nineteenth century. Looking through the census returns, most likely sometime between 1841 and 1851. What became of the first Mr Butterfield is uncertain. He is listed in the 1841 census, but not the 1851 census, suggesting that he may have died during the course of the decade in between. However although there are a number of William Butterfields in the death records between these dates, none of them died in Ilkley. We must assume that perhaps he moved out of the town, and

Mr William Butterfield stood next to the drinking fountain at the rear of White Wells. — Much was made of the 'undiluted beverage from the heart of the moor', and while it may be easy to mock such notions, the water at White Wells is exceptionally pleasant. It passes stringent modern safety requirements and contains no chemicals that are generally added to the mains supply elsewhere. The water passes through modern filters as an added precaution, but other than that it is from the same source as the one Mr Butterfield promoted.

Although the drinking fountain is not dated it is believed that it pre-dates the two baths inside White Wells, and was probably in use when the original bath at the top of the hill behind White Wells was in existence.

Contrary to a popular belief, this drinking fountain has never dispensed 'chalybeate' or 'iron' water. This notion is simply a matter of confusion with the 'canker well' on the Grove in Ilkley town centre, and another 'chalybeate' spring, discovered in 1883, at the top of Hebers Ghyll.

went to live with relatives elsewhere, leaving his son William behind to continue the work at White Wells.

When the 'Wells House Hydropathic Company' took over the running of White Wells in the 1850's, the second Mr Butterfield continued being employed in the role of bathman.

In 1872 the Ilkley Local Board took over White Wells from the 'Wells House Hydropathic Company', and a Dr Harrison paid the rent on the building. However this was somewhat short lived, because by 1875, the minutes of the Local Board meetings inform us that it was Mr Butterfield himself who was paying the rent, rather than being employed by someone else. He applied to the Local Board to pay the sum of £15 for the 'season' of 1st April to 1st November. This was rejected, and the sum of £17 was demanded instead. This was a considerable reduction in the amount of rent from the £30 Dr Harrison had been paying for a half year's rent only a few years beforehand.

In May 1877, the minutes of the Local Board meeting reported in the *'Ilkley Gazette'* informs us that the rent was further reduced for Mr Butterfield:

> **Water rent of the Old Wells:** *A discussion arose respecting the water rent of this place, which Mr Beanlands observed had been a blessing to thousands.*
> *Mr Hirst, the Clerk, said the present occupier, (Mr Butterfield) had told him he could not pay more than £12 a year.*
> *On the motion of Mr Beanlands, seconded by Mr Robinson, the rent was fixed at this amount."*

An indication of the decline in the popularity of 'Taking the waters' at White Wells.

The water supply at White Wells had been disrupted somewhat by the Local Board's 'improvement' schemes, which in 1873 had tapped into the source of the White Wells supply and reduced the amount of water available. (See Chapter Five: The Development of the Hydro's and the Expansion of Ilkley. For a description of the various waterworks and improvements undertaken by the Local Board.)

In the late 1870's Mr Butterfield was warned by the Local Board not to charge visitors for using the drinking fountain. An accusation he denied. The same accusation was levelled against him again in the 1880's and he was told to desist from this practice once more.

A photograph from the late nineteenth century shows the second Mr Butterfield stood next to the plunge bath in the western side of White Wells. This dates from the early 1890's when Mr Butterfield was in his seventies. (He died in 1893). In another photograph, Mr Butterfield is shown stood next to the drinking fountain to the rear of White Wells.

Mr William Butterfield stood next to the plunge bath in the western side of White Wells. — This photograph was taken in the 1890's, when Mr Butterfield was in his seventies. (He died in 1893.) It is likely that by the 1890's his son, also called William, would have been in charge of the proceedings at White Wells.

Mr Butterfield's father, who was also called William, had become the bath man at White Wells in about 1820, while it would appear from the census returns that the Mr Butterfield in the photograph became the bath man some time between 1841 and 1851. What became of the original Mr Butterfield remains something of a mystery.

Following the death of his father in 1893, William Butterfield (the third generation William,) who was in his thirties, took over the tenancy and the running of White Wells.

In the early twentieth century visitors to the premises were given a colourful description of the history and the properties of the waters. The baths were promoted as being Roman by an 'orator' who entertained the visitors. Contrary to the implication given by postcards of the time that Mr Butterfield gave the descriptions of the Wells and the water therein; the oration was in fact given by a gentleman called David Scott, a native of Halifax, who became involved with White Wells around 1901 when he was aged about sixty six. (In August 1903 the *'Ilkley Gazette'* featured an article in which the oration by Mr Scott was described. See Chapter Six: Out of the nineteenth and into the Twentieth Century.)

David Scott who gave the oration was described as an 'old utopian' (perhaps today he would be called a 'character'). He entertained visitors to White Wells with his flamboyant descriptions, and turned the shower pipes on and off for those wishing to bathe, while the younger Mr Butterfield, by then in his forties, was responsible for the general running of White Wells and the provision of refreshments to visitors and the payment of rent to the Ilkley Urban District

Facing page: Last in the family line associated with White Wells. Mr William Butterfield stood next to the plunge bath in the eastern side of White Wells. This photograph was taken in the early years of the twentieth century, and shows the third generation William Butterfield. He remained in charge of White Wells until he was about fifty eight years old in 1918. What became of him after this date also is something of a mystery.

By the turn of the nineteenth and twentieth centuries, the plunge bath in the eastern side of White Wells had become overgrown. (Another photograph from this era shows a notice next to the overgrown bath that requests visitors 'not to pluck the ferns'!)

And a postcard was also inscribed with the verse:

Roman Bath, Ilkley
Reader: be by me advised;
Flee the nostrums advertised;
By patent medicine dealers,
Throw your draughts and pills away,
Come to Ilkley Wells and Stay;
O'er the breezy moorlands stray,
Take a douche bath every day;
These are Natures healers.

The unknown poet signed off J.M.F.

The shower pipes remained above the bath though the supply pipe on the outside of the building was eventually severed during the course of various work undertaken to improve White Wells in the early twentieth century.

The Old Roman Well, White Wells, Ilkley.

Council. A position he retained until he was about fifty eight years old. His tenancy of White Wells expired on 31st December 1918. However it seems he was in no particular hurry to vacate the property. (Though Mr Butterfield lived in the town, not actually at White Wells.) At the meeting of the IUDC Finance Committee on 29th January 1919 it is recorded that: *"Mr Butterfield, tenant of the White Wells, whose tenancy expired on the 31st December last, having been requested to deliver up possession of the premises, and having failed to do so, the clerk was instructed to take such proceedings as are necessary for recovering possession of the said premises."*

What 'proceedings' were taken is unclear, but tenders for the catering at White Wells were being accepted in April 1919.

A local story concerning the original Mr Butterfield, (but not recorded until as late as the eighteen nineties) is heard from time to time. It tells of the 'Butterfield Fairies'. According to the tale, early one bright warm summer morning Mr Butterfield was making his way up the moor to White Wells to open up for the day. As he approached the building a sudden calm befell. Everything went still and quiet. Nothing stirred. Mr Butterfield took out his large iron key to open the bathhouse but as he inserted it into the lock a strange thing happened. The key suddenly became wobbly. It was like rubber, bending about in the lock. Eventually he managed to open the door and gain access to the building. Upon entering, a weird sight met his eyes. In the plunge bath and oblivious to him watching, a number of strange green creatures were frolicking in the water. Almost immediately they became aware of Mr Butterfield, who said "Hello there!" to them, they frantically scrambled out of the bath, climbed the walls and ran away up the moor. (It should be remembered that there were no roofs on the bath houses at this time, these were added in the 1850's.) When the creatures had disappeared out of sight, the birds started singing again and everything returned to a state of normality; and Mr Butterfield then went about his daily business.

There are variations to the story too. For example one version suggests Mr Butterfield noticed a change in how bright and vivid the colours of the moor seemed to become during the course of his experience, and in contradiction the birds started chattering even more loudly. While another dates it as 1815, five years **before** the Butterfield family involvement at White Wells began. Another version suggests that the events took place on midsummer morning. Apparently fairies and the like celebrate on 'St John's Eve', which is the night before the daybreak of midsummer morning.

What the creatures he supposedly saw were, what caused the key to become wobbly in the lock or the birds to become silent or even if there is any factual basis to the story at all remains open to conjecture –and certainly impossible to prove two centuries or so later!

It has been suggested that the creatures were green lizards in great abundance. However while small lizards are not unknown on the moor, such a large gathering of them in one place would be highly unusual to say the least. –And in any case Mr Butterfield would no doubt have been very familiar with lizards, especially if the local lizard population was so much higher than it obviously is today for this theory to have any validity. (Besides, the presence of lizards alone would not account for the wobbly lock.)

What is interesting is that in the nineteenth and early twentieth centuries some people claim to have seen fairies, elves, goblins and the like, whereas now some people claim to see UFO's and 'aliens'. It would seem that some people often see what they want to see and tap into the popular culture of the times in which they live.

To answer an oft asked question, it is a fact that during our tenancy at White Wells to date (and on many visits to the moor long before it) we have **never** seen anything we could describe as 'fairies' 'goblins' 'ghosts' 'UFO's' or 'aliens'. – Though that is not to say there aren't others who believe that they have. A lady who claimed to know about such things informed us that there is a 'troll' living under the drinking fountain behind White Wells. Though with respect to her beliefs, we have had no tangible evidence of this ourselves as yet!

So we are left with three possibilities for the Butterfield Fairies:

Something strange really did happen at White Wells.

The whole thing was contrived to dupe a gullible public. (Similar to modern day UFO hoaxes.)

The 'fairies' were invented by Mr Butterfield to help pacify any fears amongst the younger 'patients' having to undergo what for some would have been a daunting experience. Similar to the fears of some children today having to experience a visit to the doctor or dentist. – And we know from the writings of A. B. Granville that children also underwent treatment at White Wells. See his description in the next Chapter The Development of Hydropathy.

Perhaps the latter possibility concerning the 'Butterfield Fairies' is nearer to the truth of the matter than has previously been considered.

CHAPTER FOUR:
THE DEVELOPMENT OF 'HYDROPATHY'

In the 1820's Vinzenz Prissnitz (1799-1851) started to develop water treatments in the simple surroundings of his farmhouse in Grafenburg in Silesia, in what is now the modern day village of Lazne Jesenik in the Czech Republic, close to the border with Poland. Prissnitz used the term 'Hydropathy' to describe the treatments he devised. The growing popularity of this quickly spread, and 'Hydropathy' or 'Hydrotherapy' as it was also called, became something quite fashionable, particularly amongst the middle classes.

Meanwhile back in Yorkshire, at White Wells, Thomas Beanlands' son, Joseph, held the baths at White Wells for the sum of £52/10 per annum. Fifty Guineas (Though no mention of a 'farm' as well, as his father had held in 1801.) – And Mr Butterfield continued his employment as bathman.

In 1829 the 'Ilkley Bath Charitable Institution' was established by the Ilkley Curate George Fenton. This charity enabled poorer 'patients' to take the waters too. An annual Ilkley Bazaar became one of the main fundraising events for it, while subscriptions to the charity were welcomed from interested parties as well. On the front page of the *'Leeds Intellegencer'* newspaper of Thursday 10th December 1829, a list of subscribers was printed:

'Ilkley Bath Charitable Institution'

Leeds List of Subscribers.

	£	s	d
Right Hon. Earl of Harewood	1	0	0
Right Hon. Lord Ribblesdale	1	1	0
Sir Charles Ibbetson, Bart	2	2	0
William Hey	2	2	0
Miss Hey	1	1	0
Rev J.A. Rhodes	2	2	0
Mrs Rhodes	2	2	0
Miss Rhodes, Park Place	2	2	0
The Vicar of Leeds, Rev R. Fawcett	1	1	0

The Leeds Workhouse	3	3	0
Dr Hunter	1	1	0
Dr Thorpe	1	1	0
Dr Whitehead	1	1	0
Thomas Chorley, Surgeon	1	1	0
Henry Chorley...... Do	0	10	6
John Spence.......... Do	1	1	0
John Wade .... Do	1	1	0
James Howard ...... Do	1	1	0
Charles Sykes .... Do	0	10	6
Joshua Dixon	1	1	0
John Dixon	1	1	0
Benjamin Gott Esq	1	1	0
John Gott Esq	1	1	0
Wm Gott Esq	1	1	0
George Harrey Esq	1	1	0
Mrs Tempest, Tong Hall	1	1	0
Rev Dr Busfield	1	1	0
Rev Dr Hartley	1	1	0
Rev Jacob Marsham	1	1	0
Rev Henry Robinson	0	10	6
Rev Francis Cookson	0	10	6
Rev George Fenton	0	10	6
Captain Rhodes	1	1	0
Mr Heaton	1	1	0
Robert Menzies, Esq	0	10	6
J.P. Clapham	0	10	6
Marshall Stables	0	10	6
H.H. Stansfeld	0	10	6
T.B. Pease	1	1	0
W. Aldam	1	1	0
E. Birchall	1	1	0
G. Greenwood	1	1	0
Rev W. Barnard	1	1	0
Samuel Smith, Surgeon	1	1	0
Mrs Browne, Middlethorpe	1	1	0
Ann Jowett	0	10	6
Mr Atkinson, Solicitor	1	1	0
Edward Baines	1	1	0

Bradford List of Annual Subscribers.

	£	s	d
Ellis L. Cunliffe, Esq	2	2	0
John Wood, jun.	3	3	0
Dr Outhwaite	1	1	0
Wm Sharpe, Surgeon	1	1	0
The Vicar of Bradford, Rev Henry Heap	1	1	0
Matthew Thompson	1	1	0
Richard Fawcett	1	1	0
Hollins and Stansfeld	1	1	0
Magerison and Peckover	1	1	0
Wm. Rouse and Son	1	1	0
James Wade, Son and Co	1	1	0
Wm Horsfall and Brother	1	1	0
Francis Duffield, Esq	1	1	0
Cousin, Leach and Co	1	1	0
Illingworth and Co	1	1	0

	£	s	d
George Pollard	1	1	0
John Hustler, Jun.	1	1	0
Miss Hartley	1	1	0
Mr Rand	0	10	6
Mr Wood, Sen	0	10	6
Henry Cooper	0	10	6
J. & W. Hardcastle	1	1	0
J.G. Paley	1	1	0
Colonel Tempest	1	1	0
W. Cheesbrough	0	10	6
C. Harris	1	1	0
H. Harris	1	1	0
A. Harris	1	1	0
Joshua Mann	1	1	0
Captain Priestley	1	1	0
Rev W. Cooper	0	10	6
Mr T. Cooper	0	10	6
Mr Aked	1	1	0
Mr J. Mann	1	1	0
Mr Leah	1	1	0
Wm. Nicholson	0	10	6

It is in contemplation before the Commencement of the forthcoming Season at Ilkley to erect a small but substantial Building for the Reception of Forty-two patients from the Leeds Infirmary, and Eighteen from the Bradford Dispensary Annually.

The Earl of Harewood and other benevolent Individuals have offered to contribute towards the Erection; and at a Meeting of the Committee of the Bradford Dispensary held on the Second of December, it was proposed by Dr Outhwaite, and seconded by Mr Lister, Surgeon, that the Bradford Dispensary should contribute £10. 10s in aid of the Building Fund of the Ilkley Charitable Institution; and in Consideration of the distressed State of the Funds of the Leeds Infirmary, a Friend of the Ilkley Charity has offered to advance Twenty Guineas in the Name of the Leeds Infirmary, on the understanding that the Institution shall have the power of transmitting Two of its Patients Annually to the Establishment at Ilkley, to be received upon Conditions as shall be arranged at a General Meeting of the Subscribers. The Number of Subscribers necessary to support the Bradford Department of the Establishment, and the Sanction and Approbation of the Committee of the Bradford Dispensary having been obtained to the proposed Measures, the Secretary to the Ilkley Charity will take an early Opportunity of waiting upon the influential individuals in Leeds and the Neighbourhood to solicit Subscriptions in support of a Measure, the Object of which is to enable the Leeds Infirmary and Bradford Dispensary to transmit those Patients to the Establishment at Ilkley, to whom Change of Air, and, under particular Maladies, the Use of the Ilkley Waters may, by the Medical Officers of the above institutions be considered essentially necessary. During the preceeding season, 184 Patients were relieved from the Funds of this Charity and many Cures were effected in Cases which had hitherto baffled the Skill and Professional Knowledge of the most eminent Practitioners in the Kingdom.

George Fenton, Secretary.
Ilkley, Dec 3d, 1829.

The Ilkley Charity was well supported. (One of the names from the Leeds list, H. Stansfeld, later played an important role in the development of the 'Water Cure' in the Ilkley area. See the next chapter, The Establishment of the 'Hydros' and the Expansion of Ilkley.)

The 'small but substantial building' which was to be built in time for the 'forthcoming season' (1830) is the earliest mention of the 'Charity Bath' building adjacent to White Wells. Presumably during the opening 'season' the previous year (1829), the first one the 'Ilkley Bath Charitable Institution' operated, the one hundred and eighty four patients were treated in the baths inside White Wells.

The charity bath, just like the other two baths inside White Wells, was open air. It was surrounded on three sides by a high wall, slightly higher to the rear. The fourth side comprising what would have been the changing area. This probably would have been in the upper room, which contained a fireplace. (This room is now the public toilet.) While the lower room was possibly in use as a coal store for the fireplace upstairs and those inside White Wells.

Patients came from all over the area, and clearly from this account, not only from Ilkley. Although they had to pay for their own lodgings in any one of the many lodging houses that had appeared in the town (one of the most well known of these being 'Ushers Lodgings' on Wells Road); charity dispensations were issued from the vicarage. This was on Church Street, or Kirkgate as it was sometimes called, roughly where the entrance to the 'Victorian Arcade' now stands, and was referred to colloquially as 'T' charity 'ole'. The physician employed by the charity in 1831 was Dr John Spence from the nearby town of Otley, six miles to the east of Ilkley.

Throughout the 1830's the *Leeds Intellegencer* reported on the annual meetings of the charity, detailing the incomes and expenses of the previous 'season', including the various amounts paid to Mr Beanlands, the leaseholder of White Wells, for use of the bathing facilities: In 1831 £40/00, 1833 £37/00, 1834 £39/00, 1835 £35/00. In the later years of the decade, the amounts decreased to: £19/10 in 1836, £22/00 in 1837 and £21/00 in 1838.

At the meeting of Wednesday 7th February 1838 (when the reports of the 1837 season were made), it was also noted that the Rev. G. Fenton had moved to Roystone, and as a consequence it was impossible that he could *"continue his exertions with the charity to the same extent as when he resided in Ilkley."*

In addition to his work with the 'Ilkley Bath Charitable Institution' George Fenton also established the 'Canker Well' on Green Lane in Ilkley, now the Grove. This was a chalybeate or iron water spring, from which the water was collected and used for drinking rather than bathing. Similar to the various medicinal springs which had for many years been exploited in Harrogate. (Though a 'drinking fountain' was not installed at the 'Canker Well' site until the 1880's.)

George Fenton died in 1843 and was buried in Lightcliffe cemetery.

The 'charity bath' remained in use for a number of years, but fell into decline after 1862 when the 'Ilkley Bath Charity' opened its own purpose built 'Ilkley Hospital' on the Grove.

No trace of the charity bath remains today at White Wells, though the building that once housed it still exists to the west of White Wells and is in use as a public toilet.

The 'Charity Bath' building (2009.) — The Charity bath, housed in a *'Small but substantial building'*, was constructed in time for the opening of the 1830 'season' by Ilkley curate George Fenton and by the subscribers to his 'Ilkley Bath Charity'

In the charity bath enclosure there is the remains of another drinking fountain. This is found along the south wall of the enclosure, and does not issue water today.

(The fountain was mentioned in the *'Ilkley Gazette'* in June 1924, see also Chapter Seven: Between the wars.)

It is possible that the fountain dates from when the 'Charity Bath' was built. Visitors to White Wells could drink the water free of charge if bathing too, from the fountain at the rear of the building. But they were charged to drink it if not. Having a separate drinking fountain for the use of the charity bath patients in the adjoining enclosure would have effectively segregated the different clientele from those of 'means' and those of 'limited means'.

As the use of the charity bath diminished after 1862 the fountain also fell into disuse. As a result of this, by about the 1880's it had dried up.

Nearby, on the outside of the enclosure there is a redundant water tank, which the fountain tapped into. This tank was most recently 'discovered' in 1973 during the renovations of White Wells by Mr Eric Busby. (See Chapter Ten: Eric

Busby and the Renovation of White Wells.) Despite considerable speculation about the tank being used as a reservoir that previously supplied the town, it dates from the building of the Charity Bath c1830. A conclusion drawn in 1924 when the tank was similarly 'discovered' and subsequently drained and its water outlets examined. The tank is higher than the level of where the charity bath would have been, so there would have been ample pressure to fill the bath frequently. It is about the same level as the two baths inside White Wells, so cannot have been used to store water for either of these, as there would not have been sufficient pressure to feed the two baths by gravity.

The former charity bath was converted into a toilet in 1910, bringing the adjoining outside privy inside. Photographs from the 1930's suggest that during the course of the water improvement works of the late 1920's, the stone head spout from the decorative fountain in the enclosure was removed and installed as a decorative feature in the plunge bath to the west side of White Wells instead. During the renovations of the 1970's this was moved again into the display bath, and can be seen as the feature through which water flows into the bath today.

The 1910 toilet facilities became redundant in the summer of 2005 when the current public toilet was installed in the upper room of the former Charity Bath building.

Bathing at White Wells was not particularly cheap. At the time the 'charity bath' opened the fees were: *"First Bath": three shillings per person per week. Shower bath two shillings. "Second Bath": two shillings. Third or "Poor" bath: half the above. Bathers will be allowed to drink the water gratis (free). Visitors drinking the water but not using the bath: one shilling per week. One shilling and sixpence two weeks. Two shillings and sixpence monthly. Six shillings quarterly.*

In pre decimal currency, one shilling is equivalent to five pence, while sixpence was half of one shilling, or two and a half pence in modern money. Though of course we do not have the 'Ha'penny' any more.

The fees for using the baths at White Wells may appear absurdly cheap by today's standard. But one shilling in the early 1830's would have been worth about five pounds in real terms today. When reconsidered in this context, it was in fact quite expensive to take the waters here, and would compare in price to sessions of 'alternative therapies' available on the holistic medicine scene today.

The "Shower Bath" mentioned in the scale of charges refers to the "First Bath". Which is the bath that is on public display today. As well as being used as a plunge bath there was a shower arrangement overhead. Whereby users could have either a strong jet of water onto the afflicted part, or a more gentle spray of water falling on them. Later photographs of the bath show the shower pipes still there in about 1900. Though by then the First Bath was overgrown with ferns and largely (but not entirely) disused in favour of the Second Bath, which remained in use up until the 1920's.

Contrary to another popular misconception, it is highly unlikely that the baths would have had separate designations of a ladies bath and a gentlemen's bath. This probably arises from the writings of A.B. Granville, who wrote a book first published in 1841, entitled *"The Spas of England"*. In this work the chapter *"Ilkley; or, The Mountain Spa"* Granville describes a visit to White Wells. He writes:

"Ilkley fountain, as was before stated, is high upon the side of the Rumboldmoor, (sic) consequently distant from the village perhaps three quarters of a mile; the ascent is by a rough carriage-road, until about halfway; then by a winding footpath over the rugged moorside, strewed with large and small boulder stones.

There is, halfway up the lowermost part of the hill, a range of stone houses, called Usher's lodgings, which, with an aspect to the west, are among the best here. They are generally well filled during the season by the superior order of visiters (sic), who, I hear, find the cuisine excellent.

The healing waters burst from the rocky mountain-side, in a round thick stream, at the rate, repeatedly measured by myself, of sixty gallons in a minute; the temperature, 47F; was only eight degrees lower than that of the surrounding atmosphere. It is brilliantly limpid and crystal-like; but its taste disappointed me, being, like the water at Malvern, which it resembles in other respects, neither sharp nor very sapid. From two to three pints of it are generally drunk by the visiters (sic), who take long and fatiguing walks, round about the mazes of these hills, between the several doses of the water.

But the principle use of these waters is in bathing, or still more for the application of the douche to any diseased parts of the body or limb.

There are two baths the one for male, the other for female patients. *(My emphasis). They are both open above, occupying a round area, three feet deep, surrounded by a wall. Over a centre room, placed between the two baths, there is a dressing room; but all this arrangement is quite in the rough, and the whole building looks very much like one of those stone-built shelters, or houses of recovery one meets on the Alps.*

A young girl, about eleven years of age, was being subjected to the douche, under the direction of an old primitive dame, who, besides escorting invalids on one of those useful climbing quadrupeds, an ass, – her own property, – serves as a bath-woman also. The application of the douche was made directly upon an inveterate sore in one of the young lady's legs, accompanied with an almost total loss of power of moving that limb. The douche had been repeated about a week, and the patient admitted to me that she had already derived great benefit from it. I remained until the operation had been finished, and examined the limb. It looked blue, and felt extremely cold; but she was not sensible of this; on the contrary, the inward feeling throughout the deadened limb was that of a glow – a feeling which would last, she said, about two hours, and then she was able to move the limb better.

I next submitted my own hand and wrist to the whole weight of the precipitous stream, meaning to retain the limb in that position for five minutes – the same time generally considered necessary for efficacious results; but the pain, principally at the wrist, became, at the expiration of the first minute, so intensely and particularly acute, that I withdrew it from the stream. On a second experiment the time was prolonged to four minutes. The first application imparts the sensation of cold for an instant; it then produces very acute pain for a minute and a half, and at last the sensation approaches that of tepid water.

The pulse previously to the douche, soon after mounting the steep acclivity, was 108, and soft; the heat in the palm of the hand 93F. After the douche it beat 63, and took one minute to ascend to 73 beats. The hand and wrist looked red, they became slowly warm, but upon returning home on foot they tingled, and felt inwardly hot, although the thermometer marked only 90 degrees of heat on the skin.

This spring has been resorted to for upwards of two centuries. Dr Mossman, the late Mr Moorhouse, surgeon of Skipton, and Dr Hunter, of Leeds, principally on the reports of Mr Spence, surgeon at Ilkley fountain; Dr Hunter, however, the same able physician of whom I have had occasion to make favourable mention in speaking of Harrogate, is the authority upon whom I principally rely.

Despite the fact that separate male and female bathing is mentioned in the above passage, it must be remembered that the 'douche' or shower bath was available to **all** patients taking the waters at White Wells. No such conditions for separate use of the facilities are mentioned in the scale of charges. It must also be remembered that the 'Charity Bath' which would have been in use at the time of Granville's visit, and which he doesn't mention, was a singular bath. Separate bathing facilities for male and female patients to the charity bath would certainly not have existed. They would more likely have had to bathe at separate times.

Although not mentioned by Granville, it is interesting to note that after two people had used the baths, the water was drained and the baths refilled with fresh water. A process repeated numerous times throughout the day. At the current rate of flow through modern pipes, it takes over eight hours to fill the bath today!

Mounting block outside White Wells. — The mounting block outside White Wells is unusual in that it is a 'double' block, having two sets of steps. It would have proved invaluable for the comfort of 'patients' coming and going to White Wells for their 'treatments'.

Obviously a large number of clients of both genders could be served each day, using the different changing rooms available to them. Some arrived on foot, while some travelled up the moor on donkeys. The extension to the east of the bathhouse was built at about the same time as the 'charity bath'. The upper room being described as a 'sitting room' for the convenience of visitors awaiting bathing. The room under it was in use as a stable, housing the donkeys used for transporting clientele to White Wells. Visitors today will notice that there is still a mounting block at the front of the building, between the bathhouse and café entrances. Those whom have walked up from the town may also have noticed another mounting block on Wells Road, at the junctions of Wells Road, Queens Road, Skelda Rise and Wells Promenade. This was originally positioned at the bottom of Wells Road. It lay discarded for a number of years in a field at the junction of Wells Road and Whitton Croft Road. When the Christian Science Church, built on the field, was opened in the early 1940's, the block was given back to the IUDC and it was moved to its

Mounting block on Wells Road. — Known from my own childhood as 'the steps that lead to nowhere', the mounting block was previously located lower down Wells Road. Convenient for 'patients' bound for White Wells embarking on their journey up the hill from the town.

John 'Donkey' Jackson. — One of the town's familiar characters in the late nineteenth century was John Jackson. From 1868 he ran a donkey hire service from the town up the moor to White Wells on the moors, earning himself the nickname 'Donkey' Jackson by virtue of his trade.

He died in January 1907, in his early eighties, having given up his donkey business only the year before.

present position. Donkey transport to and from White Wells was provided by various people throughout the nineteenth century, but most famously between 1868 and 1906, by John 'Donkey' Jackson. (Note: Donkey *Jackson* **Not** Donkey *Johnson*, which is a common misnomer.) A well known local character whom operated a transportation service to and from the Wells. (As well as to other destinations around the town.) He was assisted during the 1870's by a Mr C.J. Milligan.

'Donkey' Jackson lived on Bridge Lane in Ilkley, until the roof of his humble abode collapsed in the late eighteen nineties and he had to move into Castle Yard near the Manor House. The original steps up to his old house on Bridge Lane still exist today. 'Donkey' Jackson continued his trade until 1906. He died in early 1907, aged 81.

'Donkey' Jackson's brother, 'Blind Tom', was employed as a gatekeeper on Wells Road. His job being to open and close the gate to allow those journeying up and down the moor ease of passage, while keeping the sheep confined to the moor.

CHAPTER FIVE:

THE ESTABLISHMENT OF THE 'HYDROS' & THE EXPANSION OF ILKLEY

THE 1830's saw the rise in popularity of 'Taking the Waters'. (– And in 1837, the beginning of the Victorian era that lasted for the remainder of the nineteenth century, and just into the twentieth.) A guide published in 1835 listed forty four lodging houses and three inns in Ilkley. This accounted for about a third of the buildings in the village at that time.

By the time of the census in 1841, there were 521 residents and 257 temporary visitors. The census reports that:

> *"Ilkley is a place celebrated for the salubrity of its air, the purity of its water and the beauty of its romantic scenery in consequence of which it is much resorted to in the summer months by all classes of the community."*

Ben Rhydding Hydropathic Establishment

The 1840's saw the beginning of the expansion of the 'water cure' or 'hydropathy' in the Ilkley area.

In the early 1840's Hamer Stansfeld, (also the Mayor of Leeds in 1843) had visited Grafenburg and was attracted to the various water 'treatments' on offer there. As a consequence of this he was keen to develop hydropathy close to Leeds. Ilkley, already having a working spa in the form of White Wells, seemed the logical choice of location. Stansfeld was already familiar with White Wells and in 1843 he invited the 'water doctor' Antoine Rischanek to come to Ilkley from the Silesian area. The doctor was installed in 'Usher's Lodgings' on West View, Wells Road, and prescribed 'patients' with their water treatments to be taken at White Wells.

Also in 1843 Hamer Stansfeld set up a company with John Atkinson, Joseph Atkinson, James Marshall and Samuel Garlick. With the intention of building a large purpose build Hydropathic Establishment in the Ilkley area. A site close to the village of Wheatley 1.5km/1mile to the east of Ilkley was chosen for this venture. The foundation stone was laid on 26th September 1843. It was called

THE ESTABLISHMENT OF THE 'HYDROS' & THE EXPANSION OF ILKLEY

ILKLEY, BEN RHYDDING (HYDRO)

Ben Rhydding Hydropathic Establishment. — Hamer Stansfeld, who was the Mayor of Leeds in 1843, had visited both the Silesian region of Europe around Grafenburg, and closer to home, Ilkley. He was greatly impressed by the development and potential of the 'water cure'.

In 1843 he brought Dr Antoine Rischanek to Ilkley.

Hamer Stansfeld along with John Atkinson, Joseph Atkinson, James Marshall and Samuel Garlick formed the consortium that invested in the construction of Ben Rhydding Hydropathic Establishment.

The Hydro opened in 1844 and was one of the first such purpose built establishments in the country. It later became a hotel and was taken over by the Government's 'Wool Control' during the Second World War. It survived until the 1950's when it was demolished to make way for the 'High Wheatley' housing development that was built during the following decade.

'Ben Rhydding,' reputedly from a suggestion by Nancy Wharton of the 'Old Wheatsheaf Inn', Ilkley. The name perhaps being inspired by the old 'thythe map' field names in the area. 'Ben' perhaps from a personal name or possibly derived from 'Bean' and 'Rhydding' from an old term for a clearing. By virtue of this the village of Wheatley in time became renamed after the hydro too. Particularly after the arrival of the railway into Ilkley in 1865 and the subsequent opening of Ben Rhydding railway station the following year.

As the building progressed and date of the grand opening approached, one of the founders, Joseph Atkinson, responded to criticism of 'Hydropathy' or 'Hydratia' as it was also referred to, in the pages of the *'Leeds Intellegencer'* in March 1844:

> *"I have no wish to enter into controversy, however, for I am no further interested in the Establishment at Ilkley (Ben Rhydding) than as a shareholder, who are fifteen in number, and who were intending to erect a building before I joined them...."*

He goes on to state: "I have no reason to alter the opinion I then formed that Hydropathy (though not a panacea) when combined with dietetics, forms a system which if judiciously practiced will be found to posess great theraputic powers, well deserving of a trial in many cases, where ordinary means have failed...".

Hamer Stansfeld and his group of associates opened Ben Rhydding Hydro a little later in the year.

A newspaper report in the *'Leeds Intellegencer'* tells us that the 'Wharfedale Hydropathic Establishment' opened on Wednesday 29th May 1844. (Also known as 'Oak Apple Day'). The report also tells us that the hydro was in sixty five acres of grounds, of which twenty four were laid out in pleasure grounds by Mr Major. The building itself described as being in the *'Tudor style of Gothic architecture'* (also referred to as the 'Scottish Baronial style'.) There were two wings to the building, one for male and one for female patients.

The contractors, who obviously hadn't wasted much time in building the place, given that the foundation stone had only been laid the previous September, were Messrs Russell and Wilks of Leeds.

Ben Rhydding golf course. — Although Ben Rhydding Hydropathic Establishment had opened in 1844, the nine hole golf course did not feature until 1885, when the popularity of 'taking the waters' was in decline and the hydro reinvented itself as a 'golfing hotel' to a newer clientele. It is now a private golf club, being spared from redevelopment following the demolition of the Hydro.

THE ESTABLISHMENT OF THE 'HYDROS' & THE EXPANSION OF ILKLEY

Two hundred ladies and gentlemen attended the opening, which was split into two rooms. Mayor Hamer Stansfeld of Leeds who had initiated the grand project presided over the guests in the drawing room, while J.P. Clapham of Burley presided over the dining room. The band of the 70th Regiment played in the entrance and later in the grounds.

The establishment was under the management of Mr Strachan from the Midland Hotel in Derby, who arranged the accommodation for sixty patients.

It was said at the opening:

"The successful treatment of disease by what is termed the Hydropathic system, during its progress for the last twenty years on the Continent, and its more recent introduction into the south and west of England, and the Midland counties, has been too firmly established to require any apology for the formation of an Institution for carrying it into operation in the north of England. Though it would be preposterous to hold this system as a panacea for 'all the ills that flesh is heir to', it is admitted by many of the most talented professional men of the day to be peculiarly adapted to some of the diseases which prevail more particularly in this country, and to be in general a powerful auxiliary in the hands of the skilful practitioner."

Dr Rischanek was the resident physician. He did not hold this position for long though. About two years after the hydro had opened, Rischanek was dismissed from his post. The hydro did not have a resident physician until about a year later, when Dr William Macleod took up the post in 1847.

Dr Macleod had studied at Edinburgh with the eminent 'water doctor' Wilson. Wilson along with a partner named Gully had themselves opened 'Graffenberg House' (sic) in Malvern in 1842, two years before Ben Rhydding opened.

In 1851 Dr Macleod took on the lease of the establishment and by 1860 it had been substantially extended with the addition of a large north wing. In 1863 Dr William Macleod bought the hydro outright.

In 1865 Ben Rhydding railway station was still under construction when the Wharfedale line to Ilkley started operating. The station opened a year later, with the purpose of enabling clientele to alight and goods to be unloaded closer to the hydro than having to travel into Ilkley and backtracking to Ben Rhydding.

However following the completion of the station, it was apparently not considered grand enough for the visitors to the hydro. In 1871 Dr Macleod came to an agreement with the Joint Railway Board whom had overseen the construction of the Wharfedale line, to own Ben Rhydding station and construct buildings there to his own requirements. This was done, but unfortunately Dr Macleod died in 1875. The station was later sold back to the railway companies in 1885. Although Ben Rhydding Hydro is now long gone, the railway station which served it is still in use on the Wharfedale line as the penultimate stop before terminating in Ilkley. Though sadly none of the Victorian grandeur of Dr Macleod's station remains at Ben Rhydding. The buildings had become dilapidated and vandalised by the time of their demolition in 1973.

As the popularity of water treatments waned toward the end of the nineteenth century, Ben Rhydding reinvented itself as a 'golfing hotel'. The adjacent golf course for the hydro clientele had opened in 1885. The grand building itself remained in use up until the 1930's, though by then some of the property had been converted into private apartments. During the Second World War it was requisitioned by the Government for the 'Wool Control Board'. (As was Wells House also.) Following the war the building was derequisitioned and remained empty for a number of years. It was demolished between 1955 and 1957, and houses have since been built on the site. Only the nine hole golf course, parts of the former stables, and the lodge house, built circa 1860 remain. The last vestiges of the former grandeur of Ben Rhydding Hydropathic Establishment.

The area is still referred to as 'Ben Rhydding' however. It has not reverted back to its former name Wheatley.

Wells House Hydropathic Establishment

Just over a decade after Ben Rhydding Hydropathic Establishment had opened, Wells House was built on the edge of the moor to the south of Ilkley.

In 1853 a joint stock company was formed to establish a rival hydro to Ben Rhydding. A site formerly occupied by a cotton mill was selected with nine acres of land, belonging to local landowner Peter Middelton. At an elevation of approximately 170m/550ft above sea level, the site is at the same approximate elevation as Middleton Lodge on the north side of the valley. By 1854 the eminent architect Cuthbert Brodrick (1821-1905) had been commissioned to design the building, and the foundation stone was laid in June of that year. Brodrick had also won the commission to build Leeds Town Hall, which was opened in 1858. Interestingly, Wells House is the only one of Brodrick's buildings to have landscaped surroundings. The grounds of the building were designed by Joshua Major, who was also involved in the design of parks and gardens in Manchester, and who had also designed the grounds of Ben Rhydding Hydro a decade before.

Cuthbert Brodrick's other designs, in addition to Wells House and Leeds Town Hall (the latter opening in 1858), include the Corn Exchange in Leeds (1862) and the 'Grand Hotel' in Scarborough (opened in 1867).

THE ESTABLISHMENT OF THE 'HYDROS' & THE EXPANSION OF ILKLEY

Wells House Hydropathic Establishment. — Wells House opened in 1856, (28th May) and was designed by the eminent architect Cuthbert Brodrick. Brodrick's most famous work was Leeds Town hall, (a concurrent project to Wells House). Though he designed a number of other high profile buildings as well. These include the Corn Exchange in Leeds (1862), and the Grand Hotel in Scarborough (1867).

Interestingly Wells House is the only one of Brodrick's buildings to be in landscaped surroundings. (Designed by Joshua Major.) All of Brodrick's other projects were in town centre locations.

The opening ceremony at Wells House was on Wednesday 28th May 1856, twelve years after the one at Ben Rhydding. The building had cost £30,000. It contained eighty seven bedrooms and six bathrooms.

There were one hundred and fifty guests at the opening ceremony, which was presided over by Benjamin Briggs Popplewell Esq, the Chairman of the Board of Directors of the 'Wells House Hydropathic Company'. The band of the North Yorkshire Rifles occupied a room on the opposite side of the corridor to the main proceedings and played a variety of favourite music. Unfortunately the weather was somewhat inclement, and *"unfavourable to such an occasion"* so the guests were unable to enjoy the grounds as had perhaps been hoped.

The Wells House Hydropathic Company was very successful in its endeavours. In 1858 a report in the *'Leeds Intellegencer'* newspaper of Saturday 13th March states:

Leeds Town Hall.

THE ESTABLISHMENT OF THE 'HYDROS' & THE EXPANSION OF ILKLEY 39

"Ilkley Wells Hydropathic Establishment. – A general meeting of the proprietors of this institution was held at Ilkley on Wednesday. The report showed a considerable profit since the opening, but the directors recommended that, instead of declaring a dividend, the surplus should be applied to meet a debt due on capital account. After some discussion the recommendation was adopted."

The Wells House Hydropathic Company had also taken over the lease of White Wells and its spring for the sum of £60 per annum. (Wells House held the lease until 1872, when the Ilkley Local Board took it on.) Roofs were installed over the baths at White Wells to enable year round use of the facilities, obviously with the approval of the landlord Squire Peter Middelton. Perhaps some of the debt due on the Wells House Hydropathic Company capital account in 1858 was by virtue of the improvements carried out. However the adjacent 'Charity Bath', operated by the 'Ilkley Bath Charitable Institution' did not have a roof installed over its bathing facilities. It remained open air.

Mr Butterfield retained his position as 'bathman' at White Wells and continued in his job.

The 'Corn Exchange', Leeds.

The 'Grand Hotel', Scarborough (photograph 2009). — Following family visits to Scarborough as a youngster, I always thought that despite its larger size, the 'Grand Hotel' and Wells House (or 'The College' as it was then) were strikingly similar. –Each enjoying elevated views and both having a vague similarity about them. As an adult I discovered this was no coincidence, due to the architect being one and the same: Cuthbert Brodrick.

When it opened in 1867, the 'Grand Hotel' was one of the largest in Europe. Interestingly it has four turrets symbolising the four seasons, twelve floors symbolising the twelve months, fifty two chimney pots symbolising the weeks, and three hundred and sixty five rooms symbolising the days of the year. By comparison, Wells House is quite small and makes no such symbolic statements.

In 1859, Charles Darwin visited Ilkley. (See the section about his visit later in this chapter.)

Wells House continued in use as a hydro during the remainder of the nineteenth century. Though toward the end of the century, when hydrotherapy was in decline, the privately run Ilkley Moor Golf Club nearby provided a convenient diversion that the guests of the Hydro could pay to use. Following the First World War Wells House was in use as a hotel. In 1938 it was renamed 'New Wells Hotel' by a Mr Raymond Smith whom had bought the property. At the start of the war the following year, Wells House was (as well as Ben Rhydding Hydro) requisitioned by the Government's 'Wool Control Board' as a finance, statistics and rationing centre. This lasted until 1946 when it was sold to a Captain Parlour, whom intended to use the building as a teacher training establishment for the Society of Jesuits. However this plan failed and the building stood empty for two years until another Government Department, the Ministry of Labour and National Service, took it over, to use as a hostel for European volunteer workers. In 1950 it was purchased by the West Riding County Council and in 1954 opened as the Ilkley College of Housecraft. More latterly becoming the Bradford and Ilkley Community College, until that too closed in 1999 and the building was sold off to private developers. Fortunately Wells House, unlike its rival Ben Rhydding Hydro, was not demolished but instead has since been extensively redeveloped on the interior to create luxury apartments. Though the former 'winter garden' extension which itself replaced the skating rink was demolished. The large glass atrium covering the central courtyard is a modern addition. The surrounding buildings from the college extensions were demolished during the redevelopment phase and replaced with housing designed to be 'in keeping' with the area.

Other Hydros in Ilkley

Other hydros opened in Ilkley during the mid-nineteenth century. These included: 'The Craiglands' (1859, – though the building was later considerably extended), at the junction of Cowpasture Road and Crossbeck Road, still a hotel today, including modern features and extensions alongside the Victorian additions; and 'The Troutbeck' (1863), on Crossbeck Road, in use as a hotel until the late 1980's when it was converted into a residential home. During the First World War, in 1915, the 'Troutbeck' housed a number of troops from the 'Bantams', the 17th Battalion Prince of Wales' Own West Yorkshire Regiment. Two hundred and eighty men were billeted at the hotel while the remainder of the troops from the battalion were billeted to some of the other smaller hydros in the town as well as to private residential addresses.

The Troutbeck's more famous claim to fame in modern folklore being that rock icon Jimi Hendrix played a gig at the 'Gyro Nightclub' in the hotel on 12th March 1967. He managed two songs before the venue was raided by the local constabulary following a complaint from a nearby resident about the number of parked cars in the vicinity of the venue. When the police entered the hotel there were subsequent concerns about overcrowding. (And dancing on a Sunday night, but given the number of people there this would hardly have been possible). The gig promptly ended, Hendrix then packed up with the rest of his entourage and departed, leaving behind him the ensuing riot which broke out amongst the disgruntled fans! (Hendrix stayed at the Crescent Hotel during his time in Ilkley.)

'The Grove' (1870), later renamed 'The Spa' (in 1885). This was partially converted into flats during the 1920's, and in 1929 a café opened in the building.

This was operated by Mrs Williamson who in late 1930 was given the tenancy of the moorland tea pavilion and White Wells. 'The Spa' was later completely converted into flats, and a café remained in the building until it was demolished in 1989. Though the replacement building at the junction of Back Parish Ghyll Road and The Grove, by the modern bandstand is also flats with shop units at ground level.

'Rockwood' (1871) a smaller hydro on Cowpasture Road, now also flats.

A relative latecomer was 'The Stoney Lea' (1883). Again a hotel in later years, the Stoney Lea was demolished in 1981 and replaced with housing. It stood at the junctions of Ben Rhydding Road, Wheatley Road and Cowpasture Road.

'Hillside Court' (photograph 2009). — In addition to staying at Wells House in 1859, Charles Darwin also lodged at 'Hillside House' during part of his time in Ilkley.

The building was owned by Marshall Hainsworth and rooms within were rented out to visitors to the town. Hainsworth died in 1897. Later the building became 'St Winifred's', a maternity hospital where a number of Ilkley residents (including myself) were born.

'St Winifred's' closed in 1971 (16th October) and the building became an annex of the Ilkley College until 1999, when this too closed. It is now residential apartments and is called 'Hillside Court.'

The Ilkley Civic Society placed a blue plaque on the building in 2009 outlining its connection to Charles Darwin.

Smaller hydros in Ilkley included 'West View House' (1859), 'Crossbeck' (1861), 'Sunset View' (1871), 'Marlborough House' (1878) and 'Moorlands' (1897).

Though by the 1880's, and certainly as late as 1897, hydropathy was in decline and no longer the highly fashionable pursuit it had been just a few years before.

In 1859 the Reverend Canon Jackson of Leeds, who was a subscriber to the 'Ilkley Bath Charitable Institution', visited Ilkley. He was apparently quite perturbed by the conditions some of the charity's recipients were living in, and decided that a hospital would be more appropriate instead. Despite obtaining charity dispensations from 'T' Charity 'Ole', the recipients were responsible for their own board and lodgings in the town. Their allowance was five shillings a week, and some chose to spend some of this on accommodation.

An appeal was established with assistance from the Reverend Snowden of Ilkley Parish Church and funds were raised for the 'Ilkley Hospital'. This opened to the south of the Grove in 1862 and all the costs had been paid off by 1864. The hospital could accommodate fifty patients. It was the first charity hospital to be established in Yorkshire. The building was extended in 1885 to provide accommodation for a further thirty patients. In 1885 its name was changed to the 'Ilkley Hospital and Convalescent Home'. In the early years of the twentieth century, during the First World War in 1917, it became a military hospital. After which the building was run as a convalescent hospital again for much of the twentieth century. More latterly the local authorities closed it and sold it to the private sector. Fortunately the building was saved and after extensive refurbishment is now owned and run by the 'Abbeyfield' group as a residential home called 'Grove House'.

Apart from the hydros, other hotels opened in the Ilkley area during the nineteenth century. Though not as hydropathic establishments. These included 'The Listers Arms' (1825). A coaching inn (originally called the 'New Inn', it quickly became known after its first tenant, John Lister) at the junction of Cunliffe Road and Skipton Road. It remained in use as a hotel until the early 1990's when in was converted into flats. 'The Crescent Hotel' opened circa 1860 on the corner of Brook Street and Leeds Road, still in use as a hotel despite a sudden and temporary closure in March 2009. (It reopened shortly afterwards. Though its long-term future remains to be seen.) There is a possibility that the Crescent may be partially converted into flats. 'The Royal' on Wells Road opened between 1867 and 1870 and was demolished in the early 1960's to be replaced with Wells Court Flats; and 'The Middelton' (1876) later renamed 'The Ilkley Moor', it was destroyed by fire in 1968 and was subsequently demolished to make way for housing. However the public bar survived and is known as the

'Grove House' (photograph 2009). — Opened in 1862 the 'Ilkley Bath Charitable Institution' hospital was the first purpose built charity hospital in Yorkshire.

During the First World War it was used as a military hospital treating injured Belgian troops. Following hostilities, it became a convalescence home for much of the remainder of the twentieth century. Under local authority ownership it served as a residential home, before being empty for a few years at the end of the 1990's. It was bought by the 'Abbeyfield Group' and after extensive renovations opened as 'Grove House' in the first decade of the twenty first century.

'Ilkley Moor Vaults' on Stockeld Road. Though colloquially this pub is known as 'The Taps'. A reference to its original function as the 'tap room' or public bar of the hotel.

The materials for many of these buildings was sourced locally from quarries on Ilkley Moor. Though Squires William and Peter Middelton were against large scale quarrying on the moor, and the activity remained relatively small scale until about 1885.

Just to the side of the Cow Rock is an area cut back into the rocks. This is now popular with climbers and is where a lot of stone was quarried. Another local legend claims this was the site of the 'Bull.' A larger rock than its companions the Cow and the Calf. However there is a lack of tangible evidence to support this theory. An item reported in the *'Ilkley Gazette'* in April 1947 alludes to another article dating from 1886 in a publication called *'Illustrated'* where it is claimed the 'Bull' rock was located further down the moor, between the Calf rock and Hangingstone Road. Again there is little further evidence to support this claim either. Nevertheless the former quarry to the east of the Cow rock is sometimes referred to as 'Bull Canyon' by the same generations that refer to White Wells as 'The Roman Baths', because it is where they were told the 'Bull' rock had been.

Behind and to the west of the Cow and Calf is the former Hangingstone Quarry. This was exploited from about 1885 and into the early twentieth century. It was opened following the death of Squire William Middelton, who had resisted large scale quarrying operations on the moor, as had his father and grandfather before him had also done. (In 1843 the then Squire Middleton had written to Hamer Stansfeld regarding concerns over the exploitation of stone from the moor for the construction of the Ben Rhydding Hydropathic establishment, built on land bought from the Bolling estate. There was a quarry below the present day 'Cow and Calf Hotel', adjacent to the land that would from 1885 become the Hydro's golf course. – An area still known colloquially as 'The Raikes' from its use as a sheep 'raike', or grazing area). During the Second World War the former Hangingstone quarry behind the Cow and Calf rocks was used as a firing range by the military. Bullet holes from this can be seen on the rock faces toward the eastern end of the quarry. There were a number of smaller quarries located at various sites around the moor too, at various times. For example one to the west in the valley of Spicey Ghyll off the Keighley Gate road; and a smaller one further up the moor to the south of White Wells. This small quarry, now long disused, forms a curious crater near to the trees on the skyline up the moor behind White Wells, and is allegedly the location of some UFO sightings in the area. This former quarry is the most likely source of stone for the construction of both the original bath to the rear of the present buildings and White Wells itself. Though some of the stone used for White Wells could have been 'recycled' from the original bath building when Robert Dale constructed the current baths in 1791. Possibly including the stone block in front of the bathhouse that may have been surplus to requirements and left as a decorative feature.

As 'hydropathy' reached its peak, a local furniture maker, Mr Robinson, promoted the sale of the 'Ilkley Couch', an adjustable reclining bed, not too far removed from what would perhaps be familiar as a garden sun-lounger, though made of wood rather than the ubiquitous white plastic used today! Such furniture was very popular with the clientele of the hydros, and the 'Ilkley Couch' was available to interested individuals by private sale too.

White Wells and the Development of Hydropathy

During the middle and the latter half of the nineteenth century the popularity of White Wells slowly declined somewhat, in favour of the large hydropathic establishments that had been built to attract the wealthier middle classes.

Although White Wells came under the auspices of Wells House between 1856 and 1872, it would seem that many of the affluent middle class patients at Wells House by degree did not want to hike or ride a donkey half way up Ilkley Moor in order to undress in austere surroundings and have a cold bath, when bathing could be done in the relative comfort of the hydro in which they were staying. (Perhaps just as the Roman soldiers hundreds of years before would have been inclined to do in their fort, long before the building of any moorland baths.) Inevitably after 1872 when the Ilkley Local Board took over the lease of White Wells, the popularity of bathing at the building declined. Interestingly though, brisk walks in the fresh air of the moor were encouraged as part of the wider package of treatments involved in the 'Ilkley Cure', and often prescribed to the patients of the hydros in addition to the various water treatments on offer as well. It is likely that during the years that Wells House held the lease of White Wells, the Doctors would have been keen to promote the moorland spa, not least because roofs had been installed over the two baths enabling year round use of the facilities there. (But not over the Charity Bath which was operated by the 'Ilkley Bath Charity' and not Wells House.)

There is a suggestion that prior to the roofs being installed at White Wells bathing was seasonal. The Charity Bath's 'season' ran from April to November, and it is likely that bathing at White Wells was the same. There is also no information regarding whether during exceptionally cold winters, the water contained within the baths froze up, or whether the baths were drained. Certainly the addition of roofs would have enabled year round bathing. Without them bathing would have been a particularly harsh experience for any patients undergoing treatment during the winter! The water comes from an underground source, so flows even when the temperature is below freezing point on the surface, and the addition of roofs provide additional insulation for any water contained within the baths. Certainly we have had no experience of the baths freezing up during the coldest of winter months, even when there has been frost and snow on the ground outside. – And there are no reports of this even from the harshest of winters, notably 1933, 1947 and 1963.

Charles Darwin Takes the Waters:

'Hydropathy' enjoyed a wide variety of followers. In 1859 at the time of the publication of his seminal work *'On The Origin of Species'* the eminent scientist Charles Darwin (1809-1882) was staying in Ilkley.

Darwin had suffered from bouts of various ailments after his return from the *"Beagle"* expedition (1831-1836). Though not all were necessarily directly as a result of it. From 1837 and particularly 1838 to 1840 these became worse. He suffered headaches and migraines, nausea, vomiting, exhaustion, insomnia, indigestion, palpitations, mental depression, swellings and eczema. These symptoms continued throughout the 1840's and in 1849 Darwin went to stay at Malvern, where he became a frequent visitor, partaking in Dr Gully's 'Water Cure'. A decade later, at the age of fifty, Darwin came to Ilkley. (His daughter Annie had sadly died during a visit to Malvern, and seeking a change of venue, he chose Ilkley instead.)

For two weeks between the beginning and middle of October 1859 Darwin stayed at 'Wells House Hydropathic Establishment'. In the middle of October he moved lodgings to 'North View House', where he was joined by his wife. This building still survives, renamed 'Hillside Court', it is to be found at the junctions of Crossbeck Road and Wells Road, near the cattle grid at the edge of the moor, and overlooking 'Darwin Gardens Millennium Green.'

The building was owned by Marshall Hainsworth and known variously as 'Hainsworth's Lodgings,' 'Wells Terrace', 'North View House', and 'Hillside House'. During the twentieth century the building was in use as 'St Winifred's', a maternity hospital, (until 1971) where a number of Ilkley residents were born. From the early 1970's until 1999 it formed the 'Hillside House' annex of the Bradford and Ilkley Community College, before being transformed into apartments.

(The nearby paddling pool was created from the former 'Hainsworth's pond' in the mid 1920's.)

It is believed that during his stay in Ilkley Darwin made the journey up to White Wells in order to 'Take the Waters'. Though there is no direct evidence to either confirm or refute this claim, it is reasonable to suggest that he probably did visit the property at sometime during his two months stay in Ilkley. Wells House had recently taken the lease of White Wells (in 1856) and roofs had been installed over the bathhouses to enable the year round use of its facilities. In the autumn of 1859 when Darwin was in Ilkley, the doctors at Wells House would likely have been keen for their clientele to use the newly improved facilities that were on offer at White Wells. (Indeed the previous year, in 1858, the directors of Wells House had opted to pay off a debt due on the capital account instead of paying a dividend to the shareholders. Debts possibly incurred due to the various 'improvement' work undertaken by the company with the permission of the landlord Squire Peter Middelton?) – And for clientele staying in nearby lodgings instead of on the main Wells House site, as Darwin was for some of the time he spent in the town, White Wells would have been a likely venue for some of the treatments the patients had to endure. Although Charles Darwin didn't describe his own treatment in great detail, he did give a general overview in various letters sent during his stay in the town. He wrote of his belief that:

> *"The Water Cure has done me much good; but I fell down on Sunday morning and sprained my ancle (sic), and have not been able to walk since and this has greatly interfered with the treatment.*
>
> *It is a curious life here: we sit down 60 or 70 to our meals, and in the evening, there is either singing, or acting...or proverbs, etc. I have got amongst a nice set, and get on very comfortably and idly. The newspaper, a little novel-reading, the Baths and loitering kills the day in a very wholesome manner. Did you ever hear of the American game of Billiards...?"*

In another letter he wrote that his fall apparently caused:

> *"a series of calamities; First a sprained ancle (sic), and then badly swollen whole leg and face, much rash and fearful succession of boils...4 or 5 at once...We have been here above 6 week, and I feel worse than when I came, so that I am not in a cheerful state of mind."*

When his wife returned home to 'Down House' in Kent in November 1859 Darwin left 'North View House' and returned to Wells House under the care of Dr Adam Smith. Whom Darwin described as being *"sensible, but he is a Homeopathist"*. He also gave Darwin the impression that he *"cared very much for the fee and very little for the patient"*.

Charles Darwin left Ilkley on 7th December 1859, just as the storm of controversy surrounding his newly published theory of evolution was breaking.

Darwin's visit to the town is examined in the book *'Darwin in Ilkley'* by Mike Dixon and Gregory Radick, published in 2009.

The Development of Ilkley

While Darwin pondered the evolution of the natural world (and by the previous account pondered his various ailments as well) Ilkley was evolving

THE ESTABLISHMENT OF THE 'HYDROS' & THE EXPANSION OF ILKLEY

too. Transport links into the town took a major step forward when the railway arrived in 1865 connecting Ilkley to Otley, Leeds and Bradford. (Though the route to and from Bradford was via Apperley Bridge until 1877, when the line extension via Shipley to Guiseley was opened.)

The railway line west of Ilkley, to Skipton via Addingham, Bolton Abbey and Embsay opened in 1888. (As far as Embsay in May 1888, and finally to Skipton by October of that year.) Ilkley railway station was extended to the north to accommodate platforms three and four, and the large retaining wall along railway road was built. The line up to Skipton and the one down Wharfedale to Otley remained in use until the 1960's when they fell victim to the infamous 'Beeching Report'.

In 1867 Squire William Middelton held the first in a series of auctions selling off numerous plots of land in and around Ilkley. Over the course of the following decade the land sales resulted in the rapid expansion of the town. The old thatched cottages on the west side of Brook Street, Skipton Road and Green lane (which became the Grove), were demolished and replaced with many of the buildings that are familiar to us today. Housing provision also expanded and the terraced streets around Wellington Road were built at this time too.

William Middelton's son Charles became the Squire in 1885 and immediately consented to the construction of Hangingstone Quarry behind the Cow and Calf rocks. Though just a few years later, in 1892, Charles Middelton sold the remainder of his estates in the Ilkley area completely, including 'Myddelton Lodge', and he left the town.

In 1869 the Ilkley Local Board was formed to administer local affairs, and immediately expressed an interest in obtaining Squire Middelton's lease of White Wells. (The local water company were keen to sell its assets to the ILB, which was done after some negotiation) and in 1872 the ILB got its wish and took over the lease of White Wells from Wells House Hydro too. Though the agreement concerning White Wells included the caveat that the Board could not interfere with Wells House's use of the spring there. Dr Harrison paid the Local Board the sum of £30 for half a year's rent on the 'Old Wells' in 1872.

The local board was also responsible for a number of public works in the Ilkley area. Some of these works included the collection of water from springs all over the moors.

If out walking on the moorland paths, you may come across old iron pipes leading to and from now redundant water collection tanks. You may also find cube shaped stones bearing the letters ILB WW on their flat tops. A number of these stones were collected up from the surrounding moor and brought to White Wells when the cobbles were laid in the 1990's. They were set at the edge

Stone markers outside White Wells. — The initials "ILB – WW" stand for "Ilkley Local Board Water Works." They date from the 1870's onwards and were originally placed at various locations on the moor. (Indeed some still are). They were used to indicate the Local Board's network of pipes associated with the various water improvement schemes undertaken by the Board. (Called the 'Maclandsborough Plan', named after the surveyor who devised the scheme.) Some of the redundant stones were collected together and placed outside White Wells by Bradford Council's Countryside Service when the cobbles were laid in the 1990's. The Local Board's moorland water collection schemes were surpassed with larger scale improvements to the water supply in the 20th Century to accommodate the expanding population of the town, and the marker stones abandoned.

of the cobbles, and can be seen at the top of the steps from the access track and near the tops of the other paths leading up to the building. The lettering on top of these stones means 'Ilkley Local Board – Water Works'. They were originally used as marker stones tracing the routes of the Local Board's pipe network on the moor.

Included in the water improvement schemes during the 1870's and 1880's (called the 'Maclandsborough Plan' after the engineer employed by the Local Board to carry out the work) was that done in the area where the access track crosses the stream at Willy Hall's Spout waterfall. Willy Hall's Spout had an estimated flow of 23,714 gallons (102,000 litres) per day in the survey of local streams, so was exploited by the Local Board. As a result the access track to

White Wells was laid in its current position. Prior to this the previous track to White Wells followed a line to the east of Willy Hall's Spout, crossing the stream at the bottom of the steep hill down the moor. There is a wide bridge in this area today.

Some of the pipes at Willy Hall's Spout were exposed following the flood of 1900, necessitating the subsequent repairs that led to the construction of the retaining wall and cobbled area still in existence today. (See the following chapter: Out of the Nineteenth and into the Twentieth Century.)

In 1873 the Local Board decided to use water from White Wells to supply houses at the moor edge. The water supply to White Wells itself was diminished by this, leading to complaints directed toward the board in the local press. It was alleged that visitors to White Wells were experiencing difficulty in using the drinking fountain to the rear of the premises. A delegation was sent from the Board to investigate this claim, and returned the information that a cup could still be filled in five seconds from the fountain, which was deemed adequate, so no further action would be taken to restore the water to its former rate of flow. Furthermore it was observed that although the reduced flow had an affect on the baths, the reduced numbers requiring bathing at White Wells did not necessitate any further action by the Board either.

Clearly we can deduce from this that the bath in the eastern side of White Wells experienced a decline in usage at this time (though it didn't become entirely redundant) in favour of the other bath in the western side of the building that remained in use up until the 1920's.

The Tarn toward the bottom of the moor, behind the 'Craiglands', was also built during the 1870's. The area, formerly a boggy patch of marsh with a pond known as Craig Dam, lent its name to the replacement Craig Tarn. As well as providing a pleasant area to stroll around or sit beside, the principle purpose of the tarn was to augment the water supply to the mill buildings which used to operate in Mill Ghyll (now a pleasant wooded area between Wells Walk and Wells promenade in the town.) In the late nineteenth and early twentieth centuries the Ilkley Tarn Band was a popular attraction at the venue, entertaining visitors at weekends during the summer months. (Until the bandstand in West View Park became a feature in the early twentieth century.)

Concern about possible flooding from the tarn was raised by the Dobson brothers, who ran the 'Craiglands Hydro'. Their criticisms of the construction methods employed on the tarn were proved correct in 1874 when the banking leaked causing flooding to the 'Craiglands', its gardens and the croquet lawn.

During the course of the water improvement schemes and the various excavations that were being made, the original pre 1791 'Well House' was discovered at the top of the hill near the trees behind White Wells. (This was 'discovered' again in 1929, during further water improvement schemes.)

The Old Reservoir

Further projects undertaken by the Local Board included acting on a recommendation to enlarge the 'Old Reservoir' housed in the curious looking building at the edge of the moor. This was done in 1873, following the Local Board's approach to the landowner, Squire William Middelton, to utilise stone and clay from on the moor to be used in the required work. The original 'Old Reservoir' had been built during the early 1850's, following an act of Parliament enabling the formation of water companies, and the development of a supply infrastructure in towns and villages across the country. By the 1870's, the 'Old Reservoir' was fast becoming inadequate to meet the needs of the expanding township of Ilkley, so various 'improvements' were necessary to augment the supply.

Other reservoirs were constructed, at Hill Top and Weary Hill, close to the Keighley Gate Road, further up the moor to the south west of the 'Old Reservoir', though these were underground reservoirs, and therefore not housed in elaborate structures as the 'Old Reservoir' had been. (A site to the east of White Wells, referred to as 'Sylvester's Peat Hole', was also considered for the construction on a reservoir, but was ultimately rejected. It is likely that this area subsequently became developed as the 'upper tarn' instead.)

By 1878, the roof of the 'Old Reservoir' was in a poor state of repair, and it was recommended that it be removed. It was wondered by members of the Board if the reservoir could be arched over instead, as the other new reservoirs had been, but it was decided instead to remove the roof for the time being.

A decade later, in 1888, the Local Board decided to re-roof the 'Old Reservoir' using concrete and iron girders. This followed a lengthy debate about the merits of selling off the stone from the building in order to pay for a concrete covering at ground level. The stone structure around the 'old reservoir' itself being largely ornamental rather than functional. Eventually it was resolved to retain the building, and concrete over the reservoir inside instead. Leaving the (unrealised) option of using the building as a shelter or a 'reading room' for visitors to the moor. The building's roof was subsequently replaced in 1889.

In 1883 a drinking fountain and a flagstaff was constructed on a cobbled area on the rise to the west of the bridge and to the south of the 'Old Reservoir' on the edge of the moor. Money for this project was put forward by a Mr Crawley of Ilkley who wanted to provide facilities for those too infirm to make the journey up the moor to White Wells in order to drink the water. 'Crawley's

THE ESTABLISHMENT OF THE 'HYDROS' & THE EXPANSION OF ILKLEY

The Lower Tarn. — The tarn was constructed in the 1870's on a marshy area of ground called Craig Dam to improve the flow of water to the buildings in Mill Ghyll in the town. (There was an earlier mill pond on Wells Road, roughly below the present day 'College Drive'/'Ivy Court' access road, on land now partly occupied by two late Victorian houses.)

A decorative fountain at the tarn, fed by gravity from a supply higher up the moor, spouted water high into the air. This was later removed though the island was allowed to remain, providing a home to ducks and other waterfowl.

Fountain' as it was known, tapped into the 'original' spring at White Wells, and was piped down the moor a distance of about three hundred metres in tin lined lead pipes, across the stream by means of the bridge, and to the fountain.

On Saturday 8th September 1883 there was an impressive opening ceremony for the fountain, which ended with three cheers and the singing of the National Anthem.

The area where the fountain stood was buried under a large mound of earth when the area was landscaped in 1970 following the construction of the underground reservoir nearby. The flagstaff had disappeared many years earlier. (The underground reservoir remains in use, and is beneath the enclosed area adjacent to the east of 'Old Reservoir' building.)

The 'Old Reservoir' continued in use for the remainder of the nineteenth century, playing its part in the supply of water for the town's growing requirements. Panorama reservoir was completed in the early twentieth century, and various other water improvement works were also carried out.

In 1935 the 'Old Reservoir' was converted into a filter station. It was reported that the level of the roof was raised three feet and four large automatic 'Bell's Filters' were installed on a reinforced concrete floor covering the old reservoir itself. The filters were capable of dealing with a flow of 360,000 gallons of water in sixteen hours.

In 2007 'Yorkshire Water', the owners of the filter station, sold it off to the private sector, and after some speculation as to whether it would become a 'visitor centre', (a proposal by some members of the 'Ilkley Parish Council') it was converted into a residential property instead.

Following the conversion it went on the market and was eventually sold in late 2008, and has subsequently been renamed 'The Old Pumphouse'.

'On Ilkla Moor Baht 'At'

The song that is synonymous with Ilkley, and indeed Yorkshire (often referred to as 'Yorkshire's National Anthem'), has its origins in the late nineteenth century.

There has been speculation as to the identity of Mary Jane, the songs only named character, and where her grave on Ilkley Moor might be found. – Although Mary Jane herself doesn't actually die in the song!

It is believed that the song originated with a church outing, possibly from Halifax, in the eighteen seventies or eighteen eighties. The group had perhaps arrived by train in Shipley or Bingley and then walked over the moor to Ilkley via 'Dick Hudsons' pub. It is a matter of speculation as to whether or not the group visited White Wells and/or the Cow and Calf rocks on their route. It seems that at some point along the walk, two members of the group, either by accident or by design, had become separated from the others. When at last they rejoined the group, much jocularity and teasing occurred. With the result that a song was improvised concerning the assumed courting activities of the young lad and lass concerned. The lyrics may have been refined during a stop at 'Dick Hudson's' pub on the way back. A very popular venue with walkers for ham and egg teas in the Victorian era. (– And indeed it still is a popular venue for walkers today.) Though perhaps being Methodists, only light refreshments may have been taken!

The song was perhaps further refined later, and used in light entertainment and musical evenings at church social gatherings, from where it spread and became more widely known.

The tune used for the song is called 'Cranbrook' by Thomas Clark (1775-1859), a shoemaker in Canterbury in the late eighteenth and early nineteenth centuries. Clark apparently enjoyed music more than making shoes, and he also enjoyed conducting as well. A pursuit he often followed in the market town of Cranbrook in Kent. The school master there, John Francis, had taught Clark to read and write (at the age of twenty eight), and it is speculated that the tune of 'Cranbrook' was composed in his gratitude to John Francis in circa 1803.

Although the tune had been written at the beginning of the nineteenth century, it was still a popular hymn tune in the late nineteenth century. A number of (particularly Methodist) hymns had been set to the tune. In fact 'Cranbrook' was also the tune of the Christmas carol 'While shepherds watched their flocks by night', which was particularly popular in Yorkshire.

Thomas Clark died in 1859, and didn't hear his tune with the lyrics of 'On Ilkla Moor baht 'At'.

The song tells the story of how, if you venture onto Ilkley Moor to pursue your courting, and you choose not to wear a hat, you will be 'bound to catch your death of cold.' Then your friends will have to bury you there, then worms will eat your remains, followed by the worms being eaten by ducks. (Suggesting that on their hike over the moors the party perhaps visited the tarn, and noted the various waterfowl.) Next the ducks will be eaten by your friends, at the top of the food chain, who will in turn have indirectly eaten you! – The song ends with the suggestion that they will have then "got their own back" on you. Altogether a good example of Yorkshire humour!

The song has evolved over the years (the last verse about "Getting us own back" being a later addition) and the opening verse has evolved from the original "Weer wor t' ban when I saw thee?" ("Where were you going when I saw you?"), into "Weer 'as t' bin sin' I saw thee?" ("Where have you been since I saw you?"). This modification occurring around the time of the Second World War.

The nuances of dialect, the variants of the song and the in depth history of it are explored in great detail in the book '*On Ilkla Mooar Baht 'At the Story of the Song*' by Arnold Kellett, published in 1998.

CHAPTER SIX:
OUT OF THE NINETEENTH AND INTO THE TWENTIETH CENTURY

In 1885 Mr Butterfield was charging sixpence for visitors to White Wells wishing to use the bathing facilities.

As the popularity of 'taking the waters' at White Wells waned and the number of bathers dropped, it was suggested that the property be demolished in favour of a terrace and refreshment rooms. Such plans were suggested as early as 1876, and repeated again over the next few years. The suggestions were still being put forward in 1887 for such a scheme to commemorate the Golden Jubilee of Queen Victoria and a decade later for the Diamond Jubilee in 1897.

There was a public outcry against such proposals, including from one of Ilkley's most celebrated former residents of the time, the Reverend Dr Robert Collyer. Collyer was born in Keighley in 1823 and grew up in Blubberhouses. He became an apprentice blacksmith in Ilkley, and later wrote a book with J.H. Turner, published in 1885, entitled *'Ilkley Ancient & Modern'* (generally regarded as **the** prime reference book for researchers of local history in the Ilkley area.)

Collyer emigrated to the United States of America where he continued his blacksmith skills in the manufacturing of hardware, and was also a lay-preacher. He later became a full time Wesleyan Minister. (He returned to visit Ilkley in 1907, for the official opening of the library. He died in America in 1912.)

In about 1892 he wrote fondly of his recollections of using the baths at White Wells:

> *"The time was well within my memory when the old White Wells held first place, and many a plunge I have had in them on a summer Sunday morning before breakfast, but the new time has brought the moors and uplands to the front, and the old wells, as we say, 'have taken a back seat.' Thousands come who do not care for the baths. They want to breathe the fresh air and wander far and wide, to drink in the beauty of the grand landscape, about to me the loveliest in the world."*

Dr Collyer hoped that White Wells, because of its age, should be allowed to remain. Fortunately wisdom prevailed and White Wells survived.

Skating on the Tarn. — Skating was for a long time a popular activity during the winter months. The local press enthusiastically reported on it, and the results of hapless individuals venturing onto thin ice and ending up knee deep in cold water! –Quite a contrast to the attitudes of today. A succession of mild winters has made the possibility of skating on the tarn more remote, and an obsession with 'Health and Safety' has made it quite unattractive. In 1996 a local police officer discouraged the activity, and described the tarn in winter as a "Death trap". However there are no records of skating on the tarn resulting in any fatal consequences. (The body of a fifty six year old Ilkley man, Mr Wallace Hudson, was found in the tarn on 8th December 1938, though this was as a result of suicide, not an accident.)

In 1909 a roller-skating rink was opened in Ilkley at the junction of Cunliffe Road and South Hawksworth Street. This provided a venue for enthusiasts to skate during the summer months as well as on the ice at the tarn in winter. The rink reportedly had a capacity for seven hundred skaters and a thousand spectators. Its popularity waned relatively quickly though, and the building was later demolished to make way for the 'West Yorkshire Road Car Co' bus depot. (This too was demolished and the site redeveloped again in the early 1990's into the 'Moors Centre' retail units.)

White Wells had to diversify in order to survive. There was also a 'shop' operating from the premises, which supplied visitors with refreshments. However despite the calls for its demolition repairs had been made to the property (£100 was spent on it in the year up to March 1889) and at a special meeting of the Waterworks Committee held in July, it was reported that:

'It was also recommended that the floors of the plunge and douche baths at the White Wells be repaired; that pen rails be fixed; that the outside wall of the shower bath be cemented; that a stove be fixed in the shop; that all woodwork be

painted; that the path in front of the old wells be repaired; that the walls of the Hospital bath be repaired.'

To what extent this work was carried out is unclear. Certainly there is evidence that railings of some sort were once fitted inside the bath in the east end of White Wells. The mounting holes can still be seen, along with remnants of iron from which such railings would have been made. Though any other repairs which may have been carried out around this time were somewhat short lived, because by the turn of the century, the bath had become overgrown with ferns. Although it was still occasionally used as a shower bath.

In August 1889, a report of the minutes of the Waterworks Committee meeting tells us that amongst the recommendations were that a notice be fixed to the drinking fountain at White Wells to inform the public that the water is free (seemingly to thwart Mr Butterfield's attempts to charge visitors to drink it); and that photographic studios be supplied and charged the rateable value. Though

The Tarn in summer. — Although the fountain had been disconnected and the island had become overgrown, the tarn remained a popular attraction year round. There were various entertainments held for visitors, and toward the eastern end a stone shelter was built, though this was later replaced with the wooden 'Cuckoo Hut' shelter about half way along the northern side of the tarn. The small island toward the eastern end of the tarn was later removed, and in August 1919 the IUDC instructed the surveyor to remove an 'old shelter' which stood at the extreme western end of the tarn.

The Lower Tarn today (photograph 2009). — The pathway leading to the tarn and shelter from Wells Road was illuminated in 1931 with the installation of street lamps. This proved especially popular during the winter months, being appreciated by skaters, allowing them to continue their activities into the evening.

The lamps along the road to and around the tarn were disconnected for a number of years, but were restored to use in May 2007. In 2009 the modern lamps were replaced with 'traditional' glass lanterns atop instead, complementing the other work that had been undertaken at the tarn by Bradford Council. This involved a considerable amount of clearance work, carried out in late 2008/early 2009 to improve the area around the tarn, though there are more trees today than a century ago. The cuckoo hut shelter, also suffering from general wear and tear (and vandalism) was repaired too.

it seems that the latter never materialised, or at least if so, it was 'unofficial' and very short lived. Formal permission for it was not subsequently granted.

Another grandiose scheme being considered by the Local Board at the time was for a narrow guage tramway of 3ft 6in to be constructed up from the town for the benefit of visitors wishing to ascend the heights of the moor. It was to have been a two-stage affair. The first leg of the journey, it was proposed, would have been underground from the railway station to the top of Wells Road, to a site adjacent to Mr Hainsworth's property. The next stage departing from roughly where the paddling pool is now sited, heading up the moor, passing to

The bandstand in West View Park. — The bandstand was built in 1904 in the small area of parkland at the top of Wells Road called 'West View Park'. Although various musical performances continued at the tarn, the bandstand proved to be a popular alternative, ultimately replacing the tarn as a venue for light entertainments. For the comfort of visitors to the bandstand, a shelter was later built over the row of seats in the left centre of the photograph.

The bandstand remained popular up until the Second World War, but after a number of years of neglect it fell into a state of disrepair and was demolished at the beginning of 1948. (See Chapter Eight: The Second World War and the Post War Years.) The nearby shelter survived until the mid 1950's before it too was demolished.

In the late 1990's West View Park was transformed into 'Darwin Gardens Millennium Green', in recognition of Charles Darwin's visit to Ilkley in 1859 and provides a popular attraction for both locals and visitors. The bandstand was on the site now occupied by the 'Darwin Gardens' car park.

the west of White Wells, and up to the top of the moor. The estimated cost of the project was £2528, for the 'smaller' scheme, that being the section from the edge of the moor to the top, and 'nearly double' for the larger scheme from the railway station to the top of Wells Road.

There was a polarised opinion within the town about the desirability of the tramway development, and clearly the 'No' camp won the day. Though the suggestion for such a scheme was still in the public mind into the early years of the twentieth century.

During the 1890's the Ilkley Local Board was replaced with the Ilkley Urban District Council (1894). As the century moved toward its close, the council, instead of demolishing White Wells, decided to carry out alterations inside the property. These incurred a rent increase of £3 per annum to the tenant. –A considerable sum in 1897.

Refreshments had been made available to visitors even before the alterations. This continued afterwards as a means of securing an income and to enable the tenant, Mr Butterfield, to pay the increase in rent and justify the improvements that had been carried out. Boards on the outside of the building announced that parties could be catered for and that items of the finest quality were available.

The former Charity Bath building to the west of White Wells was in a dilapidated state and the drinking fountain in its enclosure had been dry for quite some time. The bath that was inside the building had not been in regular use for a number of years either, since the Ilkley Hospital had replaced the former Ilkley Bath Charity in the 1860's. There was a privy at the far western end of the enclosure. (Visitors still wishing to use the somewhat derelict Charity Bath up until the alterations and improvements of the early 20th century were encouraged to use the bath still operating inside White Wells instead.)

Mr Cooper's 'Pierrot's' stage at the Tarn. — During the early years of the twentieth century, 'Pierrot' performances were a regular attraction for visitors to the tarn, though a purpose built stage and adjacent dressing room caused considerable controversy. These were subsequently removed following the 1905 'season'. The bandstand that had opened in 1904 in West View Park proved an increasingly popular venue for musical performances. However Mrs Pankhurst of the suffrage movement addressed a large crowd at the tarn on the evening of 8th June 1908.

White Wells circa 1897. — As the popularity of 'taking the waters' waned, White Wells adapted to meet the changing demands of visitors. Bathing was still available for those who wished to indulge in it, while for the growing numbers of casual visitors, refreshments were available too. In 1889 it was proposed to open a photographic studio at White Wells. However very little seems to have come of this idea. The Local Board rejected the suggestion.

The flagpole on the east gable of White Wells seems to have appeared in the 1890's, most likely for the celebrations surrounding Queen Victoria's Diamond Jubilee, which occurred in 1897. The town was decorated with many flags and bunting outside businesses and shops, and a great celebration was enjoyed by the local population. It is possible that a flag would also have been flown from the pole on the east gable of White Wells too, and the pole retained for future use.

In 1897 a suggestion was made to build hut shelters on the moors. This was considered a good idea, and fitting as a memorial of Queen Victoria's Diamond Jubilee. The design of the shelters on the coast at Saltburn-by-the-Sea were looked at, and a few years later, early in the twentieth century, (after repeated calls for them) similar shelters were subsequently constructed, firstly at the tarn and later overlooking Hainsworth's pond on the edge of the moor at the top of Wells Road. There are still shelters at these two sites today, however they are replacements for the originals. Repeated vandalism has meant that the glass in them has been long removed. The thatch was replaced by wooden shingles in 1953, and the shelter overlooking the paddling pool (formerly the area known as Hainsworth's pond until the mid 1920's when the paddling pool was built) was destroyed by fire as a result of vandalism in the early 1990's. It was rebuilt in 1995.

The 'Great Flood' of 1900

In the one hundredth year of the nineteenth century, one of the biggest disasters to hit Ilkley occurred.

Thursday 12th July 1900 had been preceded by two days of 'excessive heat'. The weather was building for a storm. The ferocity of which ensured the date became forever infamous in the history of the town as the day of 'The Flood.'

In the early afternoon there was a cloudburst above the moor and during the course of the following two hours this resulted in torrents of water flowing over the hardened ground. The water rushed into the centre of town, and it quickly overwhelmed the stream courses and the capacity of the drainage network. Rocks and boulders were washed into the town, culverts burst, livestock and poultry killed and property damaged. One estimate suggested that £100,000 worth of damage had been caused in a single afternoon.

It was not without tragedy either. A wall and shed collapsed at the rear of coachbuilder Mr Robert Brogden's premises on Chapel Lane. This resulted in damage to the foundations of his workshop, which as a consequence collapsed. His second son, twenty eight year old Alfred, who was upstairs in the property

White Wells in the 1900's. — The sign on the east gable reads: *"White Wells café. Afternoon teas & Parties catered for. Sweets and chocolate of the best quality."*

Mr Brumfitt's 'view station' direction marker post (installed in 1903) can be seen outside the porch, to the centre right of the photograph.

at the time was killed. Mr Brogden's two other sons and a blacksmith managed to escape in time. Mr Brogden himself was out of town.

Ironically, Mr Brogden had been badly affected by a previous flood in 1872, which had resulted in significant damage to his workshop in a different area of the town.

Considering the scale of the 1900 flood and the damage that it wrought, it is perhaps surprising there were not more fatalities.

White Wells was not mentioned in the reports of the flood, so it is assumed that the building remained unaffected, despite the large volumes of water rushing down every part of the moor. However other parts of the moor were affected by the flood. The bridge across Backstone Beck, to the east of the tarn, was destroyed, and the cart track up the moor to White Wells was also damaged. The area where the track crosses Willy Hall's Spout stream was washed away, exposing some of the waterworks which had been undertaken in the 1870's and 1880's.

This damage wasn't repaired until early into the twentieth century.

Into the Twentieth Century

The Victorian era ended on 22nd January 1901 with the death of the Queen at Osbourne House.

Despite national mourning and certain trepidation about the passing of the Victorian era and considerable apprehension about the new King, (he had been involved in a number of social 'scandals' in the late nineteenth century, as the then Prince of Wales, and he was almost sixty when he became King) there was an air of optimism for both the new Edwardian era, and the new century. The King did not hide the fact that quite unlike his somewhat reclusive mother, he enjoyed a lively social life and because of this was more in the public view.

The spirit of the times had changed. The public at large were embracing different attitudes to those prevalent only a generation before.

By contrast the 'science' of hydropathy, which was rooted firmly in the nineteenth century was increasingly being considered 'old fashioned'. Though it had actually been in a steady decline for about twenty years. (The King himself however, still travelled annually to Marienbad in Bohemia to 'take the waters'.)

In Ilkley damage caused by the 'Great Flood' was gradually repaired over the course of a few years. At the end of 1901, it was reported that the surveyor had examined the moor near Willy Hall's Spout, where the waterworks had been undermined and exposed by the flood, and *'considered it advisable that a rough* wall should be built, with boulders from the beck course, then filled up at the back with soil in order to protect the pipes, and restore the path at this point.'

Similarly, in March 1902 it was decided to replace the bridge over Backstone Beck that also had been destroyed in the flood.

Again there were calls to 'improve' White Wells. A gentleman called Mr A.H.Bampton was in favour of change in Ilkley, and wrote to the local newspaper that he thought *"it is incomprehensible that an old Roman bathing station should be so ill equipped with primitive baths."*

While the *'Ilkley Gazette'* itself quoted from another publication, the *'Yorkshire Daily Observer'* of Tuesday 11th July 1902, in which it had appeared under the heading

"Killing the Goose that lays the Golden Egg":

"Another energetic brain has evolved the brilliant idea of pulling down the old whitewashed cottage which has served from time immemorial as the old wells, and building on its site a series of modern baths. A bathhouse in the valley would obviously be a convenience, but the advantage of placing the establishment on the site of the old wells is that, by removing one more landmark, it would emphasise the pace of Ilkley's rise into the ranks of the Nouveau Riche."

It was decided to retain White Wells however, and to make the necessary repairs to the moor damaged in the flood, but in the case of the Willy Hall's Spout improvements, not everyone approved.

In January 1903 a letter appeared in the *'Ilkley Gazette'* about it from a correspondent calling himself 'Moorlander'. This was a lengthy letter, and regarding Willy Hall's Spout 'Moorlander' wrote:

"Six months ago at an immediate point between the Keighley Road and White Wells was a pretty ravine filled with ferns and large boulders and a cascade from the top called 'Willy Hall's Spout'. Now it is destroyed. The rocks have been cut up, and a great stone straight wall with a flat top is created, a most unsightly piece of work, and none of us know why."

At the time it was thought by some that the ulterior motive of the IUDC was to construct a 'drive' from the Keighley Gate Road to White Wells, and perhaps even beyond and across the moor. The Council received a petition of two hundred and fifteen signatures against this idea. However, the Council replied that it only intended to spend £84 in making the road five yards wide following the line of the existing track to White Wells, in order that invalids and others using bath chairs and light vehicles could reach White Wells, and that it was not the intention of the Council to *"Deface the Moor in any manner."*

White Wells prior to improvements. — Although photographs from the late nineteenth century and the early twentieth century show the rear of the building to be similar to its appearance today, a closer look reveals subtle changes that happened gradually around that time.

The two downstairs rear windows in the central section, smaller than the ones today, have shutters announcing "Teas". There are narrow steps up to the back door, but there is no window to the left of it. The supply pipe feeding the showers above the plunge bath can be seen, elevated over the drinking fountain and there is a flagpole on the eastern gable.

An earlier rear window on the upper floor had already been blocked up when this photograph was taken. (It remains blocked up today, though its outline can still be seen to the left of the bathroom window.)

Also in 1903 a gentleman called Mr George Brumfitt proposed to the Ilkley Urban District Council to erect a 'Viewstation' on the moor, in the vicinity of White Wells. His proposal was considered and approved by the Council: *"Viewstation near the White Wells, from where visitors may obtain printed cards containing a description of all objects of interest which can be seen from there approved, and that his (Mr Brumfitt's) offer to defray the cost of erecting the "station" and supplying the necessary cards for 12 months be accepted conditionally that the position of the station be subject to the approval of the Chairman of this Committee and the Surveyor".*

Mr Benson of the Council remarked that they were indebted to Mr Brumfitt for the idea, and that Mr Brumfitt was to provide the necessary apparatus for a year. The 'viewstation' itself was a post and it was decided to erect it *"in no place that would be an eyesore."* Subsequently it was placed outside the front of White Wells, where it remained for many years. The cards accompanying it updated from time to time to reflect the different additions to the landscape below. (For a detailed description of the information printed on the cards in the 1950's, refer to Chapter Eight: The Second World War and the Post War Years.)

In photographs the direction marker appears to be slightly offset relative to the frontage of White Wells. However it is in fact White Wells that is offset relative to true north. When White Wells was built it seems likely that a compass bearing may have been used to align the building to the north, but the bearing was not adjusted to allow for the declination between magnetic and true north. The result being that White Wells is slightly offset to the northwest, while the direction marker pointed to true north.

A gentleman by the name of David Scott, a native of Halifax, became involved at White Wells in 1901. (Whether or not he was also involved a few years earlier with the church outing that created the song 'On Ilkla Moor Baht 'At' is unknown, but an interesting conjecture.) He gave flamboyant 'orations' to visitors, extolling the virtues of the 'Roman' baths and the waters within. This was reported in the 'Ilkley Gazette' during August 1903:

"The Nectar of the Gods"

During the last year or two thousands of people have probably visited the Old Roman Baths and listened in open mouthed astonishment to a description of the vitalising properties of the water from the gentleman who acts as cicerone. It is a piece of unapproachable, transcendent, grandiloquent and sublime eloquence, to use language similar to that which falls in such abundance from his lips, and as we have been favoured with a transcript of the same as reeled off to a party of visitors on Wednesday, amongst whom happened to be a journalist and shorthand writer, we print it for the benefit of our readers:-

'This is the ancient, antique, archaic, time-honoured, venerable well that was discovered 600 years ago. The walls were built 250 years ago. It was roofed in fifty years ago. It is the honourable work of those noble Romans to whom we owe so much. They constructed it with a sense of integrity. The stone is in a wonderful state of preservation. The very cement seems older than the stone. They boiled it and got it to a particular consistency, and then after putting it in the stone it became harder than the stone itself. You see the form of the bath is elliptical, spoon shaped. All is harmonious, symmetrical. It is a beautiful thought in stone, frozen music. There is some nine inches below the floor the ruined tessellated pavement, but now it is in decay. It was discovered by Sir Adam de Middelton, of Middelton Hall, whose figure is in the parish church. His workmen when excavating, found to their surprise the water and debris and an entire bath with tessellated pavement. Before it was covered in it was open to the cloud-flanked dome of the

sky, the glorious turquoise heavens. We have both ladies and gentlemen taking baths. This is the very place where the secret of Lady Hygia is revealed, whose very breath is incense, and her cheeks all bloom. There is plenty of life-giving energy in these waters. So baths are best taken in the early morning. They are used every day. We have had the Ven. Archdeacon Williams, a gentleman 70 years of age. It is the inherent, essential, intrinsic quality of this Earth-laden gift of God that gives this water its importance and potency. It is vitalising, animating, exhilarating, resuscitating, enthusing, sustaining, delightful and delicious as a bath. As a douche bath it is invaluable for spinal complaints, and makes a pleasant

ILKLEY - THE WHITE WELLS FROM THE MOOR.

White Wells after improvements had been carried out. — A later photograph shows some alterations to have been made: A ventilation pipe had been added to the west gable. The flagpole on the east gable had been removed and decorative tops on two of the three chimneys were in place. Other photographs of the time suggest that the middle of the three chimneys, the one serving the kitchen, was the first to undergo this improvement, followed by the chimney to the east of the building serving the shop. –The other chimney to the west of the building was probably no longer in use by this time and explains why it was not fitted with such decoration too. An internal staircase was installed inside White Wells and this fireplace was walled up. Whether or not the staircase replaced an older one formerly in a slightly different position, perhaps rising more steeply above one of the rear windows, or whether it was a completely new feature in addition to the existing staircase rising from the bathhouse, is unclear. The date of this internal improvement work is uncertain, though it is likely to have been during the works of the late 1880's or mid 1890's.

It is likely that the external work on the chimneys was done around the time that the public toilets were installed in the former charity bath building in 1910. Access to the back door was improved, which also created a storage area below, and a window was installed to the left of the door. The other two rear windows and shutters remained and the shower supply pipe also remained …

ILKLEY AND WHITE WELLS FROM THE MOORS.

... And later again another picture shows considerable tree growth in the public toilet enclosure to the west of White Wells and a sun canopy above the window to the left of the back door. Sweets were sold through the window for many years, but it was blocked up during the renovations of the 1970's. However its outline can still be seen to the left of the back door today. At the bottom right of the photograph the rectangular cover of the water collection tank can be seen.

> *and delightful surprise. The Venerable Archdeacon the very last bath he had told me to put it on more powerfully. We can modify it so (illustrated) – temper the wind to the shorn lamb. This is the bath for rhumatism, gout, sciatica. You can drink it with impunity. It is an aid to digestion, good for dyspepsia. It is the aqua vitae, the elixir of life. It has been the great problem of the antiquarian what was the nectar of the Gods and Goddesses, but we have found it here in this water. All the essence of health and life. It contains a large quantity of latent heat and natural electricity. It will strengthen your digestive functions. There is a sense of satisfaction and pleasure in drinking this water. It is not ordinary water; it is extraordinary. One of our poets said: 'A little learning is a dangerous thing, drink deep or taste not the Pyaerian Spring.'* [1] *This is the Pyaerian Spring! There is a ceaseless inexhaustible supply.'*

---

[1] David Scott is quoting the poet Alexander Pope (1688-1744), and the poem "Essay on Criticism", written in 1709 (but not appearing until 1711) in which the "Pierian Spring" is referred to. (Obviously the misspelling occurred when the article was transcribed.) Pope himself takes the lines from a phrase written by Petronius in the ancient (1st century A.D.) 'Satyricon'. The "Pierian Spring" was the source of artistic and scientific knowledge found in ancient Macedonia, along with the home of the Gods, Mount Olympus. Therefore anyone drinking of the "Pierian Spring" would be given great knowledge.

WHITE WELLS (ROMAN BATH) ILKLEY

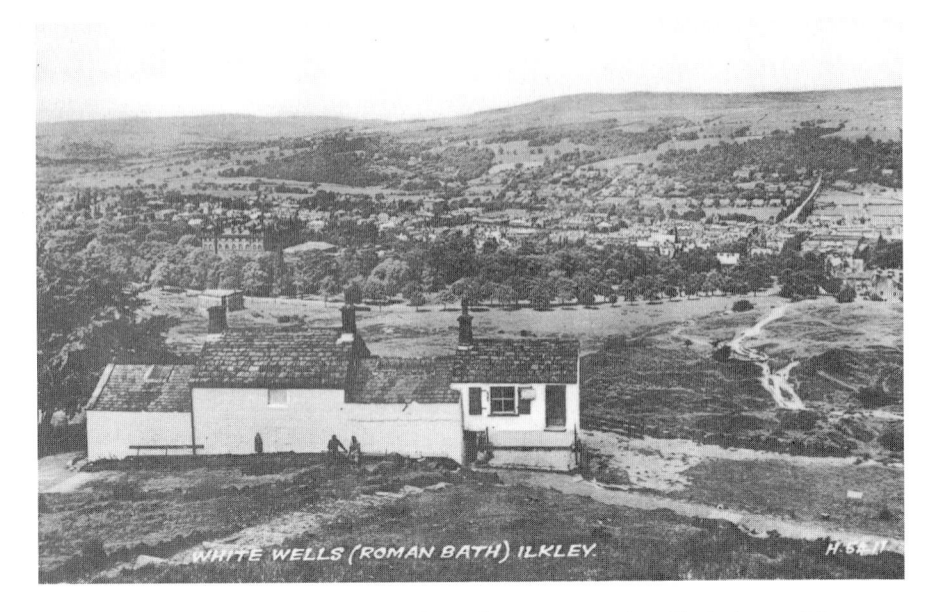

A photograph taken after the previous two shows the two rear windows blocked up, and the supply pipe to the showers had been severed, with a length of pipe left sticking out of the rear wall.

Other photographs of White Wells taken from different angles show that the window frames on the front of the building were also replaced during the early years of the twentieth century.

Bath No 2

'*The water is mellifluent, diaphanous, limpid, luminous, transparent, pellucid. It has heaven given purity and sweetness. Its chemical formula is CO_2. Put your hands in. You will find it awakens a new and pleasant sense. It strengthens the muscles and tissues. It gives lustre and brilliancy to the eyes and grace to the skin. It makes it velvety, and it removes the pimples and roughness from the countenance. It is good for the brain. Cooling and satisfying is this water. Dr Hunter [2] said it was the most valuable spring he had found anywhere. (girls dipping in the water). That is the way to get strength and energy from this water. It is strengthening to both body and mind, improving the general condition, nutrition and tone of the body, and giving increased energy and capacity for work. The eyes are the windows of the soul. Sweeter better water it was never your fortune to touch before. For the viscera of the optic nerve you could do no better, attend to that sisters beloved. Keep those dainty eyes open and bathe the human face divine with the water. Get the mellifluent globules into the orbit. You've got hazel eyes of incandescent beauty. This Bethesda beautiful, this Siloam of beauty and blessings! It is twice blessed,*

---

[2] Dr Adam Hunter had visited the wells in the early nineteenth century. See Chapter Two: Into the Nineteenth Century.

it blesses him that gives and him that takes. Are you aware "There is a tide in the affairs of men which taken at the flood leads on to fortune; omitted, all the voyage of your life is in shoals and misery"? Oh! Lovely water! Lift it to your face until it makes a glow of health and beauty. Lift it to that beauteous dome of thought. Oh for a thousand tongues to sing, the virtues of this precious spring –this splendid gift of God. A plunge in here would make you like the bridegroom rejoicing like a strong man to run a race. It would make you like giants and giantesses refreshed with new wine. Oh! The lovely water, one of God's perfect works for the benefit and blessing of his child man!'

The grand oration given to visitors was perhaps calculated more for effect than for fact. The most obvious fallacy in the performance being the claim that the chemical formula of the water at White Wells is CO_2 – Carbon Dioxide. Despite the many other things the water may or may not be, it is definitely H_2O!

Additionally there is no evidence to support the claim for earlier 'Roman Baths', supposedly discovered during excavations by 'Adam de Middelton', nor even any record of such excavations taking place. It would appear that considerable licence has been taken with the authenticity of the claim regarding a 'tessellated pavement' below the present ground level to say the least! There is simply no evidence to support this claim.

A couple of months after the above account had been published in the *'Ilkley Gazette'*, the paper carried another article on the pronouncements of the orator at White Wells. This time with an even more underlying jocular tone:

"Jottings
If any of my readers have not yet paid a visit to the Old White Wells and listened to the bathman's paralysing oration in praise of the 'mellifluent, diaphanous, limpid, luminous, transparent and pellucid' water that is said to be found there in such great abundance and possessed of the most 'vitalising, animating, exhilarating, resuscitating, enthusing, sustaining and rejuvenating' properties imaginable, they have missed a rich treat.

I have heard him on several occasions, and each time new interest attaches to his eloquent enumeration of the wonderful properties the water is said to possess. In fact after hearing him speak one comes away convinced the Bethesda and Siloam, remarkable as they were for healing, could never hold a candle to the Ilkley White Wells.

Occasionally this old utopian varies his language; the other day, for instance, the following striking passage being included: 'In my sublimest moments I sometimes think the Olympian Gods came here to spend their honeymoon.' I know nothing about the affinity of the Gods and goddesses, but if such once upon a time came here under such happy circumstances, and derived great benefit and enjoyment from their visits, I hope our ancient forefathers made plenty of money out of them, which an old lodging-house keeper informs me isn't possible nowadays."

During the early years of the twentieth century it was noted that outside White Wells there was a large collection of redundant crutches and walking sticks apparently donated from their 'cured' former owners. Visitors could look at these and be told of the remarkable properties attributed to the water.

While visitors continued to make the journey up to White Wells, more out of curiosity than an actual desire to use the baths, a number of the former hydropathic establishments in the Ilkley area promoted themselves as hotels and continued to attract visitors year round, but particularly during the summer.

As the decade progressed, other improvements and features began to appear in the area.

Panorama reservoir was opened in 1903, which greatly improved the water supply facilities for the town.

In July 1904 a bandstand opened in West View Park at the edge of the moor. (It survived for over forty years, and was demolished in early 1948.) The bandstand proved a popular venue for concerts and various musical performances at the time. Though some entertainment continued throughout the 'season' at the tarn as well. Prior to the bandstand being built, the tarn was an established venue for entertainments, including a troupe of 'Pierrots', organised by a Mr Cooper. A stage and changing area was constructed at the tarn for the use of such performers, but these quickly attracted criticism and the structures were removed following the 1905 'season'.

In 1906 Mr Cooper was refused permission to have his 'Pierrots' perform at either the tarn or at the bandstand. Instead he used a site adjoining Brook Street.

Also in 1906, Wells House celebrated its fiftieth anniversary with a large garden party held in its grounds on 23rd June, arranged by Mr Ballardie, the manager.

'Heathcote' was built on Grove Road in 1906/07. It was designed by the eminent architect Sir Edwin Lutyens, famous for many buildings of this period, but perhaps most notably for designing the national Cenotaph in Whitehall following the 'Great War' of 1914-18.

'Heathcote' is currently owned by electrical contractors N.G.Bailey, who bought the property in 1958, and is in use as offices.

John 'Donkey' Jackson died aged eighty one in January 1907. He had retired from his donkey transportation service the year before, after thirty eight years.

OUT OF THE NINETEENTH AND INTO THE TWENTIETH CENTURY

The myth of a Roman presence at White Wells was perpetuated by the *'Ilkley Gazette'*. On 30th March 1907, one of the journalists on the paper, writing under the pseudonym 'Stylus Scrivener', wrote:

"When first their medicinal properties became known no man can say, but the Romans when established here knew something of their powers of healing, and constructed the bath still in existence at the Old Well".

As well as viewing water for its medicinal benefits, real or perceived, other pastimes were gaining popularity. Swimming for leisure, exercise and sport became popular. Ilkley had had a swimming pool in the 'Victoria Hall' on Little Lane since May 1889, (and before that, a bathing pavilion had existed on the river Wharfe at Sandy Dale, on the south bank of the river, just downstream of where the suspension bridge now stands, and during the early years of the twentieth century another bathing pavilion existed on the north bank of the river, adjacent to the football pitch on the West Holmes field, opposite to the present day Memorial Gardens/Park). There were also many other developments in Ilkley during the early years of the twentieth century. Though the expansion was not as rapid as that which had followed the land sales of the eighteen sixties and seventies.

A new town hall was planned for the town, to provide a grand meeting place for the Ilkley Urban District Council. The old 'town hall' used for this purpose used to be located on the Grove in the building adjacent to the 'Canker Well' park. This building still exists, but it is now residential accommodation on the upper floors, with shops at street level. (And earlier than this, the Local Board met in offices in Brook Street.) In 1908 the present Town Hall opened. At the same time the adjacent Kings Hall was opened. (The Public Library was opened in 1907 by Dr Robert Collyer visiting from the United States).

Big issues of the day included the women's suffrage movement. Mrs Pankhurst of the 'Women's Social and Political Union' visited Ilkley on Monday 8th June 1908, and led a meeting held open air at the lower tarn on the moor. This was very well attended according to the account in the *'Ilkley Gazette'*:

"Suffragettes at Ilkley – Lively meeting at the Tarn

Miss (Mrs) Pankhurst, Miss Adela Pankhurst and other suffragettes engaged in the Pudsey Campaign have been recruiting at Ilkley during the Whitsun Holidays, and on Monday (8th June) held a demonstration at the Tarn, which some thousands of people attended. The proceedings were very lively, the interruptions consisting of bell tinkling, music hall ditties, penny trumpets, and a bugle, though the speakers managed to hold their ground and to enlist the sympathy of most present. Indeed the interruptions were most senseless, and only came from a number of young fellows who have evidently not yet learnt to realise when they are making themselves look both foolish and ridiculous"

"Bell tinkling" had been a tactic used by the suffragettes themselves when they wished to disrupt meetings earlier in their campaigns. They evidently did not take kindly to the same tactic being used against them by a small element within the crowd at Ilkley. Overall though the meeting passed peacefully, the ladies eventually got their point across, and being an essentially middle class movement the suffragettes were generally well received in Ilkley. Though over the next few years the tactics employed by the suffragettes increasingly descended into anarchy. Frequently consisting of large rowdy demonstrations in London, and the encouragement to damage property, which did little to

The 'Charity Bath' building prior to conversion into public toilets. — The 'Charity Bath' building to the west of White Wells also underwent alterations. In 1910 it was made into a public toilet. In 1911 Mr Butterfield, was given the lease of the facilities for a year for the sum of £5, on the understanding that they be kept in an acceptable condition.

Prior to the work being carried out, it appears there was a privy to the west end of the 'Charity bath' building, which was replaced during the course of the work with the facilities being installed inside the building where the former charity bath would have been. The encircling wall was altered and access made through it into the enclosure. This picture shows the 'charity bath' building prior to the work being carried out.

win sympathy for their cause. A prominent 'suffragette', Emily Davison, threw herself under the King's horse, Amner, during the 1913 Derby, and died a few days later as a result of her injuries. Naturally her funeral in London was well attended and she became a symbolic martyr to the cause.

However the attention paid to the issue of 'Women and the Vote' was distracted somewhat with the 'Great War'. It was addressed again with the result that full universal suffrage in the United Kingdom was achieved in 1928, when all women over the age of twenty one were eligible to vote for the first time. A decision coming, somewhat ironically, shortly after the death of Mrs Pankhurst. The following year, in the General Election of 1929, Ramsay Macdonald became Labour Prime Minister for the second time, replacing the Conservative Stanley Baldwin. Just how much influence the extra eligible female vote played in this is a debateable point. The Conservatives polled more votes, but Labour won more seats. Although women could now engage fully in politics, it would be a further fifty years before Margaret Thatcher became Britain's first female Prime Minister in 1979.

(Women had been granted only a limited vote with the 'Representation of the People's Act' in 1918, when all men over twenty one and only women over the age of thirty, who were householders, married to a householder or who held a university degree could vote. But equal voting rights for all women over the age of twenty one was not granted until the 'Equal Franchise Act' of 1928.

The voting age for everyone was later reduced from twenty one to eighteen in 1969.)

In 1910 the former charity bath building adjacent to the west of White Wells was converted into a public toilet. The old privy which had been situated in the west of the building's enclosure was removed and the facilities installed inside instead.

A former local resident made the headlines in 1910 when he set out on an expedition with one of the twentieth century's iconic figures. The *'Ilkley Gazette'* of 25th June informs us about this in an article entitled:

> *"To the South Pole*
> *Mr Herbert Ponting, whose fine book on Japan we reviewed a week or two ago, has now set out to find fresh fields for exploration, or really fresh ice fields, as he is one of those proceeding with Captain Scott to the Antarctic regions. Mr Ponting is the son of Mr F.W. Ponting, General Master of the Preston Banking Company until its amalgamation, who for some years resided at Westwood Lodge, Ilkley."*

Herbert Ponting returned in early 1912 after the first winter 'season' with the *'Terra Nova'* expedition, (1910-13) and before the onset of the next. Some of his

OLD WHITE WELLS, ILKLEY.

The 'Charity Bath' building following conversion into public toilets. — A photograph taken after the removal of the privy and the installation of public conveniences indicates that decorative fencing was placed around the front exterior of the former 'Charity bath' building. The sum of £8 was spent on planting shrubs at White Wells by the IUDC in 1911 …

photographs (held in the archives of the *'Royal Geographical Society'* in London) became twentieth century classics.

In 1911 the area adjacent to the new public toilet building at White Wells was planted with shrubs. Mr Butterfield was given the lease of the facilities for a year, for the sum of £5, on the understanding that they be maintained in an acceptable condition.

The improved facilities at White Wells were beneficial for the numbers of visitors coming onto the moor, and to those coming to White Wells for refreshments. At about the same time, improvements were made to the rear of the building. The area around the back door was rebuilt, providing better access to the premises, and a window to the left of the door was installed, through which refreshments were served.

In 1912 the shelter at the bottom of the moor, overlooking Hainsworth's pond attracted negative comments. One dissenter however changed his mind when he saw the views from it. The shelter became accepted and was allowed to remain. Although the structure has been replaced a number of times over the years, there is still a shelter on this site today. The present one is a replacement for the one burnt down by vandals in the early 1990's.

The *'Titanic'* sank in April, 1912; and less than a year later in early 1913 the nation received the news that Captain Scott had failed in his attempt to reach the South Pole first, and in a tragic twist of circumstances had died on the return journey, elevating him (and his men) to legendary status in the pantheon of national heroes.

The 'Winter Gardens' Annex adjacent to the 'King's Hall' in Ilkley was opened on Monday 22nd June 1914 by Councillor J. Dinsdale of the IUDC at which a large crowd was present. The date coincided with the National celebrations for the 'Official Birthday' of King George V, and the 'Trooping of the Colour'.

During the First World War (1914-1918) Ilkley Moor was still a popular destination for visitors, and Mr Butterfield continued serving refreshments at White Wells. No further mention is made in the local press of David Scott and his 'oration', but by the time of the war, Mr Scott would have been approaching eighty years of age. I have been unable to trace what happened to him with any certainty, but a gentleman of the same name and the same age (eighty three) died in Halifax, early in 1918. (David Scott was, according to the newspaper reports of his 'oration', a native of Halifax.)

... And a later photograph shows the result of the tree growth. These were planted to provide screening for the building.

Roman Baths.
The famous Plunge Bath.

The water is mellifluent, diaphanous, luminous transparent, pellucid, immaculate, and unequalled in purity. It is vitalising, animating exhilarating, resusatating, enthusing sustaining refreshing, invigorating, delightful and delicious as a bath. It is instinct with life, and is seven degrees colder than ordinary well water. It strengthens the muscles and tissues, and improves the general condition, nutrition, and tone of the body, and gives increased energy, and capacity for work

The plunge bath at White Wells. — As the popularity of bathing declined, only the bath in the western side of White Wells remained in use.

The large valve that was used to fill the bath in the 1890's (which can be seen on a previous photograph also showing Mr Butterfield stood next to the bath) was replaced with a pipe. Note also the ventilation shutter at the apex of the roof in the gable wall, the chain used to open and close it, and the row of pegs on the wall for bathers to hang their clothing on.

Typical of many postcards of this era featuring White Wells, the erroneous description 'Roman Baths' also appears on the picture.

"A UNIQUE PRESENT."

THE ILKLEY
SOUVENIR
SPOON
IN SOLID SILVER
(Hall Marked)
Registered Design.

Price 7s. 6d.,
By post (safely packed), 8s.

The Spoon has beautifully engraved in the Handle the Old Wells Drinking Fountain, and in the Bowl a View of Ilkley Bridge.

To be purchased of

C. A. Broadhead
JEWELLER, &c.,
Wells Road, Ilkley.

EXACT SIZE.

Ilkley merchandise in the late 19th and early 20th centuries. — The increasing popularity of Ilkley as a tourist destination resulted in a wide range of Ilkley 'merchandise' being put on the market. In 1900, the *'Ilkley Gazette'* printed an advertisement for "A new and interesting souvenir of Ilkley", in the shape of a silver spoon. An accompanying article read:

> "The majority of people when holiday making manage to bring something home as a souvenir of the place or places visited, and Ilkley during the course of a year being visited by thousands either in search of health or pleasure, it is only natural that souvenirs of the district in the shape of photographs, china ware and numberless fancy articles specially designed, engraved or in some way localised, should have sprung into existence. The latest addition to the pretty things of this character is a very beautiful and unique solid silver spoon which Mr C.A. Broadhead, jeweller and fine art dealer, Wells Road, has just registered and put upon the market. This lovely piece of artistic workmanship has engraved upon the bowl a view of Ilkley bridge, and at the head of the stem, which with the bowl is gold coated, there is a circle containing a representation of the District Council's seal or local coat of arms, in the shape of a view of the Old Well House, impressed upon a shield with the word 'Olicana' on the outer circle. The idea is both novel and charming and should prove not only a very pleasant but a most useful memento of a visit to this lovely and enchanting valley."

A little later in the year the advertisement was reprinted in the paper, with the additional information that one of the spoons had been supplied to His Royal Highness The Prince of Wales. –And for those wishing to purchase, the spoons were on sale for 7s/6d.

WHITE WELLS, ILKLEY.

"ILKLEY WHITE WELLS" WHISKY.

ILKLEY'S BEST WHISKY.

Recommended as a Tonic and Digestive.

Price 4/- per bottle.

BOTTLED BY THE PROPRIETORS:

BEANLANDS & SONS LTD.

Telephone 51. **14, BROOK STREET, ILKLEY.**

Whether or not "White Wells Whisky" was also on sale at White Wells, and what 'arrangement' existed between Messrs. Butterfield at White Wells and Beanlands the local grocer who promoted the product is unclear. Unfortunately it seems that there are no surviving examples of it available for tasting today! – This advertisement appeared on the front page of the *'Ilkley Gazette'* on the 17th May 1913. It was repeated the following week. In the 1920's, the whisky was re-branded, and sold by Beanlands as 'Baht 'At Whisky'.

In October 1918, a Mr Wimpenny wrote to the Ilkley Urban District Council requesting information about the tenancy of White Wells. Though he wasn't given it. Mr Butterfield's lease was going to expire at the end of December.

The IUDC instead resolved to instruct the surveyor to prepare a scheme for improving the facilities at White Wells, and submit a plan and an estimate of costs. This caused concern amongst some locals, who suspected that once again plans were afoot to demolish the property. On 18th October the *'Ilkley Gazette'* attempted to put peoples' fears at rest when an article was printed in the *'Random Jottings'* feature of the paper:

> **"The Old White Wells**
> *Many people are much exercised in mind as to what the council proposes to do in respect to the Old White Wells. The council have a scheme in hand for effecting improvements and the idea seems to have taken possession of some minds that they intend to pull the old buildings down and replace them with a more up-to-date but less picturesque structure. Nothing of the kind. All the council intend to do is to improve the tea room and refreshment accommodation and provide more shelter, but their scheme of reconstruction, if such it can be called, embraces no interference with the appearance of the White Wells as the charming moorland setting they at present present."*

By December 1918, the plan submitted to the council by the surveyor was given careful consideration. It was decided to request that the surveyor submit a modified scheme instead.

Just as another chapter in the history of White Wells was about to begin, another was closing. In December 1918 William Butterfield's tenancy of White Wells expired. There had been three generations and almost a century since his grandfather had been appointed the bathman in 1820. Again, as in the case of David Scott, I have been unable to trace what became of Mr Butterfield in the years following his departure from White Wells. One theory is that he went to live in Bradford. After the IUDC had initiated 'proceedings' against him over his reluctance to leave White Wells in early 1919, it is certainly possible that he no longer felt welcome in the town and decided to move away. The death registers for Bradford for the quarter April/May/June 1930 lists a William Butterfield who by then was seventy years old. Whether or not this is one and the same as our Mr Butterfield is uncertain. Even though the age corresponds, William Butterfield is not a particularly unusual name, particularly in a city the size of Bradford.

CHAPTER SEVEN:
BETWEEN THE WARS

During 1919 momentum was gathering with regard to establishing a shelter and refreshment rooms at or near to White Wells.

Ilkley Urban District Council who were responsible for the property advertised in the *'Ilkley Gazette'* for caterers to provide refreshments at White Wells for a limited time, 17th to 26th April inclusive, during the Easter holidays. *"Tenders to be received not later than 7th April."*

However an application to the council from a Mr T.H. Wild for the tenancy of White Wells was rejected at the beginning of April. The *Gazette* does not record the reasons for this rejection, but the council at this time were looking toward the long term future of White Wells, and was considering extending the building to the rear whilst leaving the frontage more or less as it had always appeared. At least since the mid nineteenth century when the baths were roofed over.

Soon an alternative site *"sixty yards to the south east of White Wells"* was being considered for the construction of a shelter and tearoom. However this proposal met with some resistance. The *'Ilkley Gazette'* of 27th June 1919 reported under the heading *"Opposition to the moor shelter and refreshment room"*:

"Many ratepayers do not view with any favour the council's proposal to erect a shelter and tea-room on the moor. The shelter is alright and needful in the opinion of many, but the provision of greater facilities for providing refreshments at the White Wells is thought to be introducing an unnecessary competitive element, so far as the local refreshment caterers are concerned. This is an argument against the proposal. Certainly though we are not so sure that this is the real basis of opposition. Many of those opposed to incorporation are also opposed to tea-rooms and even moorland shelters, if these things have any tendency to bring more visitors into the town, and when opposition comes from private residents only, there is somehow an unsatisfactory feeling that a desire to check or limit Ilkley's business advancement and prosperity is at the bottom of it. Not all private residents are so selfishly inclined, for some we know have done their best, and are still doing their best to give Ilkley a 'place in the sun'."

Roman Bath, Ilkley

Looking down into the plunge bath. — The plunge bath in the eastern side of White Wells also had decking in the bottom as well as on the floor of the bathhouse around it. However as use of the baths declined, they were popular instead as 'wishing wells'. In 1919 visitors were encouraged to throw pennies into the baths. It was believed that if the coins settled head uppermost, the visitors' wishes would be granted. Though it would appear that the pennies, along with the water, are absent on this photo!

The Council was still keen to build a tea pavilion, and provide further 'improvements' to the area around White Wells.

An anecdote dating from around this time suggests that White Wells was painted red, white and blue in commemoration of the end of the First World War. Closer examination of this story leads to the conclusion that this could have happened in the summer of 1919. The Armistice had been signed in November 1918, which brought about the end of hostilities. However, the Armistice wasn't ratified until 28th June 1919, with the signing of the Treaty of Versailles. (– And the United States didn't ratify their peace with Germany until 1921.) Following the signing of the Treaty of Versailles, the British Government announced national celebrations. Though many towns and communities across the United Kingdom had hoped that a date would be set for August, it was decided that it would be commemorated on the weekend of Saturday 19th July instead. Reports from that time tell of grand celebrations organised at relatively short notice. In Ilkley the celebrations started with a dance in the Winter Gardens on Friday 18th, to which former servicemen were invited, along with the widows and mothers of the 'fallen' from the town; which added a certain poignancy to the proceedings.

The main event in the town on Saturday 19th was well attended. The *'Yorkshire Post'* of 21st July reported that *"Most parts of the town were decorated with flags and streamers, and there were illuminations in the evening."* Many shops and businesses put up Union Jacks and bunting, there was a grand parade through the town, a brass band, afternoon tea served to the schoolchildren back in their own schools afterwards and sports on the Holmes field. Fireworks were also set off in the evening. All the men aged over sixty were given tobacco, while all ladies over sixty were given a quarter of tea.

Although White Wells itself is not mentioned in the reports of the celebrations, it is certainly possible that it was included, and if so, it is possible that the building was temporarily painted in red white and blue to mark the occasion.

However whether or not there is any fact in the story of temporary paintwork, visitors to White Wells at that time were encouraged to use the plunge bath as a 'wishing well', into which they could deposit their small change. It was said that *'pennies cast into the crystal bath where if they came head uppermost the visitor obtain their wish.'* How true this claim is remains unexplored, but it was obviously a good ploy to extract a few more coppers out of visitors, especially if their coins landed face down and they had to try again!

Work was carried out by the council on the moors to improve the facilities enjoyed by visitors during 1919. In November, the *'Ilkley Gazette'* reported that an island had been removed from Craig Tarn and the top tarn near White Wells had been cleared of weeds and rushes, to *"afford better skating facilities."* Though the decorative islands at the latter were allowed to remain. The sentiments of the local press being to try and create what was termed *"A winter season"*, in order that *"more visitors should be induced to come during the winter than has hitherto been the case."*

The council's initial enthusiasm for the tea pavilion was before long in doubt. By 1920 a number of councillors were against the idea and considered that

The Moorland Tea Pavilion. — Towards the end of 1918, it was suggested to make improvements to White Wells. The Ilkley Urban District Council asked the surveyor to prepare plans for such a scheme. However the plans proposed were apparently too ambitious, because the surveyor was subsequently requested to submit a modified scheme instead.

Suggestions were made to build a café to the south east of White Wells. Although controversial at the time, the plans were eventually turned into reality.
The tea pavilion opened in July 1921 by the Ilkley Urban District Council following a lengthy debate and delays. The original proprietor was Mr Wray who ran the business throughout the nineteen twenties. Shortly after opening Mr Wray reached an agreement with the IUDC to have the premises connected to the main 'town gas' supply by means of an extension from Wells Road. (White Wells was not included in the plan.)

Between 1931 and 1964 the tea pavilion was run by Mrs Williamson, who had been given the tenancy in December 1930, and from 1964 to 1971 by Mrs Gregson. Though by the beginning of the 1970's the pavilion was in a poor state of repair and had become very badly vandalised. (See Chapter Nine: Decline and Dereliction.)

The interior of the Moorland Tea Pavilion. — Both light refreshments and main meals were available, with table service, in pleasantly decorated surroundings enjoying commanding views of Wharfedale.

For the solar eclipse on 29th June 1927, *"4 o'clock ham and eggs proved quite a popular dish"* at the pavilion which had opened early for those who had ventured up the moor to witness the event, which occurred around 6am.

money could be better spent elsewhere. Particularly on the construction of council housing, an ambitious scheme for which was under proposal at the time.

It was also felt by some that a tea pavilion would provide too much competition for other traders supplying refreshments in the town. Despite the fact that refreshments had actually been available at White Wells itself for a number of years. As had been alluded to the year before in the *'Ilkley Gazette'*, when it was claimed one thousand two hundred people were served with tea on one of the bank holidays!

Nevertheless by September 1920 the woodwork of the pavilion was 'in hand' though the contractors, Messers Dean and Mennell, were apparently experiencing some difficulty in obtaining cement. The situation dragged on for quite some time without a satisfactory resolution in sight. Critics of the scheme were calling for the contractors to be dismissed, and the contract awarded to someone else, or abandoned completely.

Ultimately sufficient materials were obtained and construction began in earnest in early 1921. The tea pavilion was officially opened on 29th July 1921.

The *'Ilkley Free Press and Gazette'* reported the event:

"The tea house and shelter on the moors near the White Wells Ilkley, was formerly opened this (Friday) afternoon. For many years past it has been the custom to provide afternoon tea and light refreshment at the white washed building which form so prominent and famous a land mark on the moorside, but the need for further accommodation for this purpose was realised in many quarters before the war. The work for the new building was put in hand soon after the war. There were fears that a building was to be erected which would be some disfigurement of the beauty of the moors, but the rustic design of the new shelter is quite fitting to its situation.

The building contains a tea room 24ft long by 18ft wide surrounded by a verandah 6ft wide with a small but well equipped kitchen to the rear. Its situation, about 60 yards south east of the White Wells commands one of the finest views in the valley and its advantages are already being appreciated.

The principle room is extremely well lighted, so that from any point a full sweep of the valley can be seen. Well equipped with tables there is accommodation inside for 50 people to be served with tea at once.

Whilst later it is intended to equip the verandah in a similar manner, so that probably a further 50 people can be served.

It is intended that the furnishings from the verandah shall be of a type to accord with the rustic balcony. The principle entrance faces north, a fine rustic arch leading to the verandah and forward through the doors into the main room. Messers Dean and Mennell were the contractors.

The catering will be in the hands of Mr A.W. Wray, who has charge of the catering in the Winter Gardens during the performances by the Bijou Orchestra, and who has also had the catering at White Wells for a number of years. The building will be open during the whole seven days of the week and meals will be served at practically all hours of the day. The whole should make a very useful acquisition to Ilkley's properties and will certainly be appreciated by visitors to the town. Its opening for the August Bank Holidays is particularly appropriate. Members of the Council together with some ex-councillors, their friends and some of the officials were present at the opening.

Mr J. W. Lund, Chairman of the Council, and last year's Chairman of the Moors and Parks Committee, presided over the little ceremony, which was performed by Mr Ellis Beanlands, as Chairman of the Moors and Parks Committee this year. Mr Beanlands explained that as Chairman of that committee it fell to his duty to perform that ceremony. He had always consistently opposed the scheme, but it had been the wish of the majority of the Council that it should be carried through, and he had done his duty out of respect to his fellow councillors. One could not win *every time. On the question of incorporation he had been on the winning side, but that was not the case on this occasion.*

Afterwards the company were entertained to tea by Mr Beanlands."

One jocular suggestion for naming the tea pavilion *"Beanlands Ark"* was put forward by a commentator at the time, on the grounds that there is a "Beanlands Parade" and a "Beanlands Island" also to be found in Ilkley! The irony in the joke being of course that Mr Beanlands who had opposed the scheme, ended up performing the official opening ceremony!

Shortly after the opening of the tea pavilion the proprietor, Mr Wray, applied to the IUDC Gas Committee with a view to connecting the property to the main 'town gas' supply. 'Item 9' of the Gas Committee's meeting of 31st August 1921 records:

"An application for the extension of the gas main from Wells Road to the new refreshment pavilion was received from Mr A. Wray.

Resolved: That the extension be carried out on condition that Mr Wray will enter into an agreement to make an annual contribution equivalent to 10% of the capital outlay involved."

The minute was adopted at the general meeting of the IUDC on 7th September 1921. This was also reported in the *'Ilkley Gazette'* a couple of days later, with the additional note that: *"The agreement was confirmed at the meeting of the Council."*

Minor alterations were also carried out at White Wells too. Though the property was not connected to the 'town gas' supply. The flagpole and a sign on the east gable were removed, while decorative tops were added to two of the three chimneys. (The one on the eastern most chimney replacing a previous decorative top that had been removed a few years earlier. These alterations can be seen on photographs of White Wells dating from the time.)

Visitors to White Wells paid an admission fee to look around the overgrown shower bath and for an additional 2d could use the remaining plunge bath in the western end of the building to 'wash' in.

One visitor to White Wells, hoping to see the 'Roman baths', complained in a letter to the local press that he couldn't gain access to the plunge bath because it was in use by young ladies at the time of his visit, and he and his friend could only look at the shower bath instead!

By late 1921 there were calls for improvement work to be carried out at the upper tarn. Seemingly the clearance for skaters was only short lived, and the tarn had since become overgrown again.

A few years later, in 1924 the redundant water tank behind the former charity bath was 'discovered'. (Perhaps rather surprising considering the

The Paddling Pool (photograph 2009). — The paddling pool was created in the mid 1920's out of 'Hainsworth's Pond'. Work started in 1926, and although it ran over budget because of the decision to use stone to finish the surround instead of leaving the originally proposed brickwork, (which is underneath) it was ready to open for the start of the 1927 'season' the following spring.

The paddling pool underwent a major refurbishment in 1961.

Although the paddling pool still survives, there are concerns over public safety and possible litigation claims against Bradford Council who are responsible for the site that could possibly affect its future use.

Concerns perhaps far from the public mind when the pool was built.

work undertaken in transforming the old charity bath into a public toilet only fourteen years earlier.) The Ilkley Urban District Council arranged to have the tank drained in order that an inspection could be carried out. This was done on the evening of the 4th July, when the local fire engine, (named 'Thomas') was taken up to White Wells. Following the inspection of the water tank, it was concluded that it had, as suspected, been the supply tank for the charity bath. The description in the *'Ilkley Gazette'* also includes a reference to the ornamental fountain in the enclosure, and to the stone face spout through which the water flowed. It suggested this fountain had not been in use for some *"forty or fifty years"*, which would date it to the time when substantial water improvement works were being undertaken in the Ilkley area, including the moors, and the charity bath had fallen into disuse in the two decades following the opening of the Ilkley Charity Bath Hospital in the 1860's. It would seem that this drinking fountain had fallen out of favour at about the same time as 'Crawley's Fountain' came into being towards the bottom of the moor.

In 1926 Ilkley Urban District Council developed the area of 'Hainsworth's Pond', and created the Paddling Pool.

The *'Ilkley Gazette'* of 9th July 1926 reported on the Council's plans for a "Children's wading pool". It said:

> *"A plan, specification, and estimate of the cost of construction of a wading pool for children at Hainsworth's pond, submitted by the assistant surveyor, was approved and tenders are to be invited. Mr Porrit said that around the pool would be built a brick wall about sixteen inches high. The pool would vary from six to nine inches in depth, and around it would be a concrete path 2ft 6in wide."*

By August, Mr L.T. Learoyd's tender for the construction of the wading pool was accepted.

The original costs for the work were exceeded. By Christmas 1926 these were £456 7s 5d. This was due to the fact that it had been decided to finish the surround of the pool in stone instead of the originally proposed brick. It was ready in time for the start of the 1927 'season'. (An additional point of interest: Unfortunately Mr Learoyd's daughter Mary was tragically murdered in Ilkley in 1929, causing much speculation and intrigue in the local press. Despite there being a number of suspects, no one was charged or convicted, and the murder remains unsolved.)

A potential disaster at White Wells was averted in April 1927 when smoke was spotted in the passage underneath the 'tuck shop'. The event was also recorded in the *'Ilkley Gazette'*:

> *"The White Wells, which is always a centre of attraction for visitors at holiday times, was the scene of a fire on Sunday morning. (17th April.) Fortunately it was not serious and little damage was done. It was discovered by two Ilkley young men, who were walking on the moors about eight o'clock. They saw smoke issuing from the passage which runs underneath the shop, and discovered that a beam, which runs under the floor of the shop, was on fire. They gave the alarm from the telephone kiosk at the corner of Crossbeck Road and Mr Dean (Superintendent of the Fire Brigade) and Mr Jack Lambert (Captain) went up to the wells. They entered the shop through the window, and had no difficulty extinguishing the fire with water from the baths."*

The article also mentions the newly opened paddling pool:

> *"The new paddling pool at Hainsworth's pond came into its own with the holidays.*

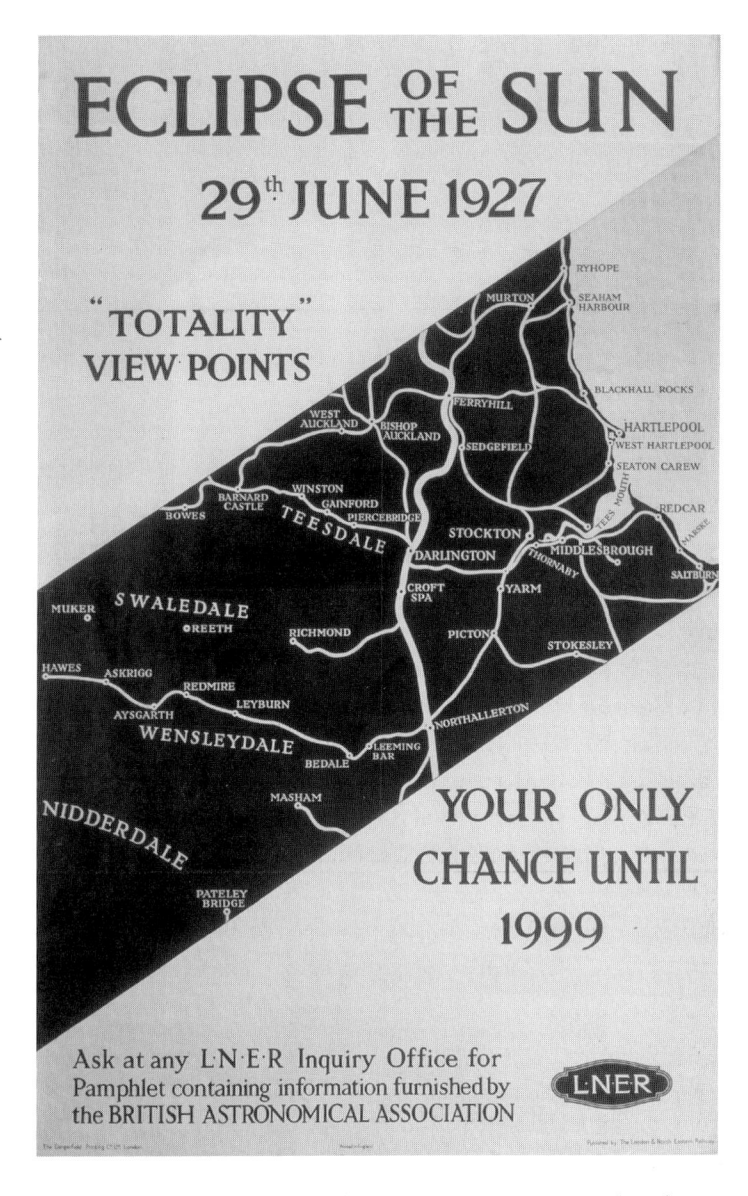

Railway advertisement for travel to the eclipse (1927). — Not mentioned on this poster, Ilkley was just outside the extreme edge of the area of the umbra, a little way below and to the left of Pateley Bridge off southern the edge of the map displayed here. As a consequence of being just outside the zone, the amount of totality of the eclipse was 99.7% in Ilkley.

Other destinations in the north of England were also advertised by different rail companies for visitors to travel to for the eclipse.

A special train carried passengers from Ilkley to Settle and Giggleswick to view the event. The train was delayed on the way, but despite anxious moments for the passengers, it arrived at its destination in time and the total eclipse was viewed under good skies. Unlike in Ilkley, where the spectacle was marred by cloud cover.

Scores of youngsters were enjoying a happy time with their toy boats on the pond heedless of the cold winds. They were paddling to their hearts content."

In June 1927 Ilkley proved a popular venue for visitors to watch the (almost) total eclipse of the sun on the morning of Wednesday 29th. Ilkley was just south of the area of the umbra, and as a consequence 99.7% of the sun was obscured. The Cow and Calf rocks had crowds of visitors, and some of the hotels put on special events lasting throughout the night, culminating with the eclipse itself, which occurred early in the morning. White Wells and the tea pavilion were also popular. Again we look to the local press for an account of the proceedings:

"Many of those who had danced all night or who had succumbed to the lure of bed, were enjoying ham and eggs at the moorland café near White Wells; indeed four o'clock ham and eggs proved quite a popular dish. But though the stretch of moors around and behind the White Wells were busier than they have ever been at this time in the morning, the great majority of Ilkley people congregated on the Cow. The eclipse occurred at around 6am and lasted approximately twenty two seconds. Eclipse parties were held through the night in the Winter Gardens and Troutbeck Hydro."

Excavations of 1929 showing the original 'Well House'. — This photograph appeared in the *'Ilkley Gazette'* in October 1929 and shows the original bath. This is located at the top of the hill immediately behind White Wells, close to the water collection tank. The 'discovery' was made during the course of work undertaken by the Ilkley Urban District Council to improve the various water works on the moors. It had been similarly 'discovered' over half a century before, during the Ilkley Local Board's water works of the 1870's.

West plunge bath showing stone face spout inflow feature. — A later photograph of the plunge bath shows that although the decking is still in place, the inflow pipe has been replaced with the stone face spout. This provided a decorative feature for the bath, and is likely to be the same spout described in 1924 as having been a feature of the dried up drinking fountain in the enclosed area to the rear of the charity bath building. The spout was probably installed in the bath circa 1929/30 when the IUDC undertook further waterworks on the moor.

When White Wells was renovated in the 1970's, the spout was relocated again and can now be seen as the inflow feature of the display bath in the eastern side of the building.

Unfortunately the event was marred by cloud. However some people travelled to Settle and Giggleswick on a special train to witness the event, and enjoyed a good view (and 100% totality).

Seventy two years later, in August 1999, the moors were again a popular venue for witnesses to a solar eclipse. Though totality in the U.K. could only be observed from Cornwall, (and that too was marred by cloud) the spectacle from the latitude of Ilkley was almost but not quite total, and provided an interesting diversion for many people on the 11th August. A similar almost total solar eclipse will be visible from Ilkley again, – on the evening of Saturday 23rd September 2090. Whether or not that too will be marred by cloud, only time will tell.

In 1929 further work was undertaken at White Wells. As part of the Ilkley Urban District Council's ongoing work into water improvement schemes for Ilkley, excavations on top of the hill behind White Wells, close to the current water collection tank, revealed the site of the original bath thought to date from the beginning of the eighteenth century.

It is likely that the stone face waterspout from the old fountain in the enclosure was brought inside White Wells during the course of this work and installed as the inflow feature on the bath in the western end of the building. By this time bathing had stopped at White Wells and the 'Roman Baths' (as they continued to be referred as) were something of a curiosity for visitors to the moor.

1931 saw the installation of the lighting around the lower tarn. This was partially in response to the popularity of the tarn for skating during the winter months. The addition of lighting, albeit limited, was apparently appreciated by both the skaters and spectators. Though some additional temporary lighting was also installed, the lamps along the road to the tarn at the western end and next to the shelter were permanent. They remain today, and were restored to use in the spring of 2007. During the summer of 2009, the modern fittings were replaced with 'traditional' glass lantern fittings instead, complimenting the other work that had been undertaken at the tarn by Bradford Council.

The Ilkley Illuminations were also established in 1931. This occurred in September, traditionally the time of the 'Ilkley Feast', and coincided with a trades fair in the town and the National 'Faraday Centenary' celebrations. Various venues around the town were illuminated for the week, including the Grove and Mill Ghyll. White Wells was illuminated too, but by means of powerful gas lights attached to brackets suspended from the guttering. The event was repeated the following year with 'improved' gas lighting at White Wells, the Parish Church and the Old Bridge. Incidentally, 1932 also was the year that Ilkley's famous peacock made its debut. Originally part of the illuminations, a

White Wells by floodlight. — Looking eerie and spectral, White Wells was lit up by gaslight in September 1931 as part of the illuminations that also saw a number of prominent buildings in the town similarly lit up. Unlike the nearby tea pavilion, which had been connected to the main 'town gas' supply shortly after it had opened a decade earlier, the gas for the illumination of White Wells was supplied in canisters. The illuminations coincided with the traditional 'feast' week, starting on the first Sunday after 14th September, a large 'Trades Fair' and the national 'Faraday Centenary.' (Ironic then that gas instead of electricity was used). The illuminations caught the public imagination, and the event was repeated throughout the decade. The 'famous' Ilkley peacock made its debut in the illuminations of 1932. A direct descendant of this peacock now forms part of the annual Ilkley Christmas illuminations, and usually features on the island at the top of Brook Street.

For the V.E. Day celebrations in May 1945, White Wells was floodlit again, though the pre-war popularity of the Ilkley Illuminations each September was not revived. Mains gas, along with electricity and a landline telephone, was not connected to White Wells until the mid 1990's.

direct descendant of it is now an annual feature of the towns Christmas Lights, having pride of place on the traffic island at the top of Brook Street.

At Christmas 1934 the Bradford based department store 'Busby's' (which had had a smaller branch in Ilkley since 1918) arranged a visit to Ilkley Moor from 'Santa Busby Claus', which included Santa demonstrating toy boats in the paddling pool. The event proved so popular that the following year 'Busby's' repeated the event, with Santa 'appearing' from behind the rocks near White Wells, then riding down the moor to the bandstand in West View Park. This too proved popular with many Ilkley children. –Santa was giving away money and sweets!

Signpost at White Wells damaged by a storm. — This photograph appeared in the *"Ilkley Gazette"* of 1st November 1935. The caption accompanying it read:

> *"The famous signpost at the White Wells Ilkley marking the points of the compass was blown down in the recent gales. The signpost was a well known landmark, and this, together with the cards in the case adjoining, proved most useful in helping visitors to identify various points of interest in the surrounding district."*

The signpost (dating from 1903) was restored to the upright position.

Following years of debate by the Ilkley Urban District Council regarding the poor bathing facilities in Ilkley, (or rather lack of them since the closure of the somewhat rustic Victoria Hall Baths in the 1920's) the Lido opened in May 1935, coinciding with the Silver Jubilee celebrations of King George V. Designed by local surveyor Mr Skinner, the lagoon shaped pool proved a popular attraction through the summer months. As indeed it still does. It remains one of only a few inland lidos in the United Kingdom. It is in what has become known as the 'Art Deco' style, popular and typical of the era. (So named after the *'Exposition des Arts Decoratifs et Industriels Modernes'* held a decade earlier in Paris in 1925, that showcased the style in many aspects including architecture, art, furnishings and jewellery; and it was a style reflected in Hollywood movies of the time.)

The direction marker at White Wells. — Despite being damaged during a storm in late October 1935 (see previous photograph), the finger post outside the front of White Wells pointing out the directions North, South, East and West was replaced. A card describing the various points of interest was available for visitors to refer to, updated periodically to accommodate the changes unfolding in the town below. Originally held in a box on the finger post, it was realised that perhaps the card was more suited to being kept in a box inside the porch of White Wells instead! (A badly damaged copy of one such card, dating from the mid 1950's, is referred to in Chapter Eight: The Second World War and the Post War Years.)

The direction marker survived until the appalling levels of vandalism inflicted on the building prior to the restoration by Eric Busby, and now after many years without its presence, a direction marker will hopefully be replaced again outside White Wells in 2010.

Also in 1935 improvement work was carried out at the old reservoir building on the edge of the moor. This involved the installation of large water filters and the roof of the building had to be raised in order to accommodate them owing to their size. Another water filtration plant was also constructed in Panorama Woods, to service the water supply flowing from the nearby Panorama reservoir.

In 1936 Wells House Hotel was still offering treatments to its clientele. For 3/- per treatment, clients could choose from: Russian vapour, Oatmeal, Pine, Brine, Sulphur, or Seaweed compresses, which also included massage. Ladies, the advertisement informed, were accommodated daily between the hours of 2pm and 5pm.

In 1938 the *'Ilkley Gazette'* reported on an old stone block, lying abandoned in a field at the bottom of Wells Road. The report stated:

" An Old Stone.

Lying in the field where it had apparently been tossed as of no further use is a squared stone the original purpose of which is likely to be soon forgotten. Once however it served an important office. It was a mounting stone, and stood in Wells Road near the corner of the buildings at present occupied by Mr H. Kaberry antique dealer, which was then the Ilkley Library. It was used to enable those seeking to enjoy the benefits of the baths at White Wells to mount the donkeys which conveyed them there. Dr T. Johnstone recalls this purpose well and mentioned this week that in addition to this stone in Wells Road there was the companion mounting stone which can still be seen at White Wells. This is a double stone, with steps on each side and was used for dismounting on arrival and for remounting on the return journey from the moor to the village.

Perhaps the Ilkley Council in its wisdom will consider the present discarded stone in the field really worth preserving in some rather more imposing position because of its association with an Ilkley of long gone by."

In 1939 the foundations of the 'Christian Science Church' were laid on the site, and in 1940 the *'Ilkley Gazette'* reported again on the stone:

"The trustees of the Christian Science Church offered to give to the Council a stone mounting block from the grounds of the church in Wells Road. The offer has been accepted with thanks and the Chairman of the Moors and Parks Committee authorised to fix a suitable site for the re-erection of the block."

The mounting block was subsequently moved to a new site, where it can still be seen today, on the island at the junction of Wells Road, Queens Road, Wells Promenade and Skelda Rise, opposite Wells Court Flats.

'CATCH ME IF YOU CAN!'

High Jinks on Ilkley Moor with Father Xmas.

"1/- Each for the First 20 Children to tig me!" Says Father Xmas.

Santa Busby Claus's Bedtime Story:—

Cheerio, Boys and Girls,

What a time we are going to have to-morrow. I'm coming over Ilkla Moor baht 'at on an 'orse, with a pocketful of shillings and a sack of toffee—whoopee!—at one minute to ten Greenwich mean time generous.

If all goes well, and I don't get stuck in the mud, I will suddenly bob up from behind a boulder, full of beans, somewhere within a stone's throw of the White Wells. (Famous in history because a Roman warrior, Olly Hardy, had a bath there. After this memorable event the wells were whitewashed and the district was called Olicana).

As soon as the first boy or girl spots me I'll disappear again and bob up somewhere else. I'm a very good dodger. You'll have to get up early in the morning if you're going to win a shilling and catch me bending. You had better get together and charge me, and just see what a good runner I am. Try to catch me before I take a flying leap on to my horse, and away I go, clomp, clomp, clomp, over the waterfall and down the hill to the bandstand, where I had such a grand welcome last year.

When I get to the bandstand I will hold my court, and please don't push, because I specially want to meet all the little children who could not get near me last year. I will stay at the bandstand until I have had a word with every one of my little friends, then up and away down Crossbeck Road and Cowpasture Road, down to the roundabout—Brook Street Circus without a clown. Round we go, and then to the station, where I shall catch the 11-32 train for Bradford. I've got to get back to my Home from Home at Busbys' in good time, or Mother Christmas will be giving me a dog's life. I've left her in charge while I'm away. Whoopee! That's why I'm looking forward to to-morrow—it's my morning off!

Cheerio, I'll give you a run for your money to-morrow, on Ilkla Moor baht 'at!

Lots of love and toffee,   SANTA BUSBY CLAUS.

Come to BUSBYS' TOY TOWN in Bradford.

You must see **FATHER CHRISTMAS' LOG CABIN** and **MAGIC CHIMNEY**, the **TEDDY BEARS' PICNIC** and **FATHER CHRISTMAS' REVIEW OF THE TROOPS** and the **Wonderful TOY DISPLAYS.**

Front page advertisement in the *'Ilkley Gazette'*, 6th December 1935, for 'Busby's' Department store. The text on the advert reads:

"'CATCH ME IF YOU CAN'
High jinks on Ilkley Moor with Father Xmas.
"1/- Each for the First 20 Children to tig me!" Says Father Xmas.
Santa Busby Claus's Bedtime Story:-

"Cheerio Boys and Girls,

What a time we are going to have tomorrow. I'm coming over Ilkla Moor Baht 'At on an 'orse, with a pocketful of shillings and a sack of toffee.- Whoopee! **At one minute to ten Greenwich mean time generous.**

If all goes well, and I don't get stuck in the mud, I will suddenly bob up from behind a boulder, full of beans, somewhere within a stone's throw of the White Wells. (Famous in history because a Roman warrior, Olly Hardy, had a bath there. After this memorable event the wells were whitewashed and the district was called Olicana.)

As soon as the first boy or girl spots me I'll disappear and bob up somewhere else. I'm a very good dodger. You'll have to get up early in the morning if you're going to win a shilling and catch me bending. You had better get together and charge me, and just see what a good runner I am. Try to catch me before I take a flying leap onto my horse, and away I go, clomp, clomp, clomp, over the waterfall and down the hill to the bandstand, where I had such a welcome last year.

When I get to the bandstand I will hold my court, and please don't push, because I specially want to meet all the little children who could not get near me last year. I will stay at the bandstand until I have had a word with every one of my little friend's, then up and away down Crossbeck Road and Cowpasture Road, down to the roundabout – Brook Street Circus without a clown. Round we go, and then to the station, where I shall catch the 11.32 train to Bradford. I've got to get back to my Home from Home at Busby's in good time, or mother Christmas will be giving me a dog's life. I've left her in charge while I'm away. Whoopee! That's why I'm looking forward to tomorrow – It's my morning off!

Cheerio, I'll give you a run for your money tomorrow, on Ilkla Moor Baht 'At!

Lots of love and toffee, SANTA BUSBY CLAUS.

Come to BUSBY'S TOY TOWN in Bradford.
You must see **FATHER CHRISTMAS' LOG CABIN** and **MAGIC CHIMNEY**, the **TEDDY BEAR'S PICNIC**, and **FATHER CHRISTMAS' REVIEW OF THE TROOPS** and the **wonderful TOY DISPLAYS.**"

Following the popularity of this event, the *'Ilkley Gazette'* of the following week, 13th December 1935, carried a report of it on the back page:

"There was a big crowd of Ilkley children on the moors on Saturday morning to welcome Father Christmas, or as described 'Santa Busby Claus'. He had given warning through the columns of the 'Ilkley Gazette' that he would appear from behind the rocks near the White Wells.

There was a mist over the moors, but the children were quite determined not to allow him to escape without being spotted, and some had even taken binoculars to make quite sure, so that altogether Santa Claus and the children had a lively time before he reached the bandstand.

He gave shillings away in addition to toffees at the White Wells and coming down the hill on horseback tried to sail ships on the paddling pool, but found the water too low for successful demonstration.

Other toys were demonstrated at the bandstand, where more toffees were distributed, and after a triumphant parade into Ilkley he called at Messrs Busby's shop in Brook Street, and departed by train to Bradford".

CHAPTER EIGHT:
THE SECOND WORLD WAR AND THE POST WAR YEARS

THE years of the Second World War (1939-1945) were perhaps the darkest the country had faced in its history. The threat of invasion by Nazi Germany was very real. Certainly in the early years of the war when the Atlantic convoys were being attacked and much of mainland Europe, including the channel ports, were under German occupation, the United Kingdom was considerably isolated.

It was fortuitous that after the Dunkirk retreat by British forces in 1940 and air supremacy by the RAF in the Battle of Britain, that Germany decided to turn its attention to the Eastern front against Soviet Russia (in June 1941) instead of invading England. (Despite the devastating 'Blitzkrieg' attacks on major cities in the U.K., particularly London.)

In military terms, not invading the United Kingdom was arguably one of the greatest strategic errors the Nazis made. Instead this enabled Britain and, as the war progressed, her western allies to launch raids on Nazi occupied Europe, and ultimately the decisive counter offensive commencing with the 'D-Day' operations in 1944, from British soil.

In Ilkley and Wharfedale life went on. On the one hand much as it always had. People still skated on the tarn in winter and swam in the new lido (and the river) in the summer. The police still charged people for drinking beer 'out of hours' in pub raids, seemingly a minor, somewhat quaint and relatively trivial issue, considering what was happening in the rest of Europe.

On the other hand, Ilkley played its part in the war effort alongside every other community in the country. Not only were local men sent to fight, money was also raised. People were encouraged to invest in national savings bonds. The Ilkley Chamber of Commerce, and the 'War Weapons Week' committee led by Percy Dalton, took out a front page advertisement in the *'Ilkley Gazette'* on 16th May 1941 encouraging support for the 'War Weapons Week' campaign which was to run from Saturday 17th to Saturday 24th May. The advert used an image of White Wells and quoted the last verse from Rudyard Kipling's patriotic poem *"For all we have and are"*, written a generation earlier in 1914. (Kipling died

The former Hangingstone Quarry. — The rocks at the eastern end of the former Hangingstone quarry bear testament to the area being used as a firing range during the Second World War. – They are covered in bullet holes! (Photograph 2009.)

Incidentally, an article appearing after the war in the *'Ilkley Gazette'*, in 1946, tells us that some of the markings on Ilkley Moor's Badger Stone are also bullet holes which appeared following target practice during the Second World War, and suggests that future generations might not realise this, and attribute them to being contemporary with the original markings on the stone!

in January 1936, more than three years before the start of the Second World War.)

The final total raised during 'War Weapons Week' was over one million pounds. This was equivalent to just over £54 per head of population in the Ilkley area. An enormous sum of money by the standards of the day. Nationally, Ilkley had beaten Heckmondwike into second place with the amount raised. The unprecedented response to the appeal caused Percy Dalton to send a telegram to the Prime Minister Winston Churchill stating:

> *"You asked for tools to finish the job. Ilkley asked for four motor torpedo boats. We are sending 19. All records broken. Over £54 per head of population. We may be baht 'at; we are certainly baht brass!"*

What the Prime Minister made of the last sentence is unrecorded! (Though Downing Street did acknowledge the achievement during the following week.)

A large 'thermometer' was erected at the top of Brook Street, which was updated each day throughout the week by painting in the total amount rising.

In 1942 there was a 'Warship Week', in 1943 'Wings for Victory', and in 1944 'Salute the Soldier'. These campaigns raised millions of pounds nationally for the government to use towards the war effort; and encouragement to invest in Government savings bonds continued after the war too; as the country had to repay its debts to the United States of America for equipment used under the U.S. Government's 'Lend Lease' scheme. This national debt was paid in annual instalments (though in some years it was deferred) with the consequence that the debt wasn't fully paid off until the end of 2007.

Despite the use of White Wells in the 'War Weapons Week' advertisement in 1941, the building itself had actually been painted in more sombre colours for the duration of the war. This was to make it blend in with the surrounding moorland and thus prevent it being used not so much as a target in itself, but to prevent it being used as a navigation aid to enemy pilots attacking nearby Leeds and Bradford. It was mentioned in the *'Ilkley Gazette'* in 1942 as having been painted, described as *"Now having a somewhat tarnished purity for reasons of camouflage;"* and more significantly it was mentioned by William Joyce in one of his infamous speeches transmitted from Germany during the war.

William Joyce was born in New York in 1906 of Irish American ancestry. He had engaged in fascist activities in Britain as a 'British Subject', and spent the war in Germany from where he frequently broadcast propaganda and sinister threats on the radio to listeners in Britain. He earned the soubriquet "Lord Haw-Haw" due to his plummy upper-class accent. In his broadcasts he mentioned locations all over Britain. In one he menacingly announced: *"And don't think because you have painted White Wells black, we don't know where you are…"*

The sources of information, from which he theatrically tried to intimidate the British population included Nazi spies operating in the country. About whom the wartime slogan "Careless talk costs lives" warned the public to be mindful of what they said.

Following hostilities William Joyce was executed for treason in 1946.

I am grateful to former Ilkley resident Mrs Marjorie Hill of the Bay of Plenty, New Zealand for her wartime recollection of "Lord Haw-Haw's" announcement.

Although White Wells had been painted and had a 'somewhat tarnished purity' for the duration of the war the nearby tea pavilion, run by Mrs

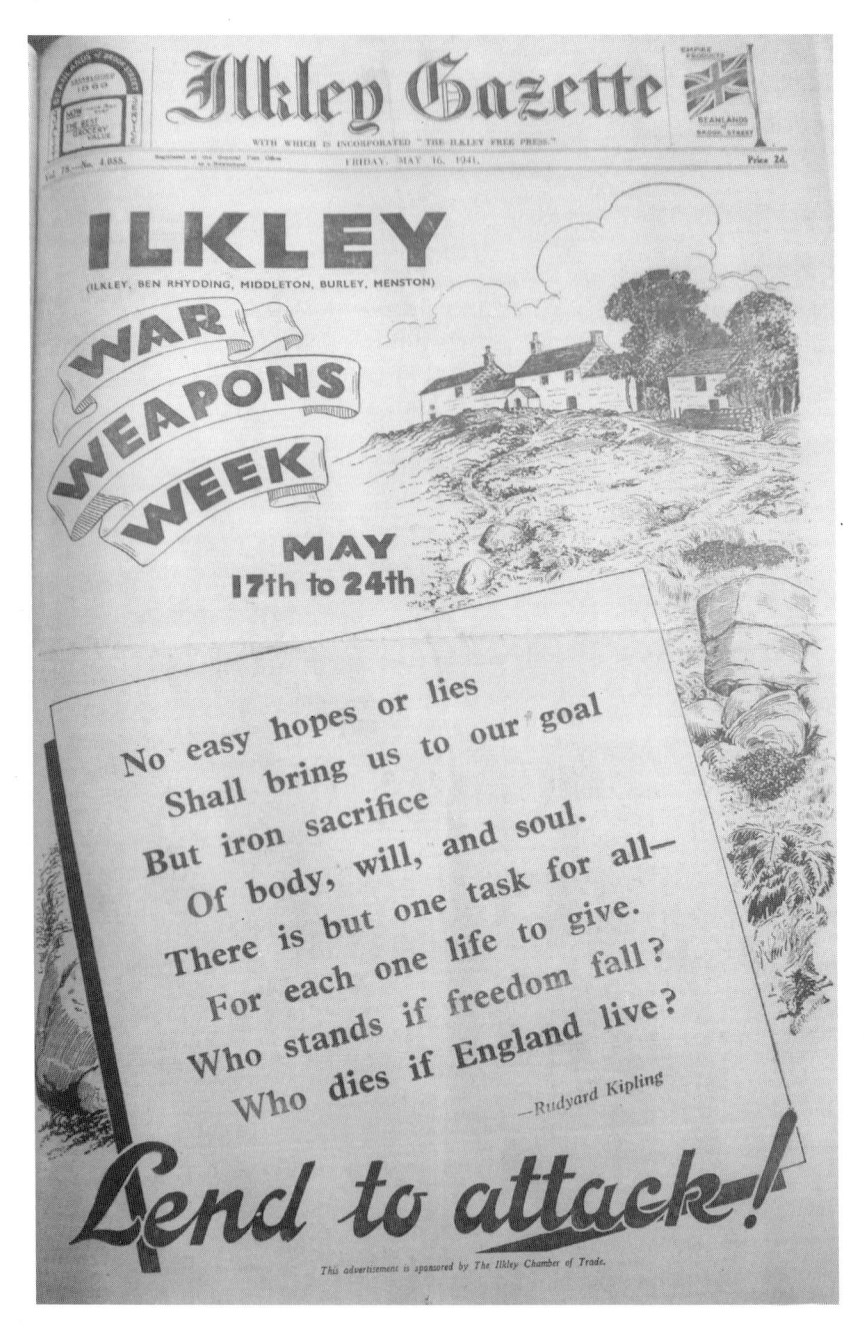

'War Weapons Week' advertisement. — The *Ilkley Chamber of Trade and Commerce* and the 'War Weapons Week' committee, led by Percy Dalton, raised vast sums of money locally in the form of 'war bonds'. Communities all over the United Kingdom were encouraged to invest money in the bonds, which in turn was used by the Government to buy weapons and hardware for the national war effort.

Williamson, continued to open. Though because of the subsequent austerity brought on by war, some things were in short supply and not always available. "We've no minerals!" became something of a catchphrase of Mrs Williamson at that time.

During the war Ilkley Moor was used as a military firing range. It was also the scene of three aircraft crashes. The first of these occurred early in the war when a two seater 'plane crashed to the west of Keighley gate. The single occupant was killed. The second was a bomber, which made a forced landing on the moor shortly afterwards. It was returning from a raid on St Nazaire and came down to the east of the Keighley Gate Road. Fortunately all survived. The third crash resulted in six fatalities. This occurred on 31st January 1944 on the ridge to the south west of the swastika stone. (Approx 2.5km/1.75miles to the west of White Wells.) It involved a 'Halifax' bomber. The crew comprised of five Canadians and one Scottish member, based at RAF Dishforth in North Yorkshire, as part of 1664 Heavy Conversion Unit RAF Bomber Command. Bad weather had closed in and the aircraft was off course by approximately forty

'War Weapons Week' Committee. — The great and the good of Ilkley who between themselves organised the 'War Weapons Week' campaign in the town and surrounding area. From left to right: Mr H. Sykes (hon secretary), Mr A.S. Maston (Chairman, Menston Savings Group Committee), Mr D. Nealy (Burley hon. Secretary), Mr A.C. Voight (Chairman of the Menston Committee), Mrs Ryder Runton (Vice-Chairman, Ilkley), Mr S.H. Plumbly (Regional Assistant Savings Commissioner), Mr Percy Dalton (President of the War Weapons Week), Mr W.H. Lee (hon. Campaign Secretary), Mr G.W. Clough (Chairman, Ilkley), Mr J. B. Boden (hon treasurer), Mr Percy Crossley (Chairman, Savings Group Committee, Ilkley), Mrs Illingworth (Chairman of the Burley Committee), Mr W. Parr (Postmaster), and Mr H. Benfield (assistant hon. Secretary).

Percy Dalton took his position in the centre of the photograph. (On his left [holding a hat] is Mr G.W. Clough, who was the Manager of the 'New Cinema' on Railway Road in the 1940's. I am grateful to my Dad, Edwin Hunnebell, for pointing out his old boss to me!)

Wartime at the Tea Pavilion. — I am grateful to Mr C. Youhill of Leeds for his recollection of wartime visits to the tea pavilion as a child, and for the use of this photograph taken at that time. The group outside the pavilion is (left to right): Mrs Hannah Youhill, (Mr Youhill's mother), Mrs Williamson's son John, Frank Gardner, (friend of Mr Youhill), Mrs Williamson, and Mr C. Youhill as a child.

I have heard a lot about Mrs Williamson from visitors to White Wells, and she has been a recurring figure throughout my research for this book. However until Mr Youhill sent me this photograph, I had never seen a picture of her. –Only the one in my minds eye. She looks exactly as I imagined her and perhaps because of this seems to look out across the years with a beguiling familiarity.

miles. The pilot dropped the aircraft through thick cloud in order to try and get a navigational fix on their position, and tragically crashed into the moorside mistakenly believing that he was flying at a higher altitude than was actually the case.

On 31st January 2006, sixty two years after the crash, a permanent memorial was unveiled on the moor at the site.

At the end of the war in Europe, VE Day (8th May 1945) was a public holiday. Bonfires were lit all over the country, and Ilkley was no exception. Large crowds gathered on the Holmes fields next to the river, and public buildings were illuminated. White Wells was not left out of the proceedings. The edition of the *'Ilkley Gazette'* issued on 11th May reported on the celebrations. It jubilantly proclaimed:

War Memorial Appeal (1946). — Following the hostilities of the Second World War, the image of White Wells that had been used in 1941's 'War Weapons Week' advert was used again. This time with an appeal to raise money for a memorial to local personnel who had died in the service of the country. The Memorial Gardens on the south side of the river between the 'Old' and 'New' bridges were created during the 1950's as a result, and are familiar to us today as 'The Park'.

"Not only has the blackout completely gone and 'the lights come on again', not only can we print news about weather while the subject is yet 'news', not only can we have bonfires and floodlight public buildings but- the White Wells are white again! Most people had been noting the fact and telling each other for a week or two, but it is the floodlighting which really brought to attention its restored pristine beauty. An anonymous contributor has even sent us the following ode on 'Our White Wells':-

> Our White Wells, it wore its battle dress
> And did its duty well.
> Once more it shines out in its white purity,-
> And we thank God all is well."

Photograph for the Ilkley Town Guide, 1948 edition. — During the austere years immediately following the Second World War, Ilkley was keen to regain its popularity as a tourist destination.

A competition was organised to find a photograph that would grace the cover of a new Ilkley Town Guide to be published in 1948. The winning photograph (above) was taken by Mr H.M. Storey (who also had a number of other photos entered in the competition). The photograph was reproduced in the *'Ilkley Gazette'* in January 1948.

The Late 1940's

In the austere years immediately following the war, Ilkley was keen to re-establish itself as a popular tourist destination. Calls were made to re-open the Ilkley Moor Golf Course, which had fallen into disuse, but this didn't happen.

A guide book for 1948 featured a photograph of White Wells, taken by a Mr H.M.Storey of Bradford. His was the winning entry in a competition organised by the Ilkley Chamber of Trade for the guide book.

The bandstand in West View Park, which had stood since 1904, was demolished. Use of the bandstand had been in steady decline, and with the interruptions of war between 1939 and 1945 it had become somewhat derelict and superfluous in the 'brave new world' that followed. Towards the end of 1947, concern was growing about the state of West View Park, and it was reported in the local press:

> *"Unsightliness.*
> *Another matter which the Council might consider in the immediate future is the unsightliness at the present time of what is officially designated as 'West View Park' and known more familiarly to local residents as 'The Bandstand'. For those who reach the moor by Wells Road this is the first sight which greets them, and a most untidy spectacle it is. Tufts of grass are growing in the asphalt surface of the area around the bandstand, and the windows are broken. The popularity of concerts in West View Park faded long ago, and it is doubtful if concerts will ever be arranged there again. In such circumstances there seems to be no justification for the bandstand to remain, or indeed for the shelter*[1] *in its present form. The shelter may be used occasionally, but hardly for the purpose for which it was originally intended. The Moor and Parks Department has much to feel proud about in Ilkley, and it will not be beyond its skill to make this part of the town more pleasant to the eye than it is at present."*

The 1950's:

During the 1950's social attitudes were changing. The 'Festival of Britain' (1951), had showcased everything 'modern' and the emphasis was on technology improving daily domestic lives.

Queen Elizabeth II began her reign in February 1952 following the death of her father, King George VI, and her (televised) Coronation ceremony was held

---

([1] The shelter referred to was located just to the south of the bandstand, built for the benefit of concert audiences. It too was demolished a few years later, in the summer of 1954. It should not be confused with the small wooden shelter overlooking the paddling pool.)

The bandstand was subsequently demolished in January 1948.

The removal of the bandstand. — In January 1948, the *'Ilkley Gazette'* printed this photograph of the demolition of the bandstand. Contrary to popular belief, the bandstand was not removed between the wars, nor did it survive into the 1950's or even the 1960's, as this evidence clearly demonstrates. However the adjacent shelter was demolished a few years later in the summer of 1954.

Interestingly, despite the towns desire to regain its place as a popular tourist destination, the bandstand was considered superfluous in the brave new world. A replacement bandstand was eventually built on the Grove in the town centre to mark the Millennium. (Though this was actually completed in 2001.)

the following year. Along with the news that Mount Everest had successfully been climbed by a British led expedition, and New Zealander Edmund Hillary and Nepali Sherpa Tensing Norgay had become the first to climb the mountain and return to tell the tale and show the world their photographs.

An era of optimism for the new 'Elizabethan Age' began.

Post war rationing ended (1954), and people were generally becoming more affluent.

Nuclear power was being explored as a means of providing sustainable cheap electricity, as well as the ultimate form of defence against the growing perceived 'threat' of communism.

There was civil unrest with the 'anti-war' protests over the Suez Crisis, and people seemed more prepared to be critical of authority and 'The Establishment'.

Vandalism, which had been a minor nuisance for decades, became an increasing menace. The tea pavilion café near White Wells was repeatedly broken into throughout the decade. A trend which, along with vandalism, would result in the ultimate demise of the café in the early 1970's.

When the last part of Ben Rhydding Hydro was demolished in 1957, the building was described as *"A monument to a departed age."* Which seems to sum up the changing attitudes of the 1950's. Attitudes that changed even further during the decade that followed.

Throughout the 1950's White Wells and the tea pavilion nearby were seldom mentioned in the local press. Except when they were broken into or associated with tragedy.

Break-ins and the theft of stock was a frequent occurrence at the tea pavilion, and at the Lido café too.

In October 1952 someone broke into the tea pavilion and attempted to burn it down. Mrs Williamson arrived to open the premises on the morning of Sunday 26th October, and found evidence of a deliberate fire. Access had been

The Paddling Pool overflowing. — A problem when the moorland streams were in full flood was that the paddling pool overflowed with water. This photograph dates from November 1951. A decade later, in the early 1960's, work was undertaken to reduce the possibility of this happening.

gained by means of the intruder breaking a pane of glass in the front door of the café, then opening the lock on the inside of the door. Part of a wall in the kitchen was burned through, and two of the tables in the café were burned as a result. Though the damage was largely restricted to the kitchen area, which was considerably charred. Nothing was reported missing from the café. Fortunately the fire did not catch hold of the wooden fabric of the building. Ilkley police were called to investigate the incident.

In 1953 the Ilkley Urban District Council looked into the possibility of obtaining burglary insurance, but eventually decided against it.

The moorland shelter overlooking the paddling pool had its thatched roof removed by the council, and replaced with wooden shingles. Similarly the shelter at the tarn was likewise improved. However petty vandalism at the two sites continued, as it still does today.

During the summer of 1954, the shelter in West View Park was demolished. Six years after the bandstand.

In August 1954, the *'Ilkley Gazette'* reported that Ben Rhydding Hydro would be demolished. This commenced the following year.

In November 1955 there was another fire, this time in the storage room next to the public toilets at White Wells. The minutes of the Council meeting of that month tell us:

"The I.U.D.C. surveyor reported on a fire which had occurred in the building adjoining the public conveniences in the vicinity of White Wells, Ilkley on Saturday 8th October 1955, and estimated that the damage amounted to £170. The surveyor further reported that the doorway to this building had been boarded up to avert any further damage or accident". No further light was shed on this incident, as to whether it was accidental or deliberate.

In February 1956 the tea pavilion was in the spotlight again. The pavilion closed during the winter months, but a body was found inside by a group of walkers who had noticed a broken window in the building. The *'Ilkley Gazette'* reported the event:

"The body of a man which on Tuesday (14th) was found lying near a gas oven in the café near White Wells on Ilkley Moor has been identified as John Seymour Peterson (51) of no fixed address.

Peterson, who came from the Liverpool district, was known in the Wharfedale area and for a time lived in Ilkley and Burley Wood Head.

The café in which the body was found is closed for the winter. The discovery was made by hikers on the moor, who were resting on the café veranda. They

Repairing one of the moor shelters. — This photograph dates from 1953, and shows the shelter overlooking the paddling pool undergoing work to improve its roof. Originally the shelter had a thatched roof, which had been replaced over the years, but by the 1950's it was decided to 'improve' on this by replacing the thatch with wooden shingles. Similarly the shelter at the tarn also underwent improvement.

> *noticed a smell of gas and, looking through a window, saw the body of a man lying inside. The police were informed and the body removed.*
>
> *Later, Ilkley Council who own the café sent workmen to replace two broken windows.*
>
> *Peterson was identified by a relative the following day. An inquest was to be held in the Lecture Hall, Ilkley this (Friday) afternoon."*

A verdict of *"Death from asphyxia from carbon monoxide poisoning, self administered whilst the balance of mind was disturbed"* was returned.

Later in the year, in October 1956, Mr Arthur Williamson, husband of the café proprietor died. Mr Williamson was seventy five years old and was well respected in the town. The week after his death the following obituary was printed in the paper of 2nd November:

> *"Mr Arthur Williamson (75) of 'Eastleigh', Chantry Close, Ilkley, who died in hospital on Saturday was a native of Stalybridge where his father was for 40 years*

schoolmaster. Mr Williamson was articled with a Dukinfield firm of accountants and afterwards worked for firms in Goole, Hull and Bradford. He had made his home in Ilkley since 1921 and his love of walking made him familiar with every part of the moor and the surrounding countryside. In the First World War he served with the Royal Corps of Signals. Cremation took place at Skipton on Tuesday."

What the obituary didn't mention was that Mr Williamson opened White Wells and the small 'tuck shop' to visitors at weekends while his wife, Jesse, ran the tea pavilion nearby. Following his death the key for visitors to look around White Wells was obtainable from the tea pavilion. Not an ideal situation, which resulted in White Wells being closed for the most part. Slowly the building became more dilapidated, and very little work was undertaken to maintain the fabric of the building.

The demolition of 'Ben Rhydding Hydropathic Establishment.' — It had been announced in August 1954 that the former Hydro was to be demolished. The building had been used by the 'Wool Control Board' during the Second World War but, unlike Wells House, it had remained empty for a number of years following its derequisitioning. This photograph shows the demolition work commencing in February 1955.

The last of Ben Rhydding Hydro. — In contrast to the somewhat rapid construction of Ben Rhydding Hydro over a century before, the demolition was a lengthy process, not being completed until 1957, as this photograph, from October of that year, shows.

Visitors to the tea pavilion and White Wells in the mid 1950's could refer to a card held in the porch entrance to the bathhouse, giving a description of what could be seen from the vantage point outside White Wells. Similar cards had been available from a box attached to the direction indicator for a number of years, but were obviously more vulnerable to the elements, so were moved inside the porch instead. The description on the card available circa 1955 is given below, with notes in brackets, where the landmark has altered since, or an additional point of interest can be clarified. Where the text appears in brackets, ( ), this is where the text on the original, and badly damaged card, is unclear and I have inserted what is likely to have been printed appropriate to the context of the description.

The View from the Old White Wells View Station

The Old White Wells are situate on the Northern slope of Rombalds Moor, about half a mile South of Ilkley. They face nearly due North, and are at an altitude of 700 feet above sea level. The level of the river Wharfe at Ilkley bridge, a mile distant, is about 235 feet above sea level. (a).

116   THE HISTORY OF WHITE WELLS

All distances stated are measured in a straight line across the map.

In the first place, it may be convenient to indicate the more prominent buildings in the foreground of the view. Commencing high on the left, at about the same level as the White Wells, the first building is the 'Semon Convalescent Home' (b), which can be identified by a small spire at the near corner and a large chimney in the centre. A little nearer to us is a fair-sized building with two bay windows fronting towards us, and a verandah fronting up to the moor. This is 'Hill Top Home' (c). To the right of this are several detached villa residences, with towers and spires of various kinds, the most prominent tower being that attached to a large residence named 'Arden Lea', now in use as a Railwaymen's convalescent home (d). Beyond, can be seen the red roofs of the villas lower down, on the North side of the Grove.

The palatial square building further right, with a new wing added 1954, and the most prominent erection from this position, is Ilkley College of Housecraft (e). Probably,

Repairs at Willy Hall's Spout. — In 1955 Ilkley Urban District Council undertook repair work on the White Wells access track. This photograph shows work in progress at Willy Hall's Spout waterfall. The retaining wall, over which the water cascades, was originally built in 1902, repairing damage that had been inflicted two years previously in the 'Great Flood', and protecting the Local Board's 'water works' which lie beneath.

It looks as if this photograph was taken just as the lads were about to have a tea break. – It appears there is steam billowing from inside their hut – from a kettle perhaps?

Summer visitors at the paddling pool. — In the 1950's and early 1960's, despite the vast changes that were happening in social attitudes generally towards 'old fashioned' things, the paddling pool remained a popular attraction during the summer months. (As did the tarn for skating during the winter.)

the plain, windowless building on the edge of the moor in a line with the College of Housecraft will excite curiosity. This was the reservoir that supplied Ilkley in the days when the place was a mere village, and is still used as a filter house and service reservoir (f). Above the trees to the right of the College of Housecraft can be seen the roof and bell tower of St Margaret's Church (g), and over that the red tiled roof of the Baptist church. A little to the right of St Margaret's church, and across the railway the 'Ilkley Moor Hotel' (h) is very prominent in the valley facing towards the moor. Right of, and quite near to St Margaret's church, is the high square tower of the building formerly known as Ilkley College, now the Wesleyan Deaconess College (i). The two prominent spires are those of the Congregational and Methodist churches, the former on the left (j) and in between them is the tower of the Parish church of All Saints. Brook Street and the railway bridge that crosses it (k) can be seen on the left of the Methodist church spire and the railway station roof a little to the right of the spire. Further away to the right will be noticed a bend in the river known as 'Crum Wheel' and wide of this are the cemetery chapels.

ILKLEY
GATEWAY TO THE YORKSHIRE DALES

Train services and fares from BRITISH RAILWAYS stations, offices and agencies

Railway advertising poster depicting Ilkley (1957). — The renowned artist Frank Sherwin (1896-1985) produced posters advertising rail travel and the delights of many destinations all over Britain. In 1957 one was produced to promote Ilkley Lido. It shows the general view looking south from the Lido, with the Cow and Calf rocks, Ilkley Moor and White Wells all visible in the background. (Some artistic licence has been taken with space limitations in the background.)

Within a few years of the poster being published, Richard Beeching (in 1963) published his infamous report recommending the closure of approximately one third of the national rail infrastructure. (Though rail closures had in fact been going on since the early 1950's, they were not on the scale of those which took place in the mid to late 1960's.) The lines from Ilkley to Skipton via Addingham and Ilkley to Arthington via Otley were subsequently closed.

Ilkley was not completely severed from the national rail network though, and the connections to Leeds and Bradford were retained. They are still used by commuters and visitors, and during the summer months, Ilkley Lido remains a popular attraction with both locals and visitors too. The indoor swimming pool adjacent to the Lido opened in 1973, and continues to provide year round facilities.

Now bring your gaze back to the buildings on the edge of the moor on your right, when 'Troutbeck Hotel' (l), will attract attention, which will be identified by its possessing a small pointed turret. Just to the right, and a little further away, is Ilkley Grammar School, which has a square tower surmounted by an "extinguisher". Right of this again is the rear of the extensive range of buildings known as 'Craiglands Hydro'. (m). The tarn, which cannot be seen from our present position, lies in a line between us and 'Craiglands'. Higher up, peeping over the edge of the moor, rather over a mile away, is 'Ben Rhydding Hydro' (n), looking with its irregular outline like a fine old Baronial castle, and just off the edge of the White Wells is the prominent corner rock known as "The Cow", about 900 feet above sea level. Its neighbour, "The Calf", is not visible from this position (o).

Turning back, and noticing objects a little further away, we see Ben Rhydding formerly called Wheatley, down in the valley below the Hydro. Straight behind Ben Rhydding village, about two and a half miles away, is Denton Park, with the Hall standing finely in the centre, and lower down a small lake and the road leading through the park to Askwith (p). Denton village is just to the left of the Hall. You may see the village school, and below it the vicarage, and the flagstaff on the church tower among the trees. Left of Denton is West Park Wood and a ravine known as Bow Beck Gill. Across this and on the hillside to the left is the village of Middleton, in line with the gasometer (q), which you will see down in the valley. Over the railway station roof and across the river is the cricket field, sports field, bathing pool and Middleton Woods. Over the tower of the Parish church can be seen the new residential district of Middleton. Right of the 'Ilkley Moor Hotel' is the road leading up to Middleton village, with the park on the left, and 'Middleton Lodge', an old Elizabethan mansion, now the home of the Passionist Fathers, at the top of the park (r). The portion of the building on the left was formerly a private chapel, which the Roman Catholics of Middleton and Ilkley were permitted to attend before the present chapel opposite the 'Ilkley Moor Hotel' was built. There is a belt of trees behind the lodge, and in this belt of trees is situate a secluded garden for religious meditation known as "Calvary". Down on the left, in a line with St Margaret's church and the Baptist church, is the golf pavilion, and the links stretch away to the left over the land mainly between the wood and the river. A special feature of the links is the fact that the course lies over Hawksworth Island, which can be seen over the College of Housecraft, an island formed by the river dividing for a short distance into two streams, and access to the island is gained by two private bridges. A quarter of a mile left of Middelton Lodge is an ivy covered house known as Tivoli. Further left again is High Austby. Lower down and in line with the Ilkley College of Housecraft is Low Austby. Over the left corner of the College of Housecraft is the village of Nesfield, in a clump of trees. Down to the left of Nesfield is Addingham Low Mill, one of the mills belonging to the big silk spinning concern of Lister and Co Ltd. (s). Left of the mill can be seen Addingham Rectory, and left of that the Church.

Still further to the left is the village of Addingham, distant 3 miles, in which the only prominent erections we can see from here are two or three mill chimneys.

Now let us take the hills which form the line of the horizon, and should be stated in the first instance that if the day be not reasonably clear you may be unable to see the more distant hills. Up on the left, beyond the Semon Convalescent Home, is High Crag on Addingham Moorside. The more distant hill further on the right commencing (on the skyline above) the Hilltop Home, and sloping down towards Bolton Abbey, which, by the way, is hidden behind the hill a little to the right of Nesfield, is the termination of Rombalds Moor. Skipton, eight and a half miles away is behind the hill about in (a line) with the Hilltop Home. Further right, away in the distance, is another range of hills. This comprises successively Rylstone, Cracoe and Burnsall Fells, and a portion of the range is also known as Barden Moor. The line of railway from Skipton to Grassington (t) runs down in the valley behind this range. The point where the range terminates on the left is called Crookrise Crag Top, and just behind are Rylstone and Norton Tower, the scenes of Wordsworth's poem of 'The White Doe of Rylstone'. A little to the right of Crookrise Crag Top, and over the winding road which can be seen leading up over the hill from Addingham to Skipton is Embsay Crag. This can hardly be distinguished unless the light is very good, because the hill rises still higher behind it, but viewed sideways Embsay Crag is a very striking feature in the landscape. The craggy point on the skyline about over Addingham Low Mill is Watt Crag, and the round hill further right, over Nesfield, is the summit of Burnsall Fell (1,661 feet), the highest point on this range, and over 300 feet higher than the hills to the north immediately opposite White Wells. The distance from where you stand to the summit of Burnsall Fell is ten and a half miles. Down on the slope of the skyline, to the right of the summit, you may see a speck of a building. This is a shooting box, and standing as it does on the crest of the hill it forms a prominent landmark for many miles viewed from both up and down the valley. The village of Burnsall lies down in the valley about a mile and a half to the right of the shooting box, and Grassington is about 3 miles beyond. It may be stated that the villages of Nesfield and Beamsley, together with Bolton Abbey and Barden Tower, are all nearly in a straight line drawn from the White Wells to Grassington. About midway between Watt Crag and the summit of Burnsall Fell you may be able with a glass to distinguish in the darkness of the hillside, about a mile on this side of the summit, a patch of lighter colour, the top line of which is straight. This is the embankment of Barden High reservoir, one of the Bradford Corporation's reservoirs. It may be well to mention Great Whernside, Buckden Pike and Simon's Seat, which are all visible from a little higher up the hill, are not to be seen from this position, as Beamsley Beacon intercepts the view. (u).

Beamsley Beacon, or Howber Hill, is the prominent corner hill behind Middleton Lodge, and is 1,250 feet above sea level. The Old Pike a little to the right and about a quarter of a mile away, is 1,341 feet, and from here can be had a view of Harrogate. Indeed, there is a glorious view in all directions from Beamsley Beacon, which in a straight line is just four miles distant from the White Wells. The solitary house in front of the little plantation down to the left of the beacon is Beacon House, and Currer Hall is a little lower down to the left. The round hill to the right of the beacon, and behind Middleton village, is called Round Hill and is 1,341 feet above sea level, the highest point of the range opposite, and slightly higher than the highest point of the hills behind the White Wells. The line of the opposite hill extends some miles further to the right, being called successively Denton, Askwith, and Weston moor. Up behind Denton Hall you will see a white shooting house. Pateley Bridge is 12 miles away, right over the village of Middleton, while Harrogate is distant 13 miles in the direction of the road that passes through Denton Park. A little left of Ben Rhydding Hydro, and in (the centre of the) opposite hillside, is the village of Askwith three and a quarter miles, while to the right of the Hydro, and high up on the edge of the far hill four and three quarter miles away is the tiny hamlet of Clifton. Midway between Ben Rhydding Hydro and the Cow rock can be seen Almescliffe Crags in the distance, nine and a half miles away, and from this (point 620) feet (v) above sea level another very fine view is to be obtained.

Points of the Compass

North: A line drawn due north from the White Wells passes over the railway station; slightly west of the summit of Round Hill (four and a quarter miles); a quarter of a mile east of Pace Gate 5 miles; three quarters of a mile east of Greenhow Hill church (ten and three quarter miles); and half mile east of Ramsgill church (15 miles).

South: A line drawn due south passes about three quarters of a mile east of Bingley church (four and a half miles); three quarters of a mile east of Queensbury church (10 miles); and one mile east of Halifax railway station (thirteen and three quarter miles).

East: A line drawn due east passes about over the Cow (7 furlongs); about over Weston church (three and three quarter miles); about over Weeton church (ten and a quarter miles); and four miles south of York Minster (30 miles).

West: A line drawn due west passes about over High Crag (one and three quarter miles); about quarter of a mile north of Silsden church (four and three quarter miles); 3 miles south of Skipton church (8 miles); and about quarter of a mile north of Barnoldswick church (15 miles).

Please replace the card in the box

"Gazette" Office, Ilkley.

Notes:

(a.): These figures are approximated. The height above sea level for the benchmark on the west gable of White Wells is 210.6 M, which is about 684ft 5in.

(b.): The Semon Home was demolished in the 1990's and replaced with housing. This can be seen looking west from White Wells.

(c.): This too has been demolished and replaced with housing.

(d.): 'Arden Lea' was built in 1881 designed by the architect T.C.Hope as a private house for Bradford draper George Thorpe. It became the 'Railwaymen's Convalescent Home' in 1915 and from 1962 belonged to the 'Marie Curie Foundation' and operated as a care home. It was converted into apartments in 2003, and renamed 'Thorpe Hall' after its original resident. The building was awarded a blue plaque by the Ilkley Civic Society in 2008, which is displayed outside the property, outlining its history.

Just to the left of 'Thorpe Hall' a white flagstaff is visible amongst the trees. This is on 'Westwood Lodge'. The building dates from 1872, and was occupied in that decade by a gentleman named Leonard Horner. In the 1890's Edward Briggs, a Bradford wool merchant owned the property, and around the turn of the century it was owned by the Ponting family. Herbert Ponting, the 'photographic artist' who accompanied Captain Robert Falcon Scott on the *Terra Nova* expedition to Antarctica lived here while the property was owned by his father.

(e.): 'Ilkley College of Housecraft' opened in the 1950's in the former Wells House Hydropathic Establishment; designed by architect Cuthbert Brodrick a century earlier. See the section on Wells House in Chapter Five: The Establishment of the Hydros.

(f.): This building was sold to a property developer by previous owners 'Yorkshire Water' and subsequently converted into a house, put on the market and sold in 2008. It is believed to date from the 1850's, following the 'Water Act' concerning public supplies, and would be consistent with the construction of Wells House nearby, though not as part of the hydro or exclusively for its use. During the 1870's, the Local Board carried out several alterations to the property, including the removal of the roof in 1878 due to it being in a somewhat precarious state of repair. The roof was replaced again in 1889 when it was decided that it was preferable as a practical feature in keeping leaves and other debris out of the water. In the mid 1930's the roof was heightened to allow the installation of filtration equipment; and in 1970 another reservoir was constructed slightly to the

THE SECOND WORLD WAR AND THE POST WAR YEARS 123

east of the property. This is located under the rectangular fenced off area to the side.

(g.): The bell tower is still visible but the roof of St Margaret's is now largely obscured by the housing development to the north east corner of Wells House.

(h.): The railway to the west of Ilkley which had opened in 1888 closed in the 1960's (as a consequence of the 'Beeching Report'), and the viaduct which carried it across the western portion of Ilkley was demolished in the early 1970's. The Ilkley Moor Hotel on Skipton Road at the junction with Stockeld Road was destroyed by fire in 1968, and the land it formerly occupied has since been built upon. However the buildings on this site are white and can be easily identified from White Wells.

(i.): This building is now apartments, and is called 'Deaconess Court.'

(j.): Today only one spire, that of Christchurch, is visible. This is the former Congregational church on the Grove. The spire of the Methodist church in Wells Road disappeared when the building was demolished in the early 1970's. The spire would have appeared directly behind Wells Court flats, easily identified from White Wells today.

(k.): The railway bridge across Brook Street was removed on Sunday 10th July 1966.

(l.): The 'Troutbeck' opened as a hydropathic establishment in 1863. During the First World War it billeted an army battalion. In the 1960's it housed the 'Gyro' nightclub, where in March 1967, rock icon Jimi Hendrix played a gig. It was converted from a hotel to a residential home in the late 1980's.

(m.): Purpose built as a hydro in 1859. Although it has had various modifications and extensions throughout its history, the 'Craiglands' is still in use as a hotel.

(n.): Ben Rhydding Hydro opened in 1844. It was demolished between early 1955 and late 1957. Consequently part of the structure remained visible from White Wells during 1955, at about the time this edition of the information card was produced. See the section on 'Ben Rhydding Hydro' in Chapter Five: The Establishment of the Hydros.

(o.): Neither the Cow or the Calf rocks are visible from White Wells. Looking across the moor in an easterly direction from White Wells, the trees going up on the skyline to the right of Hangingstone Road are adjacent to the rocky outcrop known as the 'Crocodile's Mouth'. Though this feature is not apparent from White Wells, and is better appreciated from lower down the moor. (The bridge across Backstone Beck to the east of the Tarn provides an ideal view of the 'Crocodile'.)

(p.) Denton Hall was the home of the Fairfaxes, and described as the "Finest hall that is within the dale". It was sold to the Ibbesons of Leeds, and burned down in 1734, eventually being replaced by the Georgian mansion that exists today. (The stone was obtained from a nearby quarry.) It became the seat of Marmaduke Wyvil.

The Denton Hall Estate was divided into three parts and sold off in 1919. It was bought by Lord Illingworth, who a few years later sold it to Arthur Hill.

During the Second World War it was used as a location in the 1943 Michael Powell and Emeric Pressburger film *The Life and Death of Colonel Blimp* starring Roger Livesey, and again in 1977 in the film *The Water Babies* starring James Mason. It is now owned by the electrical contracting company N.G. Bailey (Who also owns one of Ilkley's most well known buildings, 'Heathcote,' designed in 1906 by Lutyens, on Grove Road. See also note 's').

Looking slightly to the right of Denton Hall and on the skyline, the most prominent feature in this general direction today is the TV transmitter at Norwood Edge above Otley. The transmitter was built in 1962, and stands approximately 92m/300ft high.

(q.): At the time of the cards publication, the Ilkley gas works was on the site now occupied by 'Booths' supermarket at the junction of Leeds Road and Lower Wellington Road. There was a large retort house on the site, built in 1935 and demolished in the mid 1960's, that was a prominent landmark, alongside the gasometer, dating from 1892 and demolished in 1972. A second gas holder was also built at the gasworks, and was demolished when the former 'British Gas' site was redeveloped in the 1990's. 'Booths' supermarket can be identified from White Wells quite easily.

(r.): Middleton Lodge was owned by the Passionist Fathers from 1922 until the late 1990's. Although the original lodge remains, the former monastery buildings near it have been demolished and replaced with housing. Until the 1890's, Middleton Lodge was the seat of the Middelton family (along with Stockeld Park near Wetherby), the local land owners. Various Squire Middeltons were instrumental in the establishment of and the subsequent improvements to the bathing facilities at White Wells. These details are covered in the first three chapters of this book. (Note the different spellings of 'Middelton' and 'Middleton'. The correct spelling of the family name is Middelton, while the correct spelling of the lodge is Middleton, causing much confusion! However the two spellings have become variously interchanged in media reports over the years, with either being used.)

(s.): Low Mill at Addingham has also been converted into housing. The site was used as industrial units during the 1980's and in the 1990's a controversial wool scouring plant opened on the site. This was relatively short lived, and at the beginning of the twenty first century, the plant gave way to further housing redevelopment. However the former mill building still forms the centrepiece of the development.

The most obvious feature on the landscape looking in the general direction above Addingham today, are the wind turbines at Chelker reservoir. Wind turbines have been a feature next to the reservoir since the 1990's and are used to generate power to pump water from the river Wharfe into the reservoir.

In a line below Low Mill, the red roof and ornate chimneys of 'Heathcote' on Grove Road can be seen amongst the trees. 'Heathcote' was designed in 1906 by eminent architect Sir Edwin Lutyens. In 1958 'Heathcote' was bought by electrical contracting company N.G.Bailey, and it is still in use by them as offices.

(t.): The railway line between Skipton and Grassington was also a victim of the 'Beeching Report'. However the section between Skipton and Swinden Quarry near Grassington is still in industrial use, for carrying stone from the quarry to the main lines accessed from Skipton.

(u.): Great Whernside can in fact be made out from White Wells. It is visible through the gap in the trees across the valley on the slope coming down from Beamsley Beacon. It is however more apparent during the winter months, especially if there has been snowfall on the slopes of Upper Wharfedale. Though for a better view of these hills, the card quite correctly points out that this can be obtained from higher up the moor. Barden reservoir referred to opened in May 1883.

(v.): The card is unfortunately damaged and the height of Almscliffe Crag is not distinguishable in the text. However modern Ordnance Survey Maps give the height of this feature to be at approximately 190 metres, which converts to approximately 620 Feet.

CHAPTER NINE:
OUT WITH THE OLD, IN WITH THE NEW: DECLINE & DERELICTION

Although by the 1960's the moors, White Wells and the tea pavilion were still as popular as ever with both locals and visitors, attitudes and society at large were rapidly changing. The process of change had been in motion for a number of years, certainly since the start of the 1950's, but it gathered pace with the dawning of the new decade. The 1960's were the era of the cold war, JFK, Cuban missiles, Vietnam and Apollo. Science and technology were going to save the world and solve all its problems. Or destroy it in the process. The 'make-do-and-mend' philosophy of the post war era was replaced with a new optimism, and an ever increasing challenge to the old established order.

In Ilkley change was afoot as well. The 'Royal Hotel' on Wells Road was demolished and replaced with the building of Wells Court Flats in 1962; designed by Mr C. D. Biggin, of architects Walker and Biggin, Leeds. These flats are a product of their time, but by some they are considered to be 'out of keeping' with the surroundings. It is unlikely that permission for a similar construction would be granted today.

The era saw the demise of the railway that had, since 1888, connected Ilkley to Skipton and beyond. The railway bridge across Brook Street was demolished in July 1966. The line down Wharfedale to Otley was also closed. Fortunately the lines to both Leeds and Bradford were retained, and are still in use today.

The rise in the popularity of television contributed to the demise of the two cinemas in Ilkley. 'The Grove' cinema, which had opened in February 1913, and the 'Essoldo', formerly the 'New Cinema', (until 1949, when it was bought by the Newcastle based 'Essoldo' group), dating from 1928 were demolished in 1968 and 1969 respectively.

Rombalds Water Board was formed in 1962 to take on the responsibility of the town's water supply and maintenance. In an arrangement with the Ilkley Urban District Council, this also included an area of the moor around White Wells.

The paddling pool undergoing repairs (1961). — Being supplied directly from a moorland stream, the paddling pool frequently filled up with peat deposits and mud, particularly following rain. (And as seen in a previous picture, it sometimes overflowed as well.) To reduce the possibility of this happening, work was undertaken to divert the stream and arrange the inflow of the paddling pool so that water was taken from the surface of the stream while (hopefully) any unsavoury elements would be carried away through the main culvert adjacent. The success of this is somewhat subjective, even today!

Mrs Williamson who had operated the tea pavilion since the 1930's died in 1964. Her successor was Mrs I Gregson of Cottingley. She took over the tenancy in June, on a three year agreement to pay £75 per annum to the Ilkley Urban District Council; and charge 3d to visitors wishing to look around White Wells. The Council were seemingly oblivious to the fact that Rombalds Water Board had been the landlord since 1962, a situation that did not become apparent until 1968.

In November 1966 Mrs Gregson requested an extension of her tenancy. This was granted for a further three years, again with an annual rent of £75, from 8th May 1967.

In July 1968 Rombalds Water Board proposed an exchange of land on the moor. Including the area at White Wells. This provided more than a little confusion about the various areas of land actually held by the Council and Rombalds

Water Board. The council surveyor reported on the condition of the property and submitted an estimate for the cost of repairs. Which the council decided would be considered again in the preparation of the 1969/1970 estimates. The clerk of the council requested to obtain the views of the Civic Society and the Friends of the Manor House on the possible future use of White Wells. Throughout the decade very little in the way of maintenance had been carried out at White Wells. Perhaps partly through confusion with the water board about whom actually owned the property and perhaps also in keeping with the zeitgeist: White Wells represented everything 'old' instead of everything 'new', just as 'Ben Rhydding Hydro' had been considered a decade earlier.

In 1969 Mrs Gregson wrote to the Ilkley Urban District Council with a proposal to raise funds for the maintenance of White Wells.

In the minutes of the IUDC meeting of 21st April 1969 it is reported that:

"The clerk submitted a letter dated 11th April 1969 from the tenant of the White Wells Café suggesting an appeal to raise money for the repair and renovation of the White Wells, with a view to emphasising the historical importance of the buildings. The surveyor outlined for consideration suggestions for the demolition of the café building which was reaching the end of its useful life and the provision at the White Wells of facilities for serving light refreshments.

Resolved:
That the clerk be requested to explain to the tenant the suggested proposals and that these will be further considered if the suggested exchange with Rombalds Water Board is approved by the Minister."

Perhaps not the reply Mrs Gregson had anticipated.

The arrangement over a land swap with Rombalds Water Board was accommodated, and in 1970 construction began by the Board of a new underground reservoir adjacent to the filter station on the edge of the moor.

Meanwhile interested parties were enquiring to the IUDC about the future of White Wells. The minutes of council meetings from around this date show that the Civic Society was asking what form the renovations of White Wells would take, and when a start would be made.

The council surveyor submitted plans for the re-roofing of the bath houses and the conversion of the first floor into a café with part of the ground floor into a kitchen, in such a manner as to leave the two bath houses as a feature to be seen from the café. The estimated cost of this work was £2400.

It was resolved to have the surveyor prepare estimates for the repair of White Wells both with and without an integral café, and for the demolition of the old café buildings nearby.

By September 1970 the surveyor submitted a revised estimate of £900 for the repair of White Wells, while the provision of an integral café would cost an additional £2020. – And the cost of demolishing the old tea pavilion was estimated at £200.

The Civic Society added their voice to the debate by suggesting that repairs to the structure of White Wells were urgently necessary.

It was then resolved that the £900 for the immediate repairs were approved, while the additional costs to construct a café would be given further consideration at a later date.

An application with this in mind was submitted to the IUDC from a Mr Vanhinsberg and Mr Alkister for the lease of White Wells. They proposed a conversion into a high class restaurant with *"seasonal light meals and afternoon*

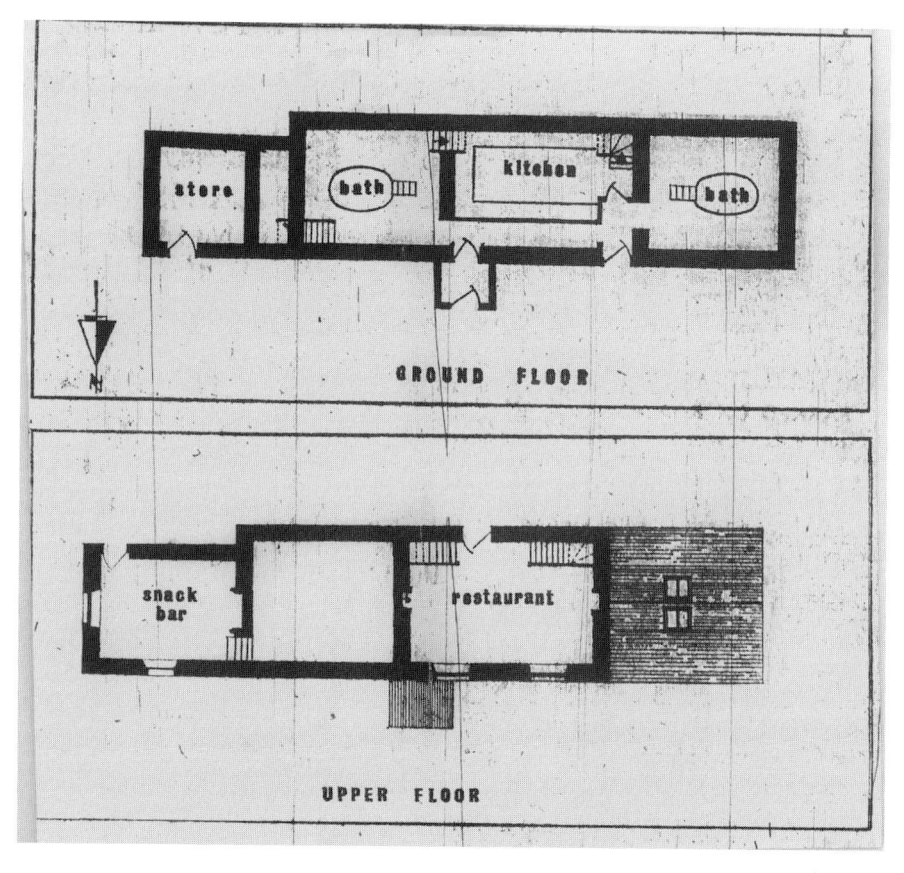

Council plans for White Wells restoration. — On 30th October 1970, the *'Ilkley Gazette'* printed plans for the future restoration of White Wells. At the time ambitious plans for a café/restaurant to be incorporated into the design were being proposed, to replace the somewhat dilapidated tea pavilion nearby.

teas". This proposal was ultimately rejected in early 1971 over concerns about inadequate car parking at White Wells and the unsuitability of the access track leading to the property for the volume of traffic the venture could potentially generate. Following this rejection, at the end of January 1971, in a letter to the *'Ilkley Gazette'*, a local resident suggested that White Wells should be converted into a youth hostel for the benefit of visitors to Wharfedale.

In February 1971, Mrs Gregson enquired as to the Council's intentions in respect of the tea pavilion, and in view of the fact that it was also in a bad state of repair had requested a reduction in her rent. The surveyor reported that the condition of the café had deteriorated to such an extent that it was almost beyond economical repair. It was resolved by the IUDC that the clerk be authorised to request Mrs Gregson to terminate her tenancy of White Wells café, and that the quarterly rent due in advance on 31st December 1970 be waived. Furthermore that the surveyor be authorised to demolish the café on the termination of the lease and report further with estimates of cost for preserving White Wells.

'Repair of White Wells begins.' — Despite the somewhat optimistic title of this photograph from the *'Ilkley Gazette'* of 12th February 1971, the 'repair' was limited to work on the roof to prevent further vandalism and break-ins at the property. However this was largely unsuccessful. Almost as soon as the work had been completed, White Wells was broken into again. A cycle which led the Council to become increasingly frustrated and calls being made for the building to be demolished.

OUT WITH THE OLD, IN WITH THE NEW: DECLINE & DERELICTION

'Hooliganism at White Wells'. — During the summer of 1971, just months after the council 'repairs', White Wells was broken into again. The roof was breached to gain access, while inside a sofa bed was installed by those responsible, amid broken bottles and further evidence of vandalism.

By March the landlord and tenant relationship between Mrs Gregson and the Council had become more acrimonious. Mrs Gregson requested reimbursement for the losses that she alleged to have sustained as a result of the council's delay in reaching a decision about the future of White Wells and the café and the termination of her tenancy. She submitted a claim for £346.11. In response the council resolved to inform Mrs Gregson that it was not proposed to make White Wells into a café and that she be offered £150 on the termination of the tenancy of White Wells café in full settlement of her claims.

Mrs Gregson did not accept the offer and the issue rolled on. By July the tea pavilion, instead of celebrating its fifty years, was standing empty. Not only was it in a bad state of repair, but it was also suffering from the effects of considerable vandalism, as was White Wells too. Prompting the *'Ilkley Gazette'* of 30th July 1971 to ask:

> "Do the latest acts of vandalism at White Wells indicate that some re-thinking is required about the future of this old landmark on Ilkley Moor, that those who said it should be demolished were right after all? Council officials have spent some time on preparing different schemes, councillors have given much thought to them and to the question of cost. It was agreed some months ago as a start to spend

£900 on making the place watertight replacing the stone roof tiles, carrying out other necessary repairs. The work had no sooner been completed before a hole was made in the roof, the door kicked in and a bed-settee installed on one of the upper floors. Stronger measures were taken to prevent people getting in. They were all to no purpose. Again a hole was made in the roof, the door forced open, and other incidental acts of vandalism carried out at the same time. Attention was also paid to the remains of the nearby café. It was thought that the last visitation had all but wrecked it, but it was demonstrated that it was still possible to do more.

The latest council suggestion under consideration is that the building could be used as a shelter for parties of children visiting nature trails on the moor, and that it could house some geological specimens and maps.

It needs little imagination following upon the recent experiences to see how much of a temptation this would be to the destructive instincts of those who have been responsible for the latest damage. Reluctantly it would seem realistic to concede that those who said the place should be pulled down were right. There seems to be little point in spending more money and time on it. The baths could be covered in, and four walls left standing to provide some shelter. The roof would not be left there very long if it was not removed."

The moorland tea pavilion near White Wells. — The tea pavilion stood near White Wells for fifty years, between 1921 and 1971. Toward the end of Mrs Gregson's tenancy (1964-1971) little had been done to maintain the fabric of the building and it was in a poor state of repair. Repeated break-ins and vandalism added to the problem and the pavilion quickly became beyond economic salvation.

OUT WITH THE OLD, IN WITH THE NEW: DECLINE & DERELICTION

The foundations of the tea pavilion today (photograph 2009). — A photo taken from a similar angle as the previous picture shows the concrete base of the former tea pavilion. All that remains of it today following the Ilkley Urban District Council's controlled burning in October 1971.

An agreement was finally reached between Mrs Gregson and the IUDC in October 1971. This is recorded in the minutes of the meeting held on the 18th, when it is noted that the sum of £250 in payment to Mrs Gregson had been agreed and that the remains of the tea pavilion could now be demolished. Time was not wasted in this endeavour. Demolition was carried out by means of a controlled burning a few days later on Thursday 21st October 1971. The '*Ilkley Gazette*' reported the event in a short paragraph tucked away on page seven, without a photograph. It said:

> "*Partly demolished by vandals, the café on the moor to the east of the White Wells was set on fire by Ilkley Council yesterday (Thursday) as the cheapest way of disposing of it.*"

White Wells fortunately survived though its future remained very uncertain. It seemed that each time the council spent money on 'repairs' or rather measures to try and keep vandalism at bay, their efforts were thwarted. Clearly this was becoming increasingly frustrating, as rate payers money was being swallowed up with nothing to show for it except an increasingly vandalised and derelict property. Little wonder then that there were calls from within the council to demolish White Wells and finally resolve the situation.

Following on from Mr Vanhinsberg and Mr Alkister's rejected suggestion in 1971 concerning the proposals to convert White Wells into a restaurant; in 1972 a gentleman named Mr C. Howell approached the IUDC with his own proposals for the property. Minute 589 of the 'Ameneties Committee' meeting of 19th March 1972 informs us:

'Min 589 White Wells.
The Clerk submitted a letter dated 19/3/72 from Mr C. Howell of Liversedge, expressing interest in using White Wells as a Dales Craft Centre, such as hand-loom weaving, wood carving, blacksmiths, pottery etc. The centre could also accommodate the proposed Field Studies Centre and continue as a museum. The building would be restored at his own cost and there would be full-time administration of the Centre. It appeared that Mr Howell proposed to make White Wells habitable for his own occupation.

Resolved:
That the applicant be informed that the council wishes to adhere to its original decision in minute 463, namely that the curator of the Manor House be authorised to administer the building and arrange with local organisations for its occasional use.

In early 1973 a Mr Hubert Dalwood proposed placing sculptures in the area around White Wells. These were to be 'modern art' sculptures, made of concrete. The Ilkley Urban District Council were split over the issue, but ultimately decided against the proposals by one vote, ten against to nine in favour, declaring that such sculptures would be *"an incongruous and discordant feature within an area of great landscape value."*

An issue that would provoke a similar response resurfaced twenty eight years later, in 2001, in the shape of the 'totem poles' at White Wells. –And again in late 2008 and early 2009 when unfounded rumours concerning the installation of 'statues' at the tarn were aired in the *'Ilkley Gazette.'*

Despite a number of people coming forward with ideas and suggestions for White Wells, and the IUDC also being anxious to do something about it, it seems they were at a loss as to just *what* that would be, and what would be acceptable to them.

The breakthrough finally came when Mr Eric Busby's proposals were given serious consideration and the restoration of White Wells could become a reality.

CHAPTER TEN:
ERIC BUSBY AND THE RENOVATION OF WHITE WELLS

ERIC BUSBY was one of the sons of Earnest Busby, the founder of the Bradford department store 'Busby's'. (There was also a smaller branch of the store in Brook Street in Ilkley, that had opened in 1918. See Chapter Seven: Between the Wars for an account of a Christmas visit to the moors by Santa Claus in 1935, arranged by 'Busby's'.) Eric had worked for many years in his fathers company, and during his retirement focused on his great passion, art. He lived in Menston, at 'Goosewell', (also a former bath house), and established an art gallery there. He had an appreciation of local history, and followed the increasing dereliction of White Wells in the early 1970's with interest.

He approached the IUDC in 1972 with a proposal of restoration for White Wells, and an offer to buy the property. His offer was declined. The IUDC, although at a loss as to what to do with the increasingly vandalised building argued that White Wells had been a 'gift' to the people of Ilkley by Squire William Middelton, and as such could not simply be bought and sold. (Arguably it was not so much a 'gift' as a commercial venture to exploit the increasing interest in 'water

Eric Busby, 1899-1983. — In the early 1970's it looked likely that White Wells would be demolished. If it had not been for the efforts of Eric Busby this undoubtedly would have happened. He proposed a restoration plan to the Ilkley Urban District Council, which was accepted on the casting vote of the Chairman, Mr Jack Spencer. The proposed restoration proceeded, and Ilkley will be forever grateful to Mr Busby that White Wells was saved and restored.

cures'.) However Mr Busby's proposals for the renovation of the building were considered and reconsidered throughout the latter half of 1972. Finally the issue came down to a vote. To either accept or reject the restoration as proposed by Eric Busby. The voting was split down the middle. With half of the councillors in favour of the first option, and half of the councillors in favour of the second. It all hinged on the casting vote of the Chairman of the IUDC in 1973, Mr Jack Spencer. To reject the proposals would almost certainly have led to the inevitable demolition of White Wells. With the weight of history perhaps pressing on his heart and mind, Mr Spencer, used his casting vote in favour of the restoration of White Wells, and gave Eric Busby the benefit of the doubt to proceed with the plans.

At the meeting of the 'Amenities Committee' on the 18th June 1973, it is recorded:

> *'Min 760: **White Wells**.*
> *Pursuant to min 709, the Clerk reported that planning permission had been obtained for the conversion of White Wells on the lines suggested by Mr Busby and that Mr Busby's estimate of the cost of converting White Wells was £9500. An improvement grant of up to £1500 would probably be available in respect of the provision of the living accommodation.*
>
> ***Resolved:***
> *That a grant of half the cost of the works when the improvement grant had been deducted but not exceeding £4000 be made to Mr Busby towards the cost of the works of conversion.*
>
> *That the Clerk be authorised to settle the terms of a lease of White Wells to Mr Busby for a term of seven years at a nominal rent of £1 per annum* [1] *with option to renew for a further seven years at a rent to be agreed.'*

The *'Ilkley Gazette'* of 6th July 1973 tells us that the vote to back Mr Busby's proposals was close:

> "When the vote was taken the Chairman announced that the voting was equal and that he would vote in favour of the amendment.
>
> This brought questions from some members and it was pointed out that without the chairman there was an uneven number of members present which suggested the vote could not have been equal unless someone abstained. There was a call for a recorded vote and this was something the chairman at first was not prepared to allow.

([1] This is probably where the notion that the tenants of White Wells still pay a 'peppercorn rent' to the council originates. Unfortunately this is another popular myth!)

After a ruling by the clerk however he changed his mind and the voting resulted as follows:

For the amendment to make a grant of up to £400: Crs Beevers, Bell, Clavering, Forest, Holden, Renton, D.Smith, Spencer, Turner. Against: Crs Brown, Davy, Emsley, Green, Marshall, Settle, Shelton, H. Smith, Wilson.

This was eight for and eight against [2] and Cr Spencer used his casting vote in support of he amendment."

At the time the approval to his plans had been given, Eric Busby wrote the following comments:

"Reclaiming of the White Wells property primary as a landmark and information centre for the Wharfedale Naturalists Society is a natural outcome from the pioneering work at the Menston Goosewell Gallery. The development is not a commercial enterprise, nevertheless it is hoped and indeed expected that it will pay its way and eventually break even, as the Menston county gallery has done, without any burden on rates, taxes or charities. It remains to be seen whether or not these simple uncomplicated aims may be achieved by the good will and shared pleasure of having preserved this historical treasure. Should others wish to share in the basic cost of this difficult task of course they will be most welcome, but there will be no public appeal and No committee control. One is encouraged and cheered by the moral support of John Thompson, Director of Art, Bradford, Keighley and Ilkley, acknowledging the help received by the advice and guidance of Mr B.E. Townend and the operational heads of the departments of the I.U.D.C. (1973), also to Mr Jack Spencer, the chairman of the Council then in office for his casting vote which saved the day.

Councillor Jack Spencer, Chairman of the Ilkley Urban District Council, 1973. — As Chairman of the Ilkley Urban District Council at the time of great uncertainty about the future of White Wells Mr Spencer had the casting vote in the debate as to whether Mr Busby's proposals should be accepted or refused. Voting was split on the issue. Fortunately he looked favourably upon Mr Busby's proposals, and perhaps with the weight of history bearing down upon him, he used both his own vote as a Councillor and his casting vote as Chairman in favour of saving White Wells. Had the vote gone the other way it is almost certain that White Wells would have been demolished shortly afterwards.

([2] It would appear that there were nine votes for and against, not the eight suggested! –With the result that the chairman had a vote in the debate, and the casting vote to decide the issue as well.)

It will take a little time for White Wells to settle down into a quiet functional pattern, no grand opening, rather a gathering together over an experimental period and at length a comfortable acceptance; a "Belonging".

Explanatory Note.

1. *To counteract vandalism it is quite necessary that part of the property should be occupied.*
2. *To conform to the requirements of the building authorities one of the baths had to be floored over at a level which allowed for damp course and underfloor ventilation.*
3. *No alteration has been made to the exterior of the buildings the new door is an opening up an old door space in the original building.*
4. *New windows are in sympathy with the 18th century design.*
5. *Light and heat are by Glo-Gas from cylinders, an overhead cable for electricity not being allowable, a buried cable would have cost approximately £4000.*
6. *Drains. Connected to mains by gravity to sound drains laid last century for adjoining toilet.* [1]
7. *The public toilets remain the responsibility of local government.*

Eric Busby, Goosewell Gallery,
Menston, Ilkley."

There was a considerable amount of work to do when the renovation of White Wells started. Residential accommodation was required, which called for the installation of an internal bathroom and bedroom upstairs in the mid-section of the building. This involved the removal of a staircase leading from the east bath house rising over the kitchen to the upper floor. Internal walls were fitted upstairs, and a new window space created for the bathroom alongside a blocked up window to the rear of the building. The stairs leading up from the entrance were also replaced and the two front entrances and small kitchen window re-opened. An internal door between the kitchen and the east bath house was installed, and the downstairs windows in the kitchen and under the stairs at the rear were also re-opened. However the most significant alteration was in the bath house in the western side of White Wells. To make the building habitable the former plunge bath had to be covered over. Rather than simply filling this

---

[1] Public toilets were installed in the former 'Charity Bath' building in 1910. Which was leased to Mr Butterfield for the sum of £5 per annum. Prior to this, photographs show what appears to have been an outside privy situated to the west of the charity bath in the original enclosure.

Interior of White Wells During renovation. — Two photographs showing the interior of White Wells during the renovation phase. These were taken in 1974.

The first photograph shows the poor condition of the plunge bath in the western side of the building. The stone face water spout had been removed and placed in the other bath in the eastern side of the building (where it remains today).

After considerable work done to repair the walls of the west bathhouse and install damp coursing, this bath was disconnected from the water supply and covered over with a raised floor (though with trapdoor access) which today forms the café.

in with concrete, it was disconnected from the supply and drained. The stone face spout through which water had previously filled the bath was removed and was installed in the other bath, where it is still in use today. A raised floor was constructed above the redundant bath. This allows for ventilation and was a requirement of the damp-coursing. Additionally a loft void was put in the roof space above to provide insulation, and two windows, one to the front of the building and one to the rear were created to provide light. The resulting room was originally envisaged as a 'sitting room', but has since evolved and is now in use as the café.

The roof of White Wells was in a poor state of repair thanks to a combination of neglect, vandalism and break-ins, so was fully repaired. A triangular space at

The second photograph shows the staircase to the upper level. This was completely replaced during the renovations. What is particularly interesting about this photograph is the fact that there is no visible evidence of the fireplace above the stairs. This was uncovered later in the restoration project (and can be seen today). The position of the fireplace suggests that the stairs have not always existed in their present location. It is likely that the staircase was installed and the fireplace blocked up during the building work carried out during the late 1880's or mid 1890's.

Access to the upper level was also gained via a staircase from the eastern bathhouse, with the steps rising through the kitchen. These steps were removed during the restoration, the wall in the corner of the bathhouse blocked up and a bathroom installed on the upper floor above the old stairwell instead.

the apex of the west gable, which had once contained an air vent, was walled up. At the back of White Wells, the rear door was replaced and the adjacent window walled up. In the east bathhouse a new staircase was installed from the former shop area adjacent to the back door, and down into the bathhouse. Replacing the badly deteriorated former one. The plunge bath was restored and safety railings installed around it, with a gate at the top of the plunge bath steps to allow access to the water if required. A decorative candelabra (salvaged from a Baptist Church) was put above the bath, and a display cabinet fitted by the kitchen door in a new dividing wall. The porch was fitted with an exterior door. Originally there had been an inner door, but the porch itself was open to the outside. It had become very badly overgrown with nettles and weeds inside it, and sheep had used it as a shelter from the elements too.

During the course of the renovation work, the underground water tank to the rear of the public toilets was 'discovered'. There was considerable speculation as to the function of the tank. It was suggested that it could possibly have been an early reservoir supplying Ilkley.

Obviously detailed research into the history of the tank had not been undertaken, otherwise it would have come to light that the tank had in fact been previously discovered in 1924. (See Chapter Seven: Between the Wars.)

In February 1975 White Wells was broken into. The intruders stole an air rifle and a total of £1 cash donated by visitors to the building's 'Fabric Fund', from a jar inside the porch. Despite the extensive renovations, the property was of course still vulnerable to break-ins, but fortunately it did not attract this activity (or the associated vandalism) to the extent that it had just a few years earlier when the property was derelict.

White Wells during renovation. — The *'Ilkley Gazette'* provided a series of photographs during 1974 showing the renovation work being carried out at White Wells. The above photo was printed in April, while the following appeared in October, when the work was almost complete.

White Wells bathhouse (1974). — Note the white railings around the bath. (Today they are black.)

The chandelier above, it was reported, came from a Baptist Chapel that was going to be demolished. Unfortunately the report didn't mention which chapel this was.

Memorial Plaque in the bathhouse porch. — During the course of the renovations a memorial plaque was installed in the wall of the bathhouse porch. The inscription reads:

"*Remembering Elsie M. Fletcher. 1886-1974. Custodian of Local History. Hon. Curator, Manor House Museum.*"

CHAPTER ELEVEN:
THE MODERN ERA

WHITE WELLS officially reopened to the public on 13th May 1976. A plaque was unveiled on the east gable of the building by the Lord Mayor. The plaque states:

> *Former bath-house built by*
> *Squire William Middleton* (sic) *for the*
> *people of Ilkley*
> *In the Eighteenth Century.*
> *Restored by Eric Busby 1972-1974.*
> **WHITE WELLS**
> *The wells were officially opened to the public on*
> *13th May 1976*
> *by the Lord Mayor*
> *Councillor Mrs Doris Birdsall Hon.M.A.*

However despite this 'official' opening, the renovations of White Wells had been largely completed by 1974, and the tenants Geoff and Barbara Lister had taken up residence and opened the bath house for visitors to look around. Though refreshments were not generally available. In 1977 Barbara Lister described living at White Wells as being like "living at *'Wuthering Heights!'*"

In 1978 Eric Busby was awarded an M.B.E. in recognition of his public services. Though by 1979 White Wells was once again unoccupied and Mr Busby who was eighty years old and no longer physically capable of running the place himself made a proposal to Bradford Council for the Libraries and Museums Department to take over as the landlords. He did not approach Ilkley Parish Council. Reflecting on his experiences in proposing and undertaking the renovations of White Wells, he wrote in 1980:

"***White Wells** – A story recorded in brief terms by Eric Busby.*

In 1972 the Ilkley Urban District Council voted in favour of the building's destruction on the grounds that it could no longer be maintained against the erosion of vandalism. The building was a horrid mess, the ancient baths desecrated by broken bottles, beer cans, litter and the walls by graffiti. Dirty matting and

White Wells opening ceremony. — The restoration of White Wells had in fact been completed for about eighteen months before the 'official' opening ceremony, involving the unveiling of the plaque on the eastern gable of the building. This was held on Saturday 13th May 1976, and was performed by the Lord Mayor, Councillor Mrs Doris Birdsall.

The picture shows Mr Busby with the Lord Mayor (in the striped top), and the newly unveiled plaque on the building in the background.

blankets on the first floor told their own story. The building fabric was riddled with dry rot.

Letters of protest appeared in the local press suggesting that the building might be converted to a residential property and that the occupier might open the property to the public on occasions. I followed this up with an offer to buy White Wells for £1000 for the purpose of adapting the building on the lines recommended in this letter.

The IUDC were not amused and I was quickly told the property could not be sold, it was a gift to the town by Squire Middleton (sic) and built on common land (their's evidently to destroy, they had already burnt down the chalet café close by at the 'upper tarn'). By this time I had got White Wells into my bloodstream, the actuating factor was largely sentimental as White Wells had been a tuck shop for long years, going back at least to my wife Margaret's childhood, mostly in South View, Ilkley, and was a place where we had often picnicked with children and where countless thousands had done before us. I also liked the building for being a focus point on the stretch of moorland roundabout, and the view from the porch being the grandest in all mid-Wharfedale in my opinion...

Subsequently there followed many meetings with the most friendly and helpful Clerk of the Council, Bertram Townend. The IUDC decided to ask me to submit a plan and I turned to a team which had been employed by me to build the Goosewell Gallery in Menston under the leadership of Stanley Webster of Haste Successors Ltd of Yeadon. From the start he told me the restoration would be a difficult task which he would not usually be willing to tackle, but that he would undertake it for me! Plans were prepared, quantities calculated, likely IUDC grants and National Restoration grants assessed, and all were duly submitted to the Council:

Voting for and against was balanced, but the Chairman used his casting vote in favour so I was committed – and excited...

The job was extremely difficult but one of the contractors cheered me up in the early days by saying he didn't see any unsurmountable difficulties. On the other hand the foreman joiner from Haste Successors said "Tha's chosen a reight bloody place this time!"

Before they took up residence the first White Wells tenants, Geoff and Barbara Lister, lived in a caravan on site for some months in order to safeguard the builders' materials as well as the property during the winter-into-spring of 1973/74, which demonstrates the way that all involved in the work became keen for it to succeed. The building was finally ready to be occupied and was open to the public in 1974, quietly and without any fuss. It was a great joy to see light shining from the windows at night and the re-establishment of a popular walking destination as part of the districts' attractions. Coincidentally this was the year of National Heritage for the preservation of buildings.

The final cost on completion was, inevitably, much higher than expected, but I was helped by gifts from some interested Canadian friends who had been born and brought up in Ilkley and a gift from Elsie Fletcher's [1] estate. It seemed appropriate to add commission on the paintings of David Anderson [2], which were currently being sold through Goosewell Gallery, to the White Wells costs.

---

[1] **Elsie Fletcher** was a respected local historian and author who lived in Menston but whose research covered a wide area in Yorkshire, including the Roman road from York which passed over Rombalds Moor. (There is a memorial stone dedicated to Elsie Fletcher in the bathhouse entrance porch.)

[2] **David Anderson** was an artist of the Glasgow School who studied in Paris in the 1900's and retired to Wells Road, Ilkley, in later life. At his death he left many paintings and his family had approached Eric to see if they could be sold at Goosewell Gallery (Eric's Menston gallery). He made the most of this 'find', and advertised and organised Press coverage, and put on several exhibitions. As a result these lovely 'Andersons' became a must-have work for local collectors in the 1970's.

In May 1976 Councillor Doris Birdsall, the Lord Mayor of Bradford, unveiled a small plaque at White Wells to commemorate the restoration. She spoke of the building being a tourist attraction and thanks were expressed to myself and the contractors.

I had always felt that the restoration had more affinity with Bradford than Ilkley, perhaps because my experience of the Easter Monday Walk[3] which was an annual event for Bradfordians, but certainly because now Bradford Metropolitan district Council had taken over the running of Ilkley and Keighley. I knew the Bradford Director of Arts and Museums, Michael Diamond, who had consulted with me on several matters relating to art. He had become interested in White Wells and thought there may be a possible tie-up with the Manor House, Ilkley, which Bradford now administered. In due course he presented this idea to the Council as a recommendation for a 1977 Jubilee Year project. Finally, in 1979 the Bradford authorities agreed that they should take over the administration and care of the building.

Bradford Council were approached with a view to taking over the responsibility or White Wells in 1979. The *'Ilkley Gazette'* reported in July of that year:

> *"If B.M.D.C. acceded to a request to take over responsibility for the running of the small museum at White Wells, Ilkley, finance of about one thousand pounds a year would be needed, the chief officer told a meeting of the Cultural Activities Panel.*
>
> *Referring to a three year plan for his division, the chief officer said the money would be needed now rather than in year three of the plan. He explained that the building had been restored and maintained by a private individual who was no longer in a fit physical condition to continue with the work, and the Council had been requested to take over responsibility."*

Bradford Council agreed to the suggestions for the Libraries and Museums department taking over, and after some decoration in the bathhouse by Bradford Council, and the addition of some 'history boards', White Wells reopened at Whitsuntide 1979, between the hours of 2pm and 6pm at weekends.

In addition the 'Wharfedale Naturalists Society' organised a small display in the room at the top of the stairs from the bath house. The flagpole, free standing on the grass to the east of White Wells, was fitted with the Society's

---

[3] What Mr Busby describes as the *'Easter walk'* could possibly be the traditional *Whitsuntide* walking race instead from Bradford to Ilkley and then back to Bradford on the road, not over the moor. Though walking over the moor was and still is a popular activity undertaken on spring and summer Bank Holidays.

curlew logo on top. (The flagpole is still there, but without the curlew atop.)

The next tenants, Fred Lancaster and his partner Sue, remained at White Wells for only a short time.

Following on from them, George and Jean Stockham became the tenants in 1981. Refreshments were served again, but on a small scale via the kitchen to bath house door. Though in particularly inclement weather customers were allowed to sit at the table in what is now the main entrance to the café. (The room which is now the café was in use as George and Jean's private sitting room.)

Jean Stockham, in contrast to the comments of Barbara Lister in 1977, likened living at White Wells to being "like living in a goldfish bowl!" A reference to the incessant 'gawpers' who out of curiosity or general nosey-ness peer through the door and windows of White Wells, even when it is abundantly clear that the place is closed!

Throughout the 1980's White Wells remained as popular as ever with both locals and visitors, though there were some concerns raised about funding and its long term future. However many people were thankful that Eric Busby had come along and had been the catalyst for the building's renovation. Sadly Mr Busby died on 1st January 1983, at the age of eighty three. Though with the restoration complete, and the tenants providing security from vandalism, most of his ambitions and plans for the building were realised within his own lifetime.

In August 1983 work was carried out at White Wells to repair the drinking fountain at the rear of the premises, and also to repair the plunge bath. The flow of water to these had stopped the previous autumn. Echoing a similar situation of almost a century before when the drinking fountain had dried up in the 1880's and required attention by the Local Board.

In 1985 the 'Ilkley Gazette' featured a report that there were concerns over the long term funding of the Ilkley Manor House Museum and White Wells. Bradford Council were anxious to put peoples' fears at rest, and gave reassurances that the future of the property was in fact 'safe'.

In May 1986 Bradford Council assessed White Wells and classified it as a 'Grade II Listed Building', effectively limiting the amount of development that could otherwise be effected. A classification which still remains in place.

David and Margaret Dawson followed George and Jean Stockham as the tenants. The Dawsons lived at White Wells until the end of 1988, when the building once again became empty.

A curious incident occurred in the vicinity of White Wells in November 1987, and was reported in the local newspaper on 13th:

"Police search after bizarre find on Moor.
Four mounted police and about a dozen volunteer countryside wardens spent most of last Friday in a fruitless search of Ilkley Moor, following a bizarre find at a local beauty spot.

The search was carried out after a walker found a book about Marilyn Monroe, containing a handwritten poem by a person named Annabel. Also found were a half empty bottle of paracetamol tablets, an empty bottle of apple juice, a box of matches and a packet of Embassy cigarettes.

Police at first feared they may have been left by someone copying Marilyn Monroe's suicide, and an immediate search of the area around White Wells, above Ilkley, was carried out with the help of police dogs.

The police say no one has been reported missing, but they were concerned that the owner of the articles may be in need of help.

An appeal has been made for anyone who has any information which might help them solve the mystery to come forward."

It would appear that nobody did, and the 'mystery' remains unsolved.

In 1989 fears were raised again about the future of White Wells. In June the 'Ilkley Gazette' reported on the situation:

"Cold Reception for White Wells Plan.
An assurance that White Wells would not be sold has been given to Parish Councillors who at their meeting on Monday disapproved a plan to privatise the historic bath-house.

Miss Pam Brittain of Nottingham wants to re-open White Wells, which has been closed since Christmas, as a hydrotherapy centre and health clinic. Bradford Council's principal officer for the Arts and Museums Department, Mr Stephen Kerry, told Councillors he was seeking their views on the proposals.

"It is our professional opinion as well as our moral conviction that White Wells belongs to the community. We simply act as stewards of it to see it is still there in another hundred years time", said Mr Kerry.

He emphasised that any contract for White Wells to be let on a commercial basis would be reviewed after six months.

Ban on Cars.
It had been said that if White Wells was let as a commercial venture there would be hundreds of cars travelling over the moor but Mr Kerry assured councillors that there would be no more cars allowed over that road than there were now. "It is not a public highway and we don't intend to encourage traffic up and down that moorland track", said Mr Kerry.

He said the use of the waters would continue to be free and that the eighteenth century building would still be used as an information centre. It could be an opportunity to bring the original use of the building like the plunge baths, said Mr Kerry.

Mr Geoffrey Finnerty, director of Legal Services with Bradford Council said Miss Brittain intended to give lectures and sell skin creams which she made in an effort to bring back some of the spa treatment. If the plan went ahead it could be that White Wells would be used again for plunge baths for the first time in one hundred years.

On the question of whether White Wells could be sold Mr Finnerty said: "I can't see the council selling any part of the moor."

Councillor Mrs Molly Renton said: "White Wells must be kept under local control and doubted whether it would make money as a commercial venture.

"Nobody is going up there to spend money on face creams. White Wells appeals to serious country lovers and walkers who love the moor", she said.

Cllr Rowland Hill said White Wells over the years had provided an attraction for the people of Ilkley and visitors and belonged to Ilkley. "I would not like to see it disturbed," said Cllr Hill who went on to thank Bradford Council for maintaining its upkeep over recent years. If they had a choice of passing the responsibility for it to the Countryside Commission he would not be against that.

Cllr Mrs Barbara Cousins, Vice Chairman of the Council said she understood White Wells which was part of Ilkley's heritage could not be sold off at any price. "It must never be allowed to go out of the local authority's control", she said.

The Parish Council in opposing the project to privatise White Wells agreed to invite residents to put forward their ideas on maintaining the building for future years.

Later this week the Department for Legal Services at Bradford Council stated that White Wells was part of the common land and as such it was unlikely that it would ever be sold off."

In the minutes of the Parish Council meeting of 3rd July, *"Councillor Hill Reported that he understood the Authority had resolved to let White Wells to a commercial tenant. He considered Ilkley was being 'conned' by the recommendation of the Bradford M.D.C. Sub-Committee as when the previous tenant left, as far as he knew, there was no advertisement for a similar tenant.*

Planning application was now in progress for a change-of-use, and Councillor Hill hoped that people who cared for this Grade II Listed Building – one of the most important listed buildings in the District – would let the Planning Department have their views. He hoped this Council would do so in due time."

150   THE HISTORY OF WHITE WELLS

In September 1989, the paper reported again on the situation at White Wells:

"Council say Yes to White Wells plan.

Plans to re-open Ilkley's famous landmark White Wells on Ilkley Moor, have been finally approved by Bradford Council's Arts and Recreation Sub-committee.
The latest move follows the Council's planners approval of a scheme initiated by Nottingham woman Miss Pamela Brittain. She together with partner, Martin Allsop, will privatise the building, closed since last Christmas, as a hydrotherapy centre, health clinic museum and café. Now the Nottingham businesswoman is finalising details of the lease of the building with Bradford Council.

Prior to the approval Miss Brittain found herself up against strong opposition to the plans in the form of environmental groups such as the Ramblers Association, Dales Society and the Council for the Protection of Rural England. They all stated that the building should not be used for commercial use."

MAGICAL WHITE WELLS TO TEST ITS POWERS

At the beginning of August 1990, Pamela Brittain and Martin Allsop were featured in an article in the *'Ilkley Gazette'*:

"Magical White Wells to Test its Powers."

"There's a certain magic which surrounds White Wells –Ilkley's historic landmark on the edge of the moors. Yet its reputed powers, claimed to have worked wonders in the past have not been used for 80 years. Until now.

For under new tenants Pamela Brittain and Martin Allsop, the secluded landmark's famous spring water, with its "special healing powers", could soon be put to the test once again.

Exploiting the powers of the natural, forever flowing water is one of the "exciting" ideas the couple have planned as they embark on a new business venture.

At the re-opening of White Wells at the weekend, Pam Brittain said, "I believe the spring water does have healing powers and, hopefully, we will be using them."

Such powers have their sceptics. Some believe in them. It is claimed the powers have a proven track record and the legend began in the eighteenth century.

It was an injured shepherd, it is said, limping off the moors with a wounded leg, who first discovered the powers behind White Wells. Having been in agony he bathed his leg in the spring waters and then, the story goes, his leg was cured.

Soon after the shepherd's story the spring waters were used for curing a form of tuberculosis. Again, in some cases, it worked wonders.

More and more people became intrigued at the powers of the waters. Curiosity prompted tests to be carried out. The results showed that its purity, tenuity and coldness gave the most benefits.

It was in 1791 that the two baths were built for people to bathe in the spring water and those baths still survive to this day. The famous spring water has never run dry.

Now, in the twentieth century and with White Wells being given a new lease of life, the people of Ilkley could be invited to bathe in the waters.

Pam Brittain said "Charles Darwin has apparently had a bath here so the people of Ilkley will be in good company."

She is a qualified beauty therapist and healer and will be putting her expertise to work with the spring waters, with sound and with skin care products which will be on sale at White Wells.

She said, "The water is very clean and is tested every eight weeks. But it is very, very cold and it is difficult to stay in long – I can assure you.

In the 80 years in which the spring water has not been used the bath has just been a museum piece. We want it to be more than that so we are bringing it back into use", she added.

White Wells will still remain as a museum with its history and legends for all to read and observe. There is also an archaeology section in the cottage style building.

And for the thirsty or hungry walker, refreshments will be provided in the new White Wells tea room. The famous spa water is on offer for anyone to drink. Yet whether it is as "exhilarating as champagne", as is claimed, is another matter.

Beauty courses for budding therapists are also in the pipeline.

In all, Pam Brittain and Martin Allsop are confident of success after coming from York.

"We are both looking forward to the business and really do believe it will take off", they said.

Pictured toasting the re-opening of White Wells with spa water are (left to right) Pamela Brittain Martin Allsop and Mr Geoff Finnerty of Bradford Council."

Pamela Brittain and Martin Allsop were subsequently appointed as the tenants of White Wells, and provided drinks and snacks along vegetarian lines.

The newspaper report of the Ilkley Parish Council disapproving plans to 'privatise' White Wells perhaps gave the impression that the property was going to be sold off to the private sector. Clearly this was not the case. Pamela Brittain and Martin Allsop intended to run their own private business from the premises, though White Wells would still be owned by Bradford Council. A very similar situation to that which had long existed, firstly with the landlords Middelton, then the Local Board, followed by Ilkley Urban District Council, and more latterly, Bradford Council. The 'Change of use' suggested in the minutes of the Parish Council meetings was a technicality to accommodate the proposals for opening White Wells as a 'hydrotherapy clinic'. Not dissimilar to its original use!

During the early 1990's, vandalism became something of a problem again on the moor. The 'cuckoo hut' shelters at the paddling pool and the tarn being in the front line of this. Tim Blythe the 'Ilkley Moor Project Officer' within Bradford Council set up the 'Ilkley Moor Action Group' with a view to undertaking various work on the moor, including the repair of the shelters. The group evolved into the 'Airdale and Wharfedale Countryside Management Project.' (Though what eventually happened to this group after 1994 when Bradford Council's Countryside Service took over the interests of White Wells is unclear.)

In 1991, it was reported that the shelter overlooking the paddling pool was in such a bad state following a fire that it would have to be demolished.

Fortunately with White Wells having tenants once again, vandalism at the property was deterred. At least until the spring of 1994. Pamela Brittain and Martin Allsop's original (and perhaps somewhat ambitious) plans for turning White Wells into a 'hydrotherapy clinic' were never fully realised, and they left in March.

Between March and the end of July, numerous concerns were raised in the local press about the fact that White Wells was closed. Vandalism and break-ins returned to plague the property, raising fears of a return to the dark days of the early 1970's. Calls were made for White Wells to be reopened, and Bradford Council pledged that this would happen. Consequently at the end of July the Council's Countryside Services Department was appointed to take over the management of White Wells from the Libraries and Museums Department and following some minor repair, restoration and decorative work, White Wells was reopened over the last weekend of July 1994. The event was mentioned in the 'Ilkley Gazette':

"One of Ilkley's Most Famous Tourist Attractions is set to Re-open This Week. Vandals and burglars targeted White Wells after the eighteenth century hydrotherapy centre on Ilkley Moor closed down in March this year when tenants Pam Brittain and Martin Allsop gave up their lease.

Bank Holiday walkers and visitors were later reported to have been unhappy that the landmark, which helped establish Ilkley as a spa town, was locked.

But it is due to open again on Saturday after the completion of renovations carried out by Bradford Council's Countryside Service –which has taken over the running of the building from the Arts Museums and Libraries Department.

These include information boards on the areas history while visitors will also be able to buy refreshments.

City Hall Councillors also meet on Monday to discuss long term plans for the site. Possibilities include the development of an upstairs bunkhouse for walkers and the creation of a Friends of White Wells Trust.

The building will be open on Saturdays and Sundays from 10am to 5pm and entry is free."

The following week a particularly interesting feature appeared in the paper about White Wells:

"Old Roman Bathhouses admit public once again."

"White Wells opens its doors to a bright new future."

Visitors to Ilkley Moor will be able to enjoy refreshments as they study the areas history at the famous landmark known as White Wells.

On Saturday White Wells was reopened as a centre offering a countryside service after renovations carried out by Bradford Council

The building was closed down earlier this year after vandals and thieves targeted White Wells which had opened as a centre for homeopathic and hydropathic remedies. Long term plans for White Wells could include the development of an upstairs bunkhouse for walkers and the creation of a Friends of White Wells Trust.

Workmen employed by Sir Adam de Middleton laying foundations for a farm are believed to have first discovered the wells – old Roman bathhouses - in about 1287.

Medicinal.

There appears to be little information about the wells until 1645 when another member of the Myddleton family had the walls of the present day building erected to protect the wells.

It was not until 1837 that the roof was put on.

Since then the wells, hollowed out of the rock, became known as two baths where visitors could bathe and drink the pure cold spring water.

The flow of water into the baths was said to possess medicinal properties for the treatment of rheumatism, gout, sprains etc.

At one time donkeys were available for hire to carry people from Bridge Lane to White Wells.

'Ilkley: Ancient and Modern' by Dr Robert Collyer and J. Horsfall Turner states: "William Butterfield, the son of another William Butterfield, who managed the baths when George the Third was King, still treats his visitors, on payment of sixpence, to a plunge, douche, spouting, or shower bath; and few would ever think of leaving Ilkley without a copious drink of the ice-cold water.

The spring supplies 90 gallons per minute; there are two dressing rooms; the bath, of oblong form, is uncovered; the water is turned off after being used by two persons; there is also a shower bath."

The reopening of the building on Saturday launches a service that will only be provided at weekends between 10am and 5pm. Entry is free."

The feature is interesting because it echoes the claims made by David Scott, some ninety years earlier, when giving visitors his "Mellifluent, diaphanous, limpid, luminous…." oration. He similarly claimed that medieval workmen had discovered the remains of an earlier 'Roman' bath (and additionally that the remains of a tessellated pavement could be found beneath White Wells.)

The source of reference the reporter used for the feature is not recorded.

Furthermore, the walls around the baths do not date from 1645 but 1791 when Robert Dale built the two baths. Nor were the baths "hollowed out of the rock". They are built of dressed stone blocks! And the roofs were not added until the 1850's when White Wells came under the auspices of Wells House Hydropathic Establishment.

Perhaps minor details in themselves, but this is how so many myths have been built up surrounding the history of White Wells over the years. It cannot be stressed enough that there is simply no evidence that there have ever been 'Roman Baths' at White Wells!

Within a year of the Countryside Service taking over the maintenance of White Wells, there followed one of the biggest innovations in the building's history. Mains gas, electricity and landline telephone were installed via a service pipe from Wells Road approximately 250 metres away and 70 metres below the level of White Wells. The Countryside Service dug the trench in which the service pipe was to be laid, through difficult and rocky ground. Eric Busby had wanted mains electricity at White Wells some twenty years earlier during the

The ideal gift for friends faraway
The Ilkley Moor Plate

This decorative 8" plate in Goss China portrays some of the treasured landmarks in and around Ilkley and Ilkley Moor. The Cow and Calf Rocks, White Wells, Church Street, and the nearby beauty spots of The Strid and Bolton Abbey. The much-loved Ilkley Coat of Arms is displayed in the centre of the plate. Price £19.95

2 sweet dishes to match –
Again carefully produced in fine bone china, these two sweet dishes (one carrying the Ilkley Coat of Arms, the other Bolton Abbey) are so modestly priced at £5.95 each, and make IDEAL PRESENTATION GIFTS.

Ideal gift ideas –
Any of these three pieces would make ideal gifts for someone living in or around Ilkley – or, in particular, *a wonderful gift idea for someone living faraway who has fond memories of Ilkley and Ilkley Moor.*

On Ilkla Moor Baht'at
The famous poem known by all true Yorkshiremen is carried on the back of the plate.

All these pieces are exclusive to **Peter Jones China**
26 The Grove, Ilkley (Tel. 816777); 26 Lands Lane, Leeds 1 (Tel. 453172).

Ilkley merchandise on sale in 1990. — 'Peter Jones China' promoted the sale of the Ilkley plate, featuring White Wells (and other attractions in the town and the local area). Their advertisement from the *'Ilkley Gazette'* in 1990 brings to mind the Ilkley merchandise that was available some ninety years earlier.

initial renovation phase, but was unable to provide it due to the costs of such a pipe and the undesirability of the alternative overhead power lines.

After the installation of the service pipe, the cobbles outside White Wells were laid in December 1995. These were installed in order to protect the pipes underneath from erosion caused by visitors' feet. However the addition of cobbles was not universally accepted as an 'improvement'. The following spring, in April 1996, the presence of the cobbles was described as 'vandalism' by some residents, and there followed correspondence in the local newspapers about it.

Despite the initial controversy generated by the cobbles, after a few months of being open at weekends and being run by volunteers, the popularity of visiting White Wells was growing again. There had been letters in the local press expressing concern when the tenants had vacated the property in March 1994 about the uncertainty of the future of the building and calls for it to be reopened again. The plunge bath provided the Countryside Service with an inspiring solution that captured the imagination.

On 1st January 1995 they organised the first 'New Year's Day Plunge'. Such was the appeal of this, it was repeated again on 1st January 1996, and likewise every year since. Usually with local newspapers photographing the 'brave' participants, and even sometimes interviews by local T.V. and radio coming to report on the event!

The 'New Year's Day Plunge' has since developed into something of a 'tradition' and the 1st of January is now the busiest day of the year at White Wells, with usually in excess of one hundred 'plungers' taking part throughout the day.

Despite the fact that White Wells had once again opened and was staffed by a team of volunteers at weekends who had reintroduced a small selection of refreshments, the building was still vulnerable. Vandalism and break-ins returned, due in part to the fact that there were no tenants actually living at White Wells. Though when the mains gas and electricity were installed in 1995, the situation improved somewhat. A security system was introduced shortly afterwards, which immediately alerts the police to any break-ins. This provides at least a deterrent if not a cure to the problem.

In 1996 the Countryside Service decided to house tenants at White Wells. Derek and Christine Arnold were appointed toward the end of the year. They opened the café at weekends in December and for the 'New Year's Day Plunge'; and then took up permanent residence at White Wells early in 1997. A wider range of refreshments and snacks became available and, significantly, an area inside White Wells was allocated as a café, rather than customers buying drinks at the kitchen door in the bathhouse. The café tables and chairs were placed in the former bathhouse to the west end of White Wells. The room which Eric Busby had created as a 'sitting room' during the renovations in the 1970's, above the former plunge bath.

Additionally the flagpole on the east gable of White Wells was re-instated and the system of flying flags when White Wells is open was introduced. This was supplemented with another smaller flagpole at the top of the steps from the access track outside the front of the premises.

Derek and Christine decorated the interior of the café with an eccentric and interesting collection of memorabilia mostly from the 1930's and 1940's. Derek was affectionately referred to as a 'character' and a 'showman' by customers,

Cobbles outside White Wells. — When the service pipe bringing mains gas, electricity and landline telephone to White Wells was laid in 1995, cobbles were also set outside the building. Ostensibly to protect the pipes from erosion caused by visitors feet. However in the spring of 1996, the presence of the cobbles caused considerable controversy, and accusations of 'vandalism' were directed toward Bradford council, insofar that the cobbles were an intrusive feature that appeared out of place with the rest of the building. The letters page of the *'Ilkley Gazette'* featured comments both for and against the cobbles, and they were retained.

Although not an original feature of White Wells, the cobbles have now 'bedded in' very well, and reduce the amount of mud brought into the café than otherwise might have been the case. The original controversy surrounding them is now largely forgotten. (Photograph 2008.)

and was something of a practical joker. Usually wearing a waistcoat and bowler hat as part of his ensemble when White Wells was open.

We got to know Derek and Christine well during their tenancy. Firstly as regular customers then by helping them out at busy times such as bank holidays, New Year's Day and when Derek and Christine were on holiday.

The Arnolds decided to leave White Wells in 1999 and retired to the east coast.

Between October 1999 and March 2000 White Wells was once again empty. For the Millennium day plunge on 1st January 2000, the Countryside Service had volunteers opening the premises.

In the New Year there were forty applications for the vacated tenancy of White Wells. The selection process whittled this down to a shortlist of the more serious candidates. In January 2000 Joanne and I learned that our application had been accepted onto the shortlist and we had an interview (at White Wells of course!). Shortly after that we were informed that we had been chosen as the successful candidates for the tenancy, and that we could start the necessary proceedings with a view to moving into the property in March.

We had the advantage of actually having the experience of running the café, and living at White Wells when Derek and Christine had been on holiday. So we already knew the routine and logistical requirements.

We took up residence on 14th March 2000, and after a preparation period of three weeks, we re-opened White Wells as a café in April 2000.

We built upon what Derek and Christine Arnold had established, while at the same time introduced our own style of decoration, and made some adjustments to the menu.

The Flags at White Wells

When we took up the tenancy of White Wells in 2000 we inherited the system of flying flags used by Derek and Christine. The idea being simple: White Wells is always open when the flags are flying, and always closed if the flags are not flying. From this basic concept we have evolved the system into the flying of different national flags on or around the weekend closest to the different national days for countries around the world. This has resulted in a lot of interest from visitors to the building, both children and adults, and we have put up a poster of national flags for reference on a wall in the café entrance. Additionally with prior notice we can fly flags by request for visitors from overseas, perhaps staying with family or friends in the area and planning a visit to White Wells during the course of their time in the United Kingdom. –Assuming we have the relevant flag in our collection of course! If not visitors are invited to supply their own flag and we will fly it for them.

In addition to the many different flags, we always fly the English flag, the Cross of St George, when we are open and usually the United Kingdom Union flag (the 'Union Jack') too.

Other special flags to look out for at White Wells include: The Yorkshire County flag, the European Union flag, and on the weekend closest to 21st October, the Royal Navy Ensign. This is flown to commemorate 'Trafalgar Day'.

Sometimes a black drape is flown above a particular national flag. This symbolises national mourning in the country being represented, for either a disaster or the death of a high profile public figure.

However the fact that we fly a wide variety of flags at White Wells over the course of a year should not be taken to imply that we necessarily agree or disagree with the situation or political opinions of the leadership or regime in any particular country being represented. The flags are flown as a point of interest only, and the fact that it is on or around that nation in questions national day and, of course, to show that White Wells is open.

One of the main events in Ilkley during the year 2000 was the opening of 'Darwin Gardens Millennium Green' on Wells Road. The former West View Park had become overgrown, and from 1997 had been the subject of a 'Millennium Project'. A group of dedicated volunteers had worked hard to clear the site, replant it and add interesting features such as the very popular maze, laid out with small flagstones each paid for by contribution.

The project was named 'Darwin Gardens', following a suggestion from local historian Frazer Irwin, to commemorate the visit to Ilkley in 1859 of the scientist Charles Darwin. Darwin had stayed at both Wells House and the nearby Hillside House, and it is believed he had also 'taken the waters' at White Wells during the course of his visit. (See the chapter Five: The Establishment of the Hydros and the Expansion of Ilkley.)

'Darwin Gardens' was officially opened on the afternoon of Saturday 24th June 2000 by the author and former Ilkley resident Jilly Cooper. A large crowd assembled in the 'Darwin Gardens' car park, that Jilly Cooper, and Dr Peter Harnett of the 'Darwin Gardens Trust' addressed. In the evening, White Wells hosted a private party attended by a number of guests, including Jilly Cooper.

CHAPTER TWELVE:
INTO THE TWENTY FIRST CENTURY

By and large the new century began where the old one had left off. With the line between the two being something of a blur. Some people considered the year 2000 to have been the start of the twenty first century, but 2000 was the one hundredth year of the twentieth century. Though to point out this simple mathematical fact was considered pedantic.

On 1st January 2001 the world did not of course end. Just as it hadn't ended at the start of the previous year. Clearly the battle of Armageddon was not unleashed upon the world either, contrary to what some prophets of doom had suggested. The most significant event of 2001, '9/11', was entirely man made.

Early in the year Britain experienced the 'Foot and Mouth' crisis, which caused widespread concern. Even Ilkley moor was not left unaffected.

THE TRIALS AND TRIBULATIONS OF 2001: 'FOOT & MOUTH' AND 'TOTEM POLES'.

The 'Foot & Mouth' Crisis

Following widespread outbreaks of foot and mouth disease in the United Kingdom, Ilkley Moor was completely closed to public access between the end of February and the beginning of August, as a measure to attempt to control the spread of the disease.

During this time straw matting soaked with disinfectant was put on the road by the cattle grids at Darwin Gardens and Westwood Lodge. The road remained in use for vehicles and pedestrians, but people were not allowed to wander onto the moor. Although we were allowed to remain in residence and still come up and go down the access track to White Wells via the closed car park and more disinfectant matting, White Wells remained out of bounds to the general public for the first time ever in its long history. We could not open and lost 100% of our livelihood for the duration of the crisis. Bradford Council, our landlords, agreed to waive our rent and council tax, but apart from that we were on our own. We had to exist on meagre unemployment benefit.

Many talks and meetings with officialdom hinted at grandiose schemes for compensation for both us and for others in a similar situation. However such schemes for financial support (for us at least) quietly evaporated when the moors reopened in August. By September the rent and council tax demands arrived instead. It took us more than the next two years to recover our losses, and get back to the position we had been in before the crisis began.

It was suggested in a letter appearing in the 'Ilkley Gazette' in late 2008, seven years after Foot and Mouth, that Ilkley Moor reopened 'early' in the crisis, enabling visitors to walk about on the moorland. This is something of a debateable point. While it is a fact that Ilkley Moor did reopen earlier than some other rural areas of the United Kingdom, the closure of the moor between February and August should not, in our opinion, be simply dismissed as a triviality, with the implication that the reopening in August was 'early' in the crisis. Especially when the closure had such a profound and devastating effect on our livelihood.

'Totem Poles':

In early 2001, before the foot and mouth crisis started, Bradford Council's Countryside Service cut down a tree in the enclosure adjacent to the public toilets. We requested some of the wood from this to recycle by means of making some 'totem poles' to stand on the paths leading to White Wells, as a point of interest for visitors. The tallest of these poles being approximately 1.3m / 4ft 6in, the smallest being approximately 75cm / 2ft 6in in height. With the others being varying heights in between. There were eight in total, with the possibility of adding a further two later. The Countryside Service considered this a novel idea and an appropriate use of the spare wood, and consented to our proposals.

Originally we had hoped to invite local schools to design the poles, in the same way that schools had been involved with some of the features in Darwin Gardens. But the foot and mouth crisis put paid to our plans. Instead during the months that the moor was closed I positioned and decorated the poles myself.

Unfortunately the poles were to become something of a contentious issue in the first month of the moor reopening. They attracted more than a little unwelcome controversy. Some members of Ilkley Parish Council were opposed to them, and it was claimed the poles were "frightening" and "terrifying" to elderly people and children. (Rather patronising, we thought, and an insult to the intelligence of the same "elderly people" whose generation had stood up to the tyranny of Adolf Hitler.) Meanwhile a religious group in the town considered one of the poles (with a 'cyclops' design) could be "evil" and that it could also have represented "the eye of Satan looking down over Ilkley". That was certainly never our intention! (And seems to us as bizarre as the idea of a 'troll' living under the drinking fountain). The poles were described on the one hand as "crude" and "amateurish", which they were, and on the other hand as "interesting" and "colourful", which they also were.

While we realised opinions would have varied about the poles, we were taken aback by the amount of venom and the 'political correctness' expressed by some individuals over the matter. In our experience we had six complaints from visitors about the totem poles, but many times that number of people who actually liked them. **Especially** children, despite the concerns of some individuals.

The local media had of course quickly taken a keen interest in the subject, and had printed a number of articles and letters both for and against the totem poles. Even the national press took an interest, but we refused to comment. It was all becoming more than a little silly.

It was suggested that the poles were cynically contrived to generate business in the wake of the foot and mouth crisis. They weren't. But such attitudes did in turn make us cynical. Especially when there was a very real possibility that our tenancy and business was at risk because of the financial situation we found ourselves in after the foot and mouth crisis.

Although we had the verbal approval of Bradford Council's Countryside Service, there was no formal 'planning permission' for the totem poles and no one from the Planning Department contacted us over the issue when the presence of the poles became apparent. We could have applied for planning permission retrospectively, and it may or may not have been granted. But we decided not to pursue the issue.

The anticipated lifespan of the poles was perhaps five years, and in any case we were not in a financial position to take the matter further at the time either, largely due to the aftermath of the foot and mouth crisis.

The totem poles survived little more than a month after the moors reopened. They were removed by the Countryside Service on Monday 10th September 2001. The day before the world was shaken by the events in New York and it became apparent that there are far more "frightening" and "evil" things in the world than a few bits of wood with silly faces painted on them outside White Wells on Ilkley Moor.

The totem poles are but a small part of the long history of White Wells, and for us at least will remain so. We have no intention of revisiting the issue again, having been well and truly, and firmly, put in our place over it. In retrospect it

'Totem poles' at White Wells. — The 'Totem poles', which were created by recycling wood from a tree that the Council's Countryside Service had to cut down in the enclosed area adjacent to the public toilets, caused more than a little unwelcome controversy when the moors reopened in August 2001, following the 'foot and mouth crisis.'

The nostrils and mouth of the face were painted red. Allegedly children ran off the moor screaming in terror upon seeing the poles, though in our experience children (in particular) liked the poles.

This one, the largest at approx 1.3m/4ft 6in, was based on indigenous Canadian west coast designs.

The New Years Day plunge, 2008. — Plunging is still a popular activity at White Wells. New Years Day is the main day for this and in 2008 one hundred and sixty seven people took the plunge throughout the day.

is something that we are neither proud nor ashamed of, and most importantly we have all since moved on from the episode.

The Ilkley Moor/White Wells 'Trust' Issue

In 2003 it was suggested that a 'trust' should be established to take over the interests of Ilkley Moor and White Wells from the landlords Bradford Council.

In January 2004 the local media reported that a petition had been established in an attempt to achieve this.

Although we thought that the idea of a 'trust' taking over the interests of White Wells was perhaps well intentioned, as the tenants of the property we were very concerned about these proposals and the possible consequences of them within a few years. We feared that if such a 'trust' came into being, the future of not only our tenancy, but the very future of White Wells itself could be seriously compromised. We did not want to see interference in our home and our business. (We'd had enough of that in 2001 with all the fuss made over the totem poles.) Furthermore we were concerned over the possibility of increased rent payments to any such 'trust', and the possibility of introducing admission charges to the bathhouse to raise income. Or even stopping visitors from using the plunge bath if they so wish on politically correct 'health and safety' grounds.

In short White Wells, we feared, may no longer be viable for tenants. We did not want to see it sold off to property developers, in the event that the 'trust' decided that it could no longer maintain the property, or see it return to the terrible state of vandalism and dereliction experienced in the early 1970's. Our own petition against a 'trust' attracted five hundred and forty three signatures, and was submitted to both the Ilkley Parish Council and Bradford Council's Executive Committee.

In the summer of 2006, over the end of June and the beginning of July, there was a large fire on Ilkley Moor. This destroyed a large tract of moorland near Keighley Gate, about two kilometres/one and a quarter miles to the south west of White Wells. As a result of this, the Ilkley Parish Council decided that Bradford Council was better placed to provide the ongoing maintenance of the moor rather than a 'trust', and this idea was presented to Bradford Council's Executive Committee for consideration. On 19th September 2006 the Executive agreed and decided in favour of retaining council control.

In 2007 a steering group was formed with a view to creating a 'Friends of Ilkley Moor' group instead of a 'trust'. Bradford Council's Countryside Service

Queue for the bathhouse, New Years Day, 2008. — Many visitors to White Wells on New Years Day come to watch the plunging as well as to take part. As a result of this, a queue usually builds up outside the bathhouse, comprising of both plungers and spectators!

Despite the misty weather on 1st January 2008, many people came up to White Wells and enjoyed the atmosphere of the day.

would still be in overall control of the moor, but the 'Friends of' group would liase with the council and work in conjunction with it and hopefully raise funds both from subscriptions and from sources that the council could not, and to supply volunteers to assist with various work on the moor.

The 'Friends of Ilkley Moor' group was launched in the spring of 2008, and endeavours to attract membership both locally and worldwide via the Internet.

Late in 2008 an announcement was made that the group had managed to secure considerable sums in funding, and proposals were made to spend some of this on 'restoration' work on the moor. Including the repair of footpaths and the removal of excess foliage around the lower tarn. Some of the work was undertaken by Bradford Council's Countryside Service.

The 'Pink Tree'

In April 2005 it was reported that a tree on the moor had been painted pink. Described as being close to White Wells immediately aroused our interest. Following the totem pole issue of 2001, we didn't want any further association with any such decoration on the moor. It transpired that the pink tree was in fact not in the immediate environs of White Wells, but close to the copse of trees near Backstone Beck, about five hundred metres to the east of White Wells.

It provided much amusement both in the local press, and to visitors on the moor. However what the motive behind it was remains a mystery. Speculation on the subject included that perhaps it was a bizarre 'April Fools' joke, or that

The installation of new water filters at White Wells (September 2009). — In September/October 2009 Bradford Council, acting upon the recommendation by its own Environmental Health Department, undertook work at White Wells to replace the water filtration system with a newer type. The new system passes water through an ultraviolet light in order to kill any bacteria that may be present and thus make the water 'safer'.

The work involved laying new pipes at the rear of White Wells and reconfiguring some of the existing pipes in order to incorporate them into the new system, housed inside the building. The drinking fountain had only worked intermittently since its pipe was cracked in the winter of 2008, and this was also repaired and connected to the new system, and the plunge bath was connected to it as well.

Work being done on the westernmost chimney of White Wells (October 2009). — Following the installation of the new water filters and a new central heating boiler, the metal cowling on top of the chimney left over from the old heating system was removed.

This photograph brings to mind the work undertaken at White Wells at the beginning of the 20th century, and provides hope that work will still be being undertaken in another hundred years.

it had something to do with someone passionate about breast cancer charities, or that it was a stunt by supporters of the UKIP political party, with a view to publicity during the general election campaign that was going on at the time.

Whatever the facts behind it, no one came forward to shed any light on the matter, and it was quickly forgotten.

Lights, Camera, Action!

In June 2005 we were approached by Yorkshire Television with a view to the possibility of using White Wells as a location set for an episode of the 1960's hospital drama series '*The Royal*'.

This involved the closure of White Wells over a three week period at the end of June and beginning of July. (For which we were reimbursed loss of earnings for the period of time the building was closed.) The first week involved the set building and preparation, the second week completing the sets and the filming itself, done over two days, (6th and 7th July), and the remainder of the time spent 'reinstating' the property back to its usual appearance. During the course of all this, we had to stay with my parents in Ilkley, as our living area had been made to resemble a rustic attic, in keeping with the 1960's theme of the episode being filmed. Likewise the café area was transformed into a 1960's style living room, complete with a false wall, which looked remarkably convincing! The entrance area was converted into a kitchen, and the former charity bath building housing the public toilet was made to resemble a house on the outside, for the exterior shots.

The meticulous attention to detail was impressive. Especially given the length of time that some parts of the set appeared on screen when the episode was transmitted in the spring of 2006.

White Wells lent itself to being a great location for television. Although for us it was a disruption to our usual routine, it was interesting to see the building transformed, the work that went into it, and the end result when it was shown on television.

The irony was not lost on us that during the 1960's White Wells was seen as a relic of a bygone era and fell into a state of disrepair; while in the 21st century, the 1960's are seen as a bygone era, viewed with a sense of nostalgia.

CHAPTER THIRTEEN:
EPILOGUE: WHITE WELLS TODAY

Taking the Plunge at White Wells Today

New Year's Day is the most widely known day for this. Though it is a relatively new 'tradition', introduced by Bradford Council Countryside Service Volunteers on 1st January 1995. Since then it has grown in popularity, and there are now usually in excess of one hundred plungers participating in this throughout the day.

'Yorkshire Day', 1st August, is another popular day for plunging. Though of course it is not a public holiday and often falls during the week, so the number of visitors is usually a lot less than on New Year's Day.

However when White Wells is open visitors can take the plunge at any time of the year. Depending upon how busy it is in the café, the plunge bath gate can be opened and the plunging supervised. Though at particularly busy times in the café, visitors wishing to plunge will be asked to either wait or call back when it is quieter. -And plunging is of course undertaken at the plungers' own risk!

There is no charge for taking the plunge, but visitors can either throw some loose change into the bath, (remember, it is believed that if the coin lands head uppermost, your wish will be granted!) buy a certificate to mark the occasion of their plunge, or support the café by purchasing drinks or snacks. Private groups can be catered for too outside usual opening times, by prior arrangement. This can include a short talk on the history of White Wells, a plunge in the bath (optional!) and refreshments provided.

When White Wells is Open

Apart from private bookings, the general rule of thumb is that White Wells is open "When the flag is flying". Which may seem somewhat ambiguous, so for all practical purposes this generally means Saturdays and Sundays 10am until 5pm, all Bank Holidays 10am until 5pm (with the exception of Christmas Day when White Wells is closed), and most Friday afternoons 2pm until 5pm.

Additionally White Wells is open during weekday afternoons in the school summer holidays though opening times can vary between 12 and 2pm until

5pm. – And at all other times "When the flag is flying". Including during other school holidays, weather and other personal commitments permitting. If the flag is not flying then White Wells is closed, and you won't have a wasted journey up the moor.

Disabled Access

Disabled badge holders can drive up the access track and park at the rear of White Wells. (There is a limited amount of parking and turning space available). On the assumption that such visitors intend to use the café during their visit. The barrier at the bottom of the access track can be opened by prior arrangement for this purpose. There is a disabled (public) toilet at White Wells and the café and bathhouse are accessible too. However by the nature of its historical design some disabled visitors may be unable to use the plunge bath or the upstairs changing area.

In ice and snow conditions the access track to White Wells is not open to vehicles.

Flags Flying at White Wells. – White Wells is open all year round – "When the flag is flying" – And although the moors provide a magnificent setting throughout, it is perhaps on bright cold days after a snowfall that the moors look their best, when they are transformed into a winter wonderland.

WHITE WELLS TIMELINE

2nd Century A.D.: The Roman fort of Olicana occupied the site where the Manor House and All Saint's Parish Church now stand.

16th Century: 1570: William Slingsby discovered 'Chalybeate' water in Harrogate and created the Tewit Well.

17th Century: 1626: Dr Edmund Deane published *"Spadacrene Anglica"*, and noted the strongest sulphur spring in Great Britain being located in Harrogate. A total of eighty seven springs were subsequently 'discovered' and exploited in the Harrogate area over the next two hundred years.

The 'legend' of the shepherd bathing his injuries in spring water on Ilkley Moor emerged during the 17th century.

1700: White Wells was built under the auspices of Squire Peter Middelton very close to this date. The bath was to the rear of White Wells on the flat ground to the south of the tumulus, near the present day water collection tank.

1702: King William III died and was succeeded by Queen Anne.

Circa 1710-1712: The water at White Wells was described as being beneficial to sufferers of scrofula and 'Kings Evil'. Noted in Leylands *"Itinerary"*.

1714: Queen Anne died and was succeeded by King George I.

Peter Middelton died. The estates were taken over by his son Marmaduke.

1727: King George I died and was succeeded by King George II.

1734: Dr Thomas Short conducted an analysis of the water at White Wells.

1757: Marmaduke Middelton died. The estates were taken over by his brother William Middelton.

1760: King George II died and was succeeded by King George III.

1763: William Middelton died. The estates were taken over by his great nephew, also called William, shortly after he attained the age of twenty one on Christmas Day 1781.

1791: Robert Dale replaced the original bath and constructed the two baths that still exist today. This was done under the auspices of Squire William Constable Middelton.

1793: Anne Harper drowned at White Wells. (15th August.)

1801: Thomas Beanlands held the "Well House and Farm" for £75.00 per annum.

Circa 1803: Thomas Clark, a shoemaker in Canterbury composed the tune of 'Cranbrook', named after the market town in Kent. It was used as a hymn tune from about the 1830's (particularly popular in the Methodist movement, though Clark wasn't a Methodist himself) and in Yorkshire the tune was popular for the Christmas carol 'While shepherd's watched their flocks by night'. Sometime during the 1870's or 1880's it became adopted as the tune to the jocular song 'On Ilkla Moor Baht 'At', created, it is believed, by a church outing from Halifax.

1809: Charles Darwin born. (12th February.)

1817: Thomas Beanlands died and his son Joseph took over the lease of White Wells.

1819: There were concerns that White Wells required improvement and repairs due to no one living on the premises.

1820: King George III died and was succeeded by King George IV.
  William Butterfield was employed as bathman at White Wells, thus beginning a family association with the property that was to last almost a century, until 1918. Though the Butterfield family did not live at White Wells.
  Dr Adam Hunter wrote about the water at White Wells around this date, and also postulated a theory that the waters at White Wells could have been exploited by the Romans.

1829: The 'Ilkley Bath Charitable Institution' was established by the Reverend George Fenton. The venture was supported by Squire William Middleton. Charity dispensations were made from the 'Charity 'ole' at the vicarage in Church Street.
  Vinzenz Prissnitz had been developing 'hydropathy' during the 1820's in Grafenburg (now the village of Lazne Jesenik in the modern day Czech Republic) and 'water treatments' were beoming increasingly popular in both Europe and Britain as well. Joseph Beanlands held the baths at White Wells for £52 & 10 shillings per annum. (Fifty Guineas.)

1830: The 'Charity' or 'poor' bath was built by the 'Ilkley Bath Charitable Institution' to the west of White Wells.
  The extension to the east of White Wells was added at about this time too, comprising of a stable on the ground floor to house the donkeys used in bringing clientele to the property, and a 'sitting room' above for those awaiting their 'treatment'.

Joseph Beanlands was paid from the funds of the charity for its use of the water at White Wells throughout the 1830's.

King George IV died and was succeeded by his brother King William IV.

1837: King William IV died and his niece Princess Victoria became Queen.

1841: *"The Spas of England"* by A.B. Granville was published. This work describes the baths at White Wells, and suggests separate male and female bathing. However there is little further evidence to support this theory upon closer analysis. It is most likely that *both* genders would have been able to use the different treatments in each of the two baths and the singular 'Charity bath', but at different times.

1842: Dr Gully opened a hydropathic establishment in Malvern, to exploit the interest in 'water treatments' there. Gully was one of the most eminent 'water doctors' of his day, and included Charles Dickens in his list of patients.

1843: Hamer Stansfeld, the Mayor of Leeds, brought Dr Antoine Rischanek to Ilkley, and installed him in 'Ushers Lodgings' on Wells Road. From here Dr Rischanek prescribed the various treatments to be taken at White Wells by his patients.

Also in this year Hamer Stansfeld along with John Atkinson, Joseph Atkinson, James Marshall and Samuel Garlick advanced their proposals for 'Ben Rhydding Hydropathic Establishment.' The foundation stone was laid on 26th September.

1844: 'Ben Rhydding Hydro' opened on 29th May. Dr Antoine Rischanek was appointed as the head physician by Hamer Stansfeld. A position he didn't hold for long.

1847: Dr William Macleod became the head physician at 'Ben Rhydding.' Dr Macleod had studied medicine with Dr Gully at Edinburgh. (See also 1842 & 1849.)

Squire William Middelton died. The local estates were taken over by his son Peter.

1849: Charles Darwin visited Dr Gully's establishment in Malvern.

1853: A joint stock company proposed a second large Hydropathic establishment in the Ilkley area. The name: 'Wells House'. The land for this venture was bought from Squire Peter Middelton. It comprised of nine acres and three dilapidated cottages that were originally part of a mill.

1854: Construction of 'Wells House' began. The foundation stone was laid in June. The building was designed by Cuthbert Brodrick, the architect who had also been chosen to design Leeds Town Hall.

1856: 'Wells House Hydropathic Establishment' opened on 28th May. The landscaped grounds designed by Joshua Major provide, interestingly, the only one of Cuthbert Brodrick's buildings to be in such a setting. (All of Brodrick's other works are in town centre locations.)

Wells House also took on the lease of White Wells. (Which it held until 1872 when the Ilkley Local Board took it over.)

1858: The Wells House Hydropathic Establishment reported a 'considerable profit' at its general meeting. However instead of paying a dividend to shareholders, it was decided to meet a debt due on its capital account.

1859: Wells House Hydro had taken over the lease of White Wells in the mid 1850's and the baths had been roofed over by this date. However the adjacent Charity bath building to the west remained open air, and under the auspices of the 'Ilkley Bath Charity', not Wells House.

Charles Darwin visited Ilkley. He stayed firstly at Wells House then moved to 'North View House' (now 'Hillside Court'), at the western end of Crossbeck Road, and finally back to Wells House again. This took place around the time of the publication of his most famous work *"On The Origin of Species."* It is believed that Darwin made the journey up the moor to White Wells to 'take the waters' at some point during his time in Ilkley, though there is no evidence to either confirm or refute this claim, it is certainly possible that Darwin visited the premises at some point during his stay in Ilkley.

Reverend Canon Jackson visited Ilkley and was appalled by the basic standards of accommodation the recipients of the bath charity were living in. He proposed to build 'Ilkley Hospital' for their benefit instead.

1860: Ben Rhydding Hydro had been substantially extended by this date.

1862: 'Ilkley Hospital' opened. This building now survives as the 'Abbeyfield' residential home, 'Grove House', on the south side of the Grove, overlooking the modern bandstand.

Following the opening of the Ilkley hospital, the charity bath at White Wells fell into disuse.

1863: Dr William Macleod bought Ben Rhydding Hydro.

1865: The railway line to Ilkley from Leeds, Bradford (via Apperley Bridge) and Otley opened.

1866: Ben Rhydding railway station opened.

Squire Peter Middelton died. The estates were taken over by his son William.

1867: The first in a series of auctions by Squire William Middelton were held, selling off substantial plots of land and property in Ilkley town centre. Over the course of the next decade Ilkley expanded and was developed into the town that is familiar today. The Grove was developed from 'Green Lane', and the terraced housing projects including Wellington Road were built.

1868: John 'Donkey' Jackson started operating his donkey transportation service to and from White Wells.

1869: The Ilkley Local Board came into being with Mr J. Thompson being appointed as its first chairman. The local water company that had been created in the 1850's was keen to sell its infrastructure to the newly formed Ilkley Local Board which, after some negotiation over the price, it did. The Board also expressed an interest in obtaining the lease of White Wells from William Middelton. (Which it secured in 1872).

1870's: The Ilkley Local Board undertook extensive waterworks on Ilkley Moor; including the creation of Craig Tarn behind the Craiglands Hydro and work at Willy Hall's Spout waterfalls and the subsequent laying of the current access track to White Wells from Wells Road.

The 'Charity Bath' by this time was largely unused, in favour of the two baths inside White Wells. The drinking fountain in the adjacent enclosure had dried up, while the one behind White Wells remained in working order.

John 'Donkey' Jackson was assisted by Mr C.J. Milligan in operating his donkey transportation service both to White Wells and around the town.

The jocular song 'On Ilkla Moor Baht 'At' was created by a church outing (believed to have been from Halifax) walking on the moors. Though the exact date is unclear, it is thought this occurred in either the 1870's or the 1880's.

1872: The Ilkley Local Board took over the lease of White Wells from Wells House Hydro.

Dr Harrison paid the Local Board the sum of £30 for half a years rent on the 'Old Wells'.

1873: Following work carried out that tapped into the White Wells supply in order to feed houses on the edge of the moor, complaints were made to the Local Board regarding the reduced flow of water available at the White Wells drinking fountain behind the building. After a visit by members of the Board, it was concluded that the supply was still sufficient. (A cup could still be filled in five seconds.)

During the course of the water works the remains of the original bath, pre-dating the 1791 replacements, were discovered at the top of the hill immediately behind White Wells. (The original bath was 'discovered' again fifty six years later in 1929 during further water improvement works on the moor.)

1875: William Butterfield paid the sum of £17 to the Local Board to open White Wells for the 'season', 1st April to 1st November.

1876: The Ilkley Local Board met with opposition to its suggestion to replace White Wells with a terrace and possibly refreshment rooms.

1877: The Railway line to/from Bradford via Shipley, Baildon and Guiseley opened.

Mr Butterfield informed the Local Board that he could not pay more than £12 a year for the rent of White Wells. The Board looked favourably at this, and permitted the rent to be fixed at this amount.

1878: Mr Butterfield was told by the Local Board that he could not charge visitors for using the drinking fountain at White Wells. An accusation that he denied.

1880's: The roof of the 'Old Reservoir' building, removed in the 1870s was replaced.

The 'Ilkley Tarn Band' was formed and played at the venue for the entertainment of visitors at weekends during the summer months.

Bathing at White Wells was still undertaken, but it was not as popular as it had been. However repair work was carried out on both baths during the 1880's,

1883: A 'chalybeate' or 'iron' water spring was discovered at the top of Hebers Ghyll Wood. This was fitted with a decorative fountain and drinking cup for the benefit of visitors to consume the water.

Another drinking fountain (called 'Crawley's Fountain', after Mr Crawley who had funded the project) was built to the south of the old reservoir building on the edge of the moor. It stood on a cobbled area, and had a flagstaff adjacent to it. The opening ceremony was on Saturday 8th September 1883, when a large crowd assembled for the occasion, which ended with a hearty rendition of "God Save the Queen". Water was fed via a pipe from White Wells to the fountain. The dried up remains of this fountain were covered over in 1970 when the underground reservoir was constructed nearby.

1885: William Middelton died. The estates were taken over by his brother, Charles. A quarry was opened behind the Cow and Calf rocks to exploit the abundance of stone. This operation continued into the early years of the twentieth century.

1887: The Ilkley Local Board suggested replacing White Wells with a memorial for Queen Victoria's Golden Jubilee. Once again the suggestion to replace White Wells was met with opposition.

1888: The railway line west of Ilkley to Skipton via Addingham, Bolton Abbey and Embsay opened.

1889: The 'Victoria Baths' opened on Little Lane in Ilkley, the 'season' ran from May to October, and effectively made the former bathing pavilion at Sandy Dale on the riverside a less attractive proposition! (However another bathing pavilion was still in use into the early twentieth century, located on the north bank of the river, adjacent to the football pitch on the West Holmes field).

A suggestion was made to open a 'photographic studio' at White Wells. This was refused by the Ilkley Local Board.

1890's: The popularity of 'Hydropathy' was in decline.

Ilkley Moor Golf Club opened on the moor to the west of White Wells. Although a private golf club, visitors to Wells House Hydro could pay to use the golfing facilities on offer.

Proposals were seriously considered following earlier suggestions for a moorland tramway. However the scheme was somewhat ambitious, and had its objectors. (The subject was still being discussed into the early twentieth century.)

Further calls were made to demolish White Wells, though it survived and in view of the decline in popularity of bathing had to diversify in order to survive. Therefore the sale of refreshments, which had been ongoing for a number of years continued.

Photographs dating from later in the decade suggest that a flagpole could have been added to the building in time for Queen Victoria's Diamond jubilee celebrations of 1897.

1892: Charles Middelton sold the remainder of his estates and left 'Myddelton Lodge' and Ilkley.

1893: William Butterfield died at the age of seventy five. His son, also called William, by this time in his thirties, held the tenancy of White Wells. A position he retained until 1918, when he left, aged fifty eight.

1894: The Ilkley Local Board was replaced by Ilkley Urban District Council.

The old vicarage (and the associated former 'Charity 'Ole') was demolished and replaced with the arcade.

1897: Work was done inside White Wells, and the rent was increased by the sum of £3 per annum.

A suggestion for hut shelters on the moor was made. These were to be a memorial for Queen Victoria's Diamond Jubilee. Designs of shelters along the promenade at Saltburn-on-Sea were looked at as possible models for the Ilkley Moor shelters.

1900's: The shower bath at White Wells was considerably overgrown with moss and ferns by this date, though the shower pipes remained overhead.

Refreshments continued being available at White Wells, from a small 'tuck shop' opened at the rear of the building.

1900: 'The Great Flood' washed away property and did considerable damage on 12th July, following a cloudburst over Ilkley Moor. Although White Wells wasn't mentioned in reports of the resulting destruction, the moorland streams simply couldn't cope with the immense volumes of water flowing off the moor and into the town. The bridge over Backstone Beck to the east of the tarn was destroyed, and the cart track up the moor to White Wells was damaged where it crosses Willy Hall's Spout. The main roads in the town were badly damaged, as was property, and in one case a building collapsed, resulting in a fatality.

1901: Queen Victoria died (22nd January) at Osbourne House on the Isle of Wight, bringing the Victorian era to an end after over sixty three years. She was succeeded by King Edward VII.

David Scott, from Halifax, a gentleman in his sixties, was employed at White Wells. He provided visitors with a colourful 'oration', extolling the virtues of the 'mellifluent' water available and its supposed properties, and a somewhat misleading description of how the Romans had constructed the baths.

1902: The bridge across Backstone Beck was replaced, and the cart track to White Wells was repaired at Willy Hall's Spout. However the latter attracted a considerable amount of controversy. The repairs involved the construction of a retaining wall (which is still in place) to carry the track across the ravine. This work was criticised in letters to the local press.

1903: The Panorama reservoir was built on the moor about 1.5km/1 mile to the west of White Wells.

Mr George Brumfitt of Ilkley suggested a 'view station' to be placed on the moor somewhere in the vicinity of White Wells. The 'view station' was to consist of a simple post pointing out the directions north, south, east and west, and information cards contained within a box attached to the post, describing prominent features on the landscape below. The post was erected outside the bathhouse porch, and remained for many years. (Until the vandalism of the late 1960's/early 1970's.) The information cards being periodically updated to reflect any new features which appeared in the valley below.

1904: The bandstand opened in West View Park. (19th July). This provided an alternative venue for musical events to be held as well as the already established venue at the tarn. However, a stage and dressing room was built at the tarn for the 'Pierrots', who continued to perform there.

1905: Mr Cooper, organiser of the 'Pierrots' who performed at the tarn, removed the wooden buildings there, following concerns that the structures were 'objectionable, a great disfigurement, and out of harmony with the surroundings.'

1906: 'Heathcote' on Grove Road was designed by eminent architect Sir Edwin Lutyens. (He also designed the National Cenotaph in Whitehall following the 'Great War'.)

1907: John 'Donkey' Jackson died, (15th January) aged eighty one.

The myth of a Roman presence at White Wells was perpetuated in the *'Ilkley Gazette'* by 'Stylus Scrivener', the pseudonym of one of the journalists working on the paper.

Mr J. Hillyard opened a pavilion belonging to the Ilkley Moor Golf Club on 13th April on the moors approx 1km / 0.75 mile to the west of White Wells.

1908: The Town Hall, Library and the 'King's Hall' were 'officially' opened in Ilkley. (24th April).

On the evening of Monday 8th June, Mrs Pankhurst addressed an open air meeting held at the lower tarn, on the subject of women and the vote.

1909: A roller-skating rink opened in Ilkley on the corner of Cunliffe Road and South Hawksworth Street (31st July). This provided participants with all season entertainment rather than just on the ice at the tarn in winter. However the popularity of the roller-skating rink was relatively short lived, and it was demolished to make way for the 'West Yorkshire Road Car Co' bus depot a few years later. (The depot was subsequently demolished too and the site re-developed into the 'Moors Centre' retail units in the early 1990's.)

1910: King Edward VII died at the age of sixty eight, only nine years into his reign which had started at the beginning of the new century, and heralded a sense of optimism. He was succeeded by King George V.

Ilkley Urban District Council recommended that public toilets should be provided at White Wells. These were housed in the former 'charity bath' building, and were completed in July.

In September, calls were made for seats to be placed on the routes to White Wells.

A former resident of Westwood Lodge in Ilkley, Mr Herbert Ponting, joined Captain Robet Falcon Scott as official 'photographic artist' on the *'Terra Nova'* expedition to Antarctica.

1911: In January the Ilkley Urban District Council recommended that the sum of £8 be spent on planting shrubs at White Wells. These provided a natural screen for the public toilets that had been completed the previous year. In April it was recommended by the council that the toilets be let to Mr Butterfield for the sum of £5 for one year, conditionally that the conveniences be maintained in a satisfactory condition.

Also around this date the access to the back door of White Wells was improved, and two of the chimneys were given decorative tops.

King George V had his Coronation on 22nd June, amid great national celebration. Locally too the event was marked with parties and a bonfire on the moor above White Wells.

1912: The moorland shelter that had been built on the slope above 'Hainsworth's Pond caused some controversy, but one critic changed his mind when he visited it and appreciated the view!

The *'Titanic'* sank in April.

1913: The nation had to come to terms with the fact that Captain Scott had failed in his attempt to reach the South Pole first. Although he did reach the pole, he died on the return journey with the other members of the polar party, and thus became one of the twentieth century's iconic figures.

The Grove Cinema opened (21st February). This cinema was demolished in 1968.

The Ilkley Grammar School swimming pool opened. (17th May).

'White Wells Whisky' was advertised in the *'Ilkley Gazette'* as being available from 'Beanlands', one of the town's prominent grocery emporiums.

Operations at Hangingstone Quarry behind the Cow and Calf rocks were being scaled down. There was concern expressed in the local press in September that quarrying still appeared to be going on, but in October the *'Ilkley Gazette'* recorded the meeting of the Ilkley Urban District Council's 'Burial Board, Moor and Parks Committee':

'Respecting the removal of loose stones from the quarry; it was stated that it was only the worked stone that was to be removed.'

The days of quarrying on Ilkley Moor were at an end.

1914: The 'Winter Gardens' Annex adjacent to the 'King's Hall' in Ilkley opened (22nd June.) The date coinciding with the 'Official Birthday' of His Majesty King George V.

1914-1918: The First World War. During which the *'Troutbeck'* housed troops from the 'Bantams', the 17th Service Battalion Prince of Wales' Own West Yorkshire Regiment, from Leeds. (February 1915). While many Ilkley men enlisted into the Duke of Wellington's Regiment.

1918: 'Busby's' opened a branch of their department store in Ilkley.

The Butterfield family involvement as bathkeepers at White Wells ended after ninety eight years with the family.

1919: Excavations of the Roman fort site behind Ilkley Parish Church were carried out by A.M. Woodward. These continued over the course of the next three years.

Ilkley Urban District Council advertised in the local press for caterers to provide refreshments at White Wells over the Easter holiday period.

Grand celebrations took place in the town over the weekend of 19th July to mark the signing of the peace treaty, formally ending the 'Great War'. (The Treaty of Versailles had been signed on 28th June, and the Government decided the event would be marked nationally in July.) An anecdote from the time suggests that White Wells was temporarily painted red white and blue in keeping with the national mood of patriotism surrounding the celebrations. Although no reference to this happening has come to light when researching press reports of the celebrations, White Wells may nevertheless have been included in this colourful way!

Visitors to White Wells were encouraged to throw pennies into the plunge bath. It was believed that if the coins settled head uppermost, the visitor's wish would be granted.

1920's: Bathing ended at White Wells.

Wells House was in use as a hotel.

Ben Rhydding Hydro promoted itself as a 'Golf Hotel'.

1921: The moorland tea pavilion opened (29th July) following considerable controversy and delays in construction. Mr A. Wray became the first to operate the pavilion and shortly afterwards reached an agreement with the IUDC for having the property connected to the main 'town gas' supply. Prior to the opening of the tea pavilion Mr Wray had served refreshments from the 'tuck shop' operating from the rear door of White Wells. Visitors to White Wells at this time paid an admission fee to look around the overgrown 'shower bath' and for an additional 2d could use the remaining 'plunge bath' in the western end of the building to 'wash' in.

1924: The former water storage tank for the charity bath was 'discovered' adjacent to the dry stone wall at the rear of the toilet block. The tank was pumped out by the Ilkley fire engine 'Thomas' on the evening of the 4th July and an inspection of the interior of the tank was undertaken. It was concluded that the tank was the original supply reservoir for the 'Charity Bath'.

The Home Secretary, Arthur Henderson, stayed at Wells House Hotel for one week during August.

1926: Hainsworth's pond was developed into the paddling pool. The original costs were exceeded, and by Christmas 1926 these were £456 7s 5d. This was due to the fact that it had been decided to finish the surround of the pool with stone instead of the originally proposed brick. The pool was built by local contractor Mr Lewis Learoyd.

1927: The paddling pool opened in time for the summer 'season.'

Early one morning two walkers noticed smoke coming from White Wells, it was emanating from the passageway underneath the shop. (17th April). The alarm was raised and the fire extinguished using water from the bath by two men from the local fire brigade who gained access through the window of the shop at the rear of the premises.

All night dances were arranged by some of the hotels in Ilkley for guests wanting to see the eclipse of the sun. (29th June). The tea pavilion at White Wells served ham and egg breakfasts at 4am for the benefit of visitors, which proved popular! The eclipse itself occurred at around 6am and although its duration was short and the weather in Ilkley was somewhat cloudy, it was a memorable occasion by all accounts.

1928: The 'New Cinema' opened on Railway Road. (28th May). The building also incorporated a ballroom. The theatre organ which was installed later did not, contrary to popular belief, rise up from below the floor in front of the screen! It was a permanent fixture. The cinema was taken over by the 'Essoldo' group in 1949, and following the rise in popularity of television over the following two decades leading to a decline in cinema audiences a trend that was reflected nationally, the cinema was demolished in 1969 to be replaced with a supermarket. The year after Ilkley's other cinema, The Grove, had also been demolished (1968).

In 1928 universal suffrage for all women over the age of twenty one was granted in the 'Equal Franchise Act'. Following a lengthy campaign that twenty years previously had seen a 'suffragette' meeting at the tarn. Now all women could vote on equal terms with their male peers.

1929: During the course of water improvement works, the original bath at White Wells was 'rediscovered' once again. (It had previously been unearthed during excavations by the Ilkley Local Board in the 1870's.) The bath is located about 1.5m/5ft below surface level, close to the water collection tank at the top of the hill near to the trees behind White Wells.

In June the General Election resulted in Ramsay Macdonald being elected as Prime Minister for the second time.

1930: In December the tenancy of the tea pavilion at White Wells was granted to Mrs Williamson of the Spa Café in Ilkley on a yearly rental. Though she and her husband did not live on the site, they were responsible for the provision of refreshments and allowing visitors to look around the baths. Mr Williamson opened White Wells at weekends, and operated the small 'tuck shop' through the back door of the building until his death in 1956. Mrs Williamson continued opening the pavilion until her death in 1964.

1931: Lighting was installed along the road leading to and around the bottom tarn.

Mr Mott of the IUDC said the cost of the street lighting installation would be approximately £165 for five lamps, three on the roadway and two at the tarn, and five hundred yards of cable.

White Wells was illuminated by gaslight during the 'Ilkley Illuminations' in September. This coincided with a major trade fair in the town and also the centenary of Michael Faraday. The 'Ilkley Illuminations' became an annual event throughout the 1930's, taking place during 'Ilkley Feast Week.' ('Ilkley Feast' was traditionally held on the first Sunday following the 14th September, and consequently the week following in the case of the 'Ilkley Illuminations').

1933: Extra illuminations were installed around the tarn in January to afford better skating facilities for those making the most of their winter pastime.

1934: After many years of debate by the IUDC about the provision of public bathing facilities in the town, construction started on the Ilkley Lido.

'Busby's' department store arranged a highly successful visit to the paddling pool by Santa Claus in the run up to Christmas, to promote the sale of toy boats etc. The event proved popular, and was repeated the following year.

1935: The Ilkley Lido opened. The Lido was designed by the local surveyor, Mr A. Skinner. The opening coincided with the silver jubilee celebrations of King George V in May.

At Christmas 'Busby's' department store arranged a return visit to Ilkley Moor from Santa Claus. He appeared amongst the rocks behind White Wells, and made his way down into Ilkley, to 'Busby's' store in Brook Street, followed by children who had been invited to engage in a game of 'tig' with him, upon which they received money and sweets.

1936: King George V died. (20thJanuary.) King Edward VIII acceded to the throne, but abdicated in December before his Coronation scheduled for the following

May. (The IUDC had, somewhat prematurely, engaged local schoolchildren to plant trees along the Holmes field adjacent to the river in November to mark Edward VIII's coronation, as this was considered the optimum time most favourable for this prior to the event that never was the following spring.) The throne was taken by Edward's brother, whom became King George VI.

A variety of compress treatments were advertised and offered to clientele of Wells House Hotel.

1938: Wells House Hotel was renamed with the prefix 'New', by Mr Raymond Smith, the new owner of the property.

1939: Wells House and Ben Rhydding Hydro were taken over by the 'Wool Control Board'. They remained under Government control during Second World War.

The Ilkley Moor Golf Club closed. The course on the moor near the Keighley Gate Road to Hebers Ghyll became abandoned.

1940's: The former Hangingstone quarry was used as a military firing range, as were other large areas of moorland.

White Wells was painted so as not to become a navigational aid to enemy pilots attacking nearby Leeds and Bradford.

'Lord Haw-Haw,' in a broadcast during the war, said: "And don't think because you have painted White Wells black, we don't know where you are..."

Just as in the First World War, a number of Ilkley men were conscripted into the Duke of Wellington's Regiment. (Including my Dad, at the age of eighteen, in 1944.)

Despite the war, the moorland tea pavilion run by Mrs Williamson continued to open. Although not always with a full range of stock. "We've no minerals!" became something of a catchphrase used by Mrs Williamson when addressing visitors to her establishment.

After the Second World War, Wells House was sold with a view to becoming a 'teacher training' establishment. This plan however fell through and the building remained empty for two years before being taken over by the Government again, this time as a hostel for European migrant workers.

Late in the decade calls were made to reopen the moor golf course, but the plans for this were never realised.

1941: An image of White Wells was used by the Ilkley Chamber of Commerce in an advertisement on the front page of the *'Ilkley Gazette'* encouraging local residents to invest in 'war bonds' during a campaign called 'War Weapons Week.' (Similar campaigns ran throughout the war, and afterwards.)

1945: By the time of the V.E. Day celebrations (8th May), White Wells had been painted white once more and was illuminated again. Parties, bonfires, beacons and fireworks formed part of the celebrations both locally and nationally.

1946: The image of White Wells used for the 'War Weapons Week' advertisement was used again on the front page of the *'Ilkley Gazette'* for an advertisement to raise funds for a war memorial.

1947: Following the Second World War, Ilkley Moor was still under the control of the Army's Northern Command, including the areas around White Wells. Notices were put in place warning visitors of unexploded bombs and a miscellany of other ordnance; mortars grenades and bazookas had been fired over the moor when it was used as a firing range during the war though not in the vicinity of White Wells. Polish troops were brought in to engage in clearance and making the moor safe again for the general public to wander on. Despite their best efforts, unexploded ordnance was still being found occasionally over a decade later.

1948: A photograph of White Wells from the south west, taken by a Mr H.M. Storey of Bradford, was chosen as the winner of a competition for inclusion in a visitors' guidebook to Ilkley.

The bandstand in West View Park was demolished, though the nearby shelter remained until the summer of 1954.

1950: Wells House was taken over by the local authority with a view to creating a college.

1952: King George VI died. (6th February). Queen Elizabeth II acceded to the throne.

The tea pavilion was broken into and a fire deliberately started. (25th October). Fortunately the fire was mainly confined to the kitchen area, with some minor damage to the café. The main fabric of the building did not catch light.

1953: The thatched roof on the moorland shelter overlooking the paddling pool was replaced with cedar wood shingles.

The Coronation of Queen Elizabeth II took place (2nd June).

The IUDC considered the possibility of obtaining burglary insurance to cover the moorland tea pavilion, White Wells and the Lido café, following a number of break-ins. However the idea was eventually rejected.

1954: 'Ilkley College of Housecraft' opened in the former Wells House Hotel building. (It later had extensions added to it along with various buildings in the grounds. It became the 'Bradford and Ilkley Community College', and eventually closed in 1999.)

The shelter remaining in West View Park was demolished during the summer months, six years after the nearby bandstand.

It was announced that 'Ben Rhydding Hydro' would be demolished. The property had been empty for a number of years following its derequisitioning by the 'Wool Control Board.'

1955: A start was made on the demolition of Ben Rhydding Hydro. The demolition was a slow process. It was not completed until October 1957. The cleared site made way for the High Wheatley housing development, which occurred over the next decade. However the Hydro's nine hole golf course, which had opened in 1885, survived and is still in use today as the private 'Ben Rhydding Golf Club'.

A fire occurred in the room adjacent to the public toilet at White Wells. (8th October.)

1956: The body of John Peterson was discovered in the tea pavilion next to White Wells by a walking group who found a broken window and the smell of gas. (14th February). The subsequent inquiry concluded that Mr Peterson had committed suicide after breaking into the pavilion (which was closed for the winter) a few days before the grim discovery.

Mr Williamson died. He had previously opened White Wells for visitors to look around and to buy sweets etc from the small 'tuck shop' while his wife ran the nearby pavilion cafe. Following his death, the key for White Wells was available for visitors to borrow from Mrs Williamson in the tea pavilion. However this was the start of the structural decline of White Wells, due in part to there no longer being a shop or supervision inside the property.

1957: A railway advertisement poster depicting Ilkley Lido by the artist Frank Sherwin was produced. In the background Ilkley Moor and White Wells are also visible.

Concerns were raised by the IUDC that the demolition of Ben Rhydding Hydro was becoming a somewhat protracted affair, and that the remaining portion of the building was in a dangerous condition. The demolition was completed shortly afterwards.

In November Mrs Williamson's tea pavilion near White Wells was broken into and a quantity of stock and crockery stolen.

1960's: New developments in Ilkley took place. The 'Royal Hotel' on Wells Road was demolished to make way for Wells Court flats, and the town's two cinemas were both demolished before the end of the decade. The railway line west of Ilkley fell victim to the 'Beeching Report', and the bridge carrying the railway west over Brook Street was demolished. The rail link to Arthington via Otley was also severed.

1962: The Rombalds Water Board was formed. (1st April). White Wells became the property of the water board, though this was apparently not fully appreciated by the Ilkley Urban District Council, who continued to charge rent to the tenant of the tea pavilion and oversaw the 3d admission charge made to visitors wishing to borrow the key for White Wells from the tea pavilion. A situation that didn't become apparent until 1968.

The TV transmitter at Norwood Edge near Otley was constructed to improve television reception in the area.

1963: The 'Beeching Report' was published (27th March) that recommended the closure of approximately one third of the national rail infrastructure. Ilkley was not overlooked, and two years later the rail links into and out of the town felt the effects of the report.

1964: Mrs I. Gregson of Cottingley was appointed as the tenant of the tea pavilion (June), following the death of Mrs Williamson.

1965: The railway link to Skipton via Addingham and Bolton Abbey, and down Wharfedale to Otley, Pool and Arthington closed under the recommendations of the 'Beeching Report'. The lines to and from Leeds and Bradford were however retained, and remain in use today.

1966: The railway bridge over Brook Street, which carried the line to Skipton was removed. (Sunday, 10th July.) An early start of around 5am was made on the demolition of the bridge to minimise disruption in the town centre.

1967: Jimi Hendrix played a gig at the 'Troutbeck Hotel', which ended in chaos after being raided by the police over concerns about overcrowding.

Mrs Gregson's tenancy of the tea pavilion was renewed by the Ilkley Urban District Council.

1968: The Rombald's Water Board suggested a 'land swap' with the Ilkley Urban District Council. This involved giving back White Wells to the Council in exchange for land at the edge of the moor on which the Water board proposed building a new underground reservoir.

The 'Grove Cinema' was demolished. Today the site is part of Ilkley's central car park.

1969: The tea pavillion tenant Mrs Gregson wrote to the Ilkley Urban District Council suggesting a fundraising scheme for White Wells. She received a reply from the Council suggesting that she should vacate the tea pavilion instead.

The 'Essoldo Cinema' (formerly the 'New Cinema') on Railway Road was demolished and replaced with 'Hillards' supermarket the following year.

1970: The tea pavilion closed. The tenant, Mrs Gregson, entered into protracted wrangling with the Ilkley Urban District Council about the termination of her tenancy and being reimbursed £350 for this. The Council instead offered her

£150 and the situation stagnated for a number of months until October 1971. Meanwhile the closed up tea pavilion became increasingly vandalised.

An underground reservoir, was constructed on the edge of the moor, next to the water filter station. The nearby 'Crawleys Fountain', which had been dry for more than a decade, was landscaped over. Leaving no trace of the fountain or its surrounding cobbled terrace at surface level.

1971: The United Kingdom replaced the former system of 'Pounds, Shillings and Pence', whereby a pound consisted of twenty shillings each of twelve pennies, with the decimal system of one hundred pennies to the pound. (15th February.) Though some decimal coins had been introduced into circulation in 1968 with the arrival of the five pence/one shilling piece and the ten pence/two shilling piece. In 1969 the fifty pence/ten shilling piece went into circulation, with the old ten shilling note ceasing to be legal tender in November 1970. (The current coins are somewhat reduced in size to these originals.)

After considerable wrangling between the Ilkley Urban District Council and the tea pavillion tenant Mrs Gregson over payment to terminate her tenancy, Mrs Gregson agreed to accept the sum of £250. Within days of the Council meeting on 18th October, when this settlement was announced, the badly vandalised tea pavilion was demolished in a controlled burning (21st October.)

St Winifred's maternity hospital closed (16th October.) Coincidentally, just days before the tea pavilion was demolished.

1972: Proposals from interested parties to restore White Wells to their own requirements were received by the Ilkley Urban District Council. However these were rejected.

1973: Finally an arrangement was made for a grant between Ilkley Urban District Council and Mr Eric Busby who had proposed a restoration plan for White Wells that the Council finally accepted.

The water tank behind the former charity bath was 'rediscovered' during the restoration of White Wells. There was speculation that this tank could have been used to supply Ilkley, however it was in fact used to contain water for use in the charity bath, a theory that was postulated (and confirmed) when the tank was previously 'rediscovered', drained and inspected in 1924.

The Ilkley Indoor Swimming Pool (adjacent to the Lido) opened on 14th June, though the 'official' opening did not take place until 21st September.

1974: The Ilkley Urban District Council was replaced by the City of Bradford Metropolitan District Council, following local Government reorganisation.

The first tenants of the newly restored White Wells, Geoff and Barbara Lister, took up residence in the property.

1975: In February, White Wells was broken into and an air rifle and cash donated to the 'fabric fund' was stolen.

1976: White Wells was 'officially' re-opened to the public (13th May) by The Lord Mayor, Councillor Mrs Doris Birdsall.

Severe drought affected all parts of the United Kingdom following one of the driest summers on record. The 'Top Tarn' near White Wells dried up, and remained dry for a number of years following, becoming increasingly overgrown. (During the mid 1980's it was cleaned out and 'restored')

1977: Queen Elizabeth II celebrated her Silver Jubilee.

1978: The first 'Ilkley Moor Fell Race' took place.

Eric Busby was awarded an M.B.E. in recognition of public services.

1979: Bradford Council's Art Libraries and Museums department took over the responsibility for White Wells.

1980's: White Wells housed a number of different tenants for varying lengths of time.

1983: Eric Busby died on 1st January at the age of eighty three.

During the summer Bradford Council undertook repairs to the drinking fountain which had been dry since the end of 1982, and also improved the water flow into the plunge bath inside White Wells.

1985: Concerns were raised regarding the future of White Wells due to possible cuts in funding in various departments of Bradford Council.

1986: Bradford Council classified White Wells as a 'Grade II Listed Building'. (May.)

1987: The police were called in to search the moor around White Wells for a missing person, whom they feared could have been copying Marilyn Monroe's suicide, following the discovery of a bottle of pills, matches and cigarettes.

1989: The suggestion that White Wells might be 'privatised' caused considerable controversy amongst the Ilkley Parish Council, who objected to the proposals. The applicants for the tenancy, Pamela Brittain and her partner Martin Allsop, suggested creating a 'hydrotherapy clinic' at White Wells, whereby clients could also buy various skin creams etc.

1990: Pamela Brittain and Martin Allsop were appointed as the tenants of White Wells and re-opened the building at the end of July. Despite ambitious plans for creating a 'hydrotherapy clinic' at White Wells, these plans were never fully realised. However snacks and refreshments along vegetarian lines were made available to visitors.

1994: Pamela Brittain and Martin Allsop left White Wells (March).

Bradford Council's Countryside Services Department took over the responsibility for White Wells from the Libraries and Museums Department (July).

The moorland shelter overlooking the paddling pool was rebuilt following its destruction in an arson attack by vandals earlier in the decade.

1995: The New Year's Day plunge was initiated by Countryside Service volunteers. It captured the imagination and has since become something of a 'tradition' which has been repeated every New Year's Day since.

Mains gas, electricity and landline telephone was installed via a service pipe from Wells Road. The cobbles were installed outside the front of White Wells to help protect the service pipes from erosion.

1996: The *'Ilkley Gazette'* featured complaints from a Parish Councillor and local residents concerning the cobbles that had been installed the previous autumn outside White Wells.

Toward the end of the year, Derek and Christine Arnold were appointed as the tenants of White Wells. They took up permanent residence at the property in early 1997.

The flagpole on the east gable of White Wells had been restored, and the system of flying flags when White Wells is open was introduced.

1999: A solar eclipse (11th August) was visible from Ilkley. However totality in the U.K. was only visible in Cornwall. Nevertheless, it provided an interesting spectacle, and crowds gathered on the moors, particularly at the Cow and Calf rocks, but also at White Wells too, echoing the previous total eclipse (of which 99.7% was visible in Ilkley) on 29th June 1927.

Derek and Christine Arnold left White Wells. (October).

The Bradford and Ilkley Community College closed the Ilkley campus in Wells House. The building was subsequently converted into luxury apartments (1999-2003) with housing in the grounds replacing the former college buildings dating from the 1950's and 60's. The landscaped frontage by Joshua Major, including two ponds, remain.

2000: Mark Hunnebell and Joanne Everall took up residence as the tenants of White Wells (14th March).

'Darwin Gardens Millennium Green' was officially opened (by the author Jilly Cooper) on the site of the former West View Park on Wells Road, following the extensive restoration of the overgrown site (Saturday, 24th June).

Jilly Cooper attended a private party hosted by Mark Hunnebell and Joanne Everall at White Wells, on the evening of 24th June, following the official opening of 'Darwin Gardens.'

2001: The national 'Foot and Mouth Disease' crisis not only affected the farming industry in the U.K., but also tourism and the general movement of people onto 'access land' and public footpaths across open countryside. Ilkley Moor and White Wells were closed to public access between the end of February and 1st August.

The 'Totem Poles' installed outside White Wells by Mark Hunnebell and Joanne Everall caused controversy. They were deemed as "terrifying" for children and elderly people and a religious group in the town described them as "the eye of Satan looking down over Ilkley". The 'Totem Poles' were subsequently removed (10th September).

2002: The exterior of White Wells was re-painted during the summer months.
Queen Elizabeth II celebrated her Golden Jubilee.

2004: A petition calling for a 'Trust' to be established to take over the interests of Ilkey Moor and White Wells was initiated. White Wells tenants Mark Hunnebell and Joanne Everall initiated a counter petition for visitors to sign against such a 'Trust', because of fears over any possible future admission charges to White Wells, increased rents and the property becoming a perpetual charity case. Or even becoming unsustainable for tenants, and being either sold off to private sector property developers or returning to a state of vandalism and dereliction.

2005: In April a 'pink tree' appeared on the moor about 500 metres to the east of White Wells. Speculation about this included the theories that it was a bizarre 'April Fool's' joke, that it was something to do with the UKIP political party (in lieu of the forthcoming General Election), or that it was something to do with the breast cancer campaign. Whatever the facts no one came forward to explain it.

The public toilets at White Wells were replaced with new facilities opening in the upper room of the former charity bath building. The former toilets installed in 1910 were boarded up, having become unsuitable for modern requirements.

White Wells was used as a location for the Yorkshire Television hospital drama series *"The Royal"*, which involved the closure of White Wells to the public over a three week period for the construction of interior sets in the entrance area, the café and the living quarters upstairs. (The plunge bath was not used as a location, but served as a store for furniture and fittings from the café.) The filming itself was done over two days (6th & 7th July) and then reinstating the property the following week. The former charity bath building was also used as a set, which involved the exterior being made to resemble a house.

2006: A permanent memorial was unveiled (31st January) at the crash site of a 'Halifax' bomber, to the south west of the Swastika stone sixty two years after the incident that claimed the lives of the six crew members on board.

On the recommendation of Ilkley Parish Council, Bradford Council's Executive Committee decide against the establishment of a 'trust' to take over Ilkley Moor and White Wells from the Countryside Service (19th September); following a fire in July that had damaged a significant area of land on the top of Ilkley Moor.

The petition against a 'trust' had been duly submitted to Bradford Council and contained five hundred and forty three signatures.

A correspondent in the *Ilkley Gazette* suggested that instead of establishing a local 'trust', control of Ilkley Moor should be handed over to the 'National Trust'. An idea that did not receive the full backing of either the Ilkley Parish Council or Bradford Council.

2007: Following the fire of 2006, Bradford Council initiated the establishment of a 'Friends of Ilkley Moor' group in an attempt to attract further funding for the moor through private subscriptions. Though Bradford Council pledged that it did not intend to relinquish overall control or responsibility for the moor or to revisit the proposal of a 'trust'; either local or the 'National Trust', as had been suggested in 2006 by an Ilkley resident in the local media.

The lighting on the access track to the tarn at the bottom of the moor and adjacent to the 'cuckoo hut' shelter at the tarn was reinstated. The old lampposts being adapted for use with modern fittings.

'Silverwell Cottage' on Ilkley moor was sold at auction by Bradford Council Countryside Service for £375,000. (21st June). The money being 'ringfenced' for use on the moor.

Following considerable speculation in the local media, conversion work started on the former Yorkshire Water filter station on the edge of the moor with a view to it becoming a four bedroom house.

Using money from the sale of Silverwell Cottage, Bradford Council Countryside Service improved the surface of the Keighley Gate Road over the moor.

2008: In January an article concerning the lighting at the tarn appeared in the *Ilkley Gazette* and the suggestion that the lamps there are 'Victorian'. (They are not, they were installed in 1931. See Chapter Seven: Between the Wars.)

The 'Friends of Ilkley Moor Group' was officially launched (19th April.)

Meanwhile the 'Darwin Gardens Trust' was struggling to attract funding or volunteers to continue its work at the Millennium green site, and approached Ilkley Parish Council with a proposal to take over the responsibility for 'Darwin Gardens' instead.

Work to convert the former Yorkshire water filter station on the edge of the moor was completed. Reverting back to its former name, 'The Old Reservoir', it went on the market during the summer months. In October the propertry was sold. It has since been renamed 'The Old Pumphouse'.

Concern was expressed in the *'Ilkley Gazette'* regarding the possible installation of 'statues' at the tarn. .

2009: Rumours that 'statues' of members of Ilkley Parish Council were to be installed at the tarn were laid to rest in the *'Ilkley Gazette'* and a suggestion made that a figure of 'Mary Jane' (a character in the song 'On Ilkla Moor Ba'ht 'At') may be placed on one of the benches at the tarn instead.

The 'cuckoo hut' shelter at the tarn was repaired.

The lamps that had been restored to use in 2007 were refitted with traditional glass lantern style tops.

Responsibility for 'Darwin Gardens Millennium Green' was given over to the Ilkley Parish Council by the former 'Darwin Gardens Trust'.

The 'Crescent Hotel' in the town centre closed in March, its future use as a hotel or the possibility of being converted into apartments, being the subject of considerable speculation. However it reopened again as a hotel shortly afterwards. It has since been suggested that it may be partially converted to residential use.

Various events were held to commemorate the two hundredth anniversary of Darwin's birth, and the one hundred and fiftieth anniversary of Darwin staying in the town at the time of the publication of *"On the origin of Species."*

Work was undertaken at White Wells by Bradford Council to further improve the water supply, and install an electronic ultra-violet light filtration system to meet increasing 'health and safety' recommendations.

INDEX

Access track (to White Wells): 51, 64, 130, 176, 179.
Aircrash Memorial: 106, 192.
Airedale and Wharfedale Countryside Management Project: 152.
Alkister, Mr (& Vanhinsberg, Mr): 129, 134.
Allsop, Martin (& Brittain, Pamela): 148, 149, 150, 151, 152, 153, 190, 191.
Almscliffe Crag: 121, 125.
Anderson, David (artist): 145.
Anne, Queen: 2, 172.
Arden Lea: 116, 122.
Arnold, Derek & Christine: 156, 157, 158, 191.
Atkinson, John: 32, 33, 174.
Atkinson, Joseph: 32, 33, 174.
Backstone Beck: 3, 64, 65, 179.
Badger Stone: 102.
Baldwin, Stanley (Prime Minister): 75.
Ballardie, Mr: 72.
Bampton, Mr A H: 65.
Bandstand (on Grove): 110, 175.
Bandstand (in West View Park): 51, 60, 72, 95, 100, 109, 110, 180.
'Bantams' (17th Service Battalion, Prince of Wales own Regiment): 41, 182.
'Beagle' expedition: see Darwin, Charles.
Beanlands, Mr Ellis (of IUDC): 87, 88.
Beanlands (grocers): 80, 181.
Beanlands, Joseph: 10, 20, 24, 173, 174.
Beanlands, Thomas: 9, 10, 20, 173.
'Beeching Report': 49, 118, 123, 125, 187, 188.
Beeching, (Dr) Richard: 118.
Ben Rhydding Hydropathic Establishment: 32, 33, 34, 35, 36, 37, 41, 45, 111, 112, 114, 115, 119, 121, 123, 128, 174, 175, 182, 185, 187.
Benson, Mr (of IUDC): 66.
Biggin, Mr C D (architect): 126.
Birdsall, Councillor Mrs Doris: 143, 144, 146, 190.
'Blind Tom' ('Donkey' Jackson's brother): 31.
Blyth, Tim: 152.
'Bottom Tarn': see Tarn.

Bradford and Ilkley Community College: 41, 42, 47, 186, 191.
Bradford Council: 59, 89, 94, 146, 147, 148, 149, 150, 151, 152, 153, 160, 163, 165, 166, 167, 190, 193, 194.
Bradford Council Arts Libraries and Museums: 143, 146, 148, 152, 153, 190, 191.
Bradford Council Countryside and Rights of Way Service: 152, 153, 154, 156, 158, 161, 162, 165, 166, 170, 191, 193.
Briggs-Popplewell, Benjamin: 37.
Brittain, Pamela (& Allsop, Martin): 148, 149, 150, 151, 152, 153, 190, 191.
Brodrick, Cuthbert (architect): 36, 40, 122, 174, 175.
Brogden, Alfred: 63.
Brogden, Robert: 63, 64.
Brumfitt, Mr George ('Viewstation' at White Wells): 63, 66, 179.
'Bull Rock': 44, 45.
Busby's (Department store): 11, 95, 99, 100, 135, 182, 184.
Busby, Eric: 25, 26, 97, 134, 135, 136, 137, 143, 144, 145, 146, 147, 154, 157, 189, 190.
'Butterfield Fairies': 18, 19.
Butterfield, William ('Bathman' at White Wells circa 1820-1851? [Born circa 1776]): 10, 11, 12, 13, 15, 18, 19, 154, 173.
Butterfield, William ('Bathman' at White Wells circa 1851?-1890. [Born circa 1818, died 1893]): 12, 14, 15, 39, 56, 58, 78, 154, 177, 178.
Butterfield, William ('Bathman' at White Wells circa 1890-1918. [Born 1860, died 1930?]): 15, 16, 17, 18, 61, 74, 76, 77, 81, 138, 178, 181, 182.
'Canker Well': see Drinking fountain on Grove.
Cartimandua, Queen: 11.
Charity Bath: 10, 23, 24, 25, 26, 28, 29, 39, 46, 58, 61, 68, 74, 75, 76, 77, 89, 90, 138, 173, 174, 175, 176, 180, 183, 189, 192, 193.

INDEX

'Charity 'Ole': 24, 43, 173, 178.
Churchill, Winston (Prime Minister): 102, 103.
City of Bradford Metropolitan District Council: see Bradford Council.
Clapham, Mr J P: 35.
'Clarks Picture House': see Grove Cinema.
Clark, Thomas: 55, 173.
Clough, Mr ('War Weapons Week Committee' & Manager of New Cinema): 105.
Cobbles (outside White Wells): 49, 50, 156, 157, 191.
Collyer, Reverend Dr Robert: 11, 56, 73, 154.
Cooper, Jilly: 159, 191.
Cooper, Mr: see 'Pierrots' at Tarn.
Corn Exchange Leeds: 36, 37, 39.
Council for the Protection of Rural England: 150.
Cousins, Councillor Mrs Barbara (of Ilkley Parish Council): 149.
Cow and Calf Rocks: 44, 45, 49, 54, 92, 118, 119, 121, 123, 181, 191.
Craig Dam / Craig Tarn: see Tarn.
Craiglands Hydro: 41, 51, 119, 123, 176.
Cranbrook: 55, 173.
Crawley's Fountain (drinking fountain on moor): 52, 53, 90, 177, 189.
Crescent Hotel: 41, 43, 194.
Crossbeck Hydro: 43.
'Cuckoo Hut' shelters: see Moorland Shelters.
Dale, Robert: 4, 5, 9, 45, 154, 172.
Dales Society: 150.
Dalton, Percy ('War Weapons Week' Committee): 101, 102, 104, 105.
Dalwood, Mr Hubert (sculptures on moor 1973): 134.
Darwin, Charles: 40, 42, 47, 48, 60, 151, 159, 173, 174, 175, 194.
Darwin Gardens (Millennium Green): 47, 60, 159, 160, 161, 191, 194.
Davison, Emily ('suffragette'): 75.
Dawson, David & Margaret: 147.
Dean, Edmund ('*Spadacrene Anglica*'): 1, 172.
Dean & Mennell (contractors): 86, 87.
Decimal Currency (introduction of): 189.
Denton Hall: 119, 121, 124.
Diamond, Michael (Bradford Director of Arts and Museums in the 1970's): 146.

Dickens, Charles: 174.
'Dick Hudson's' pub: 54.
Direction Marker at White Wells: see 'Viewstation'.
Dixon, Mike (& Radick, Gregory): 48.
Dobson Brothers (of Craiglands Hydro): 51.
'Donkey Jackson': see Jackson, John 'Donkey'.
Drinking fountain behind White Wells: 6, 7, 66, 147, 167, 176, 177, 190.
Drinking fountain in Charity Bath enclosure: 25, 61, 90, 94, 176.
Drinking fountain at Hebers Ghyll: 6, 13, 177.
Drinking fountain on Grove ('Canker Well'): 6, 13, 24, 73.
Drinking fountain on moor: see Crawley's fountain.
Eclipse of the sun (1927): 86, 91, 92, 94, 183.
Eclipse of the sun (1999): 94, 191.
Edward VII, King: 64, 179, 180.
Edward VIII, King: 185.
Electricity (supply to White Wells): 95, 138, 154, 191.
Elizabeth II, Queen: 109, 186, 190, 192.
'Essoldo' Cinema ('New Cinema'): 126, 183, 188.
Everall, Joanne (& Hunnebell, Mark): 191, 192.
Fees for bathing (circa 1830): 26.
Fenton, Reverend George: 20-23, 24, 25, 173.
Finnerty, Mr Geoff (of Bradford Council): 150, 151.
Flags (at White Wells): 62, 158, 159, 191.
Fletcher, Elsie M: 11, 142, 145.
Flood of 1900: see Great Flood.
Foot and Mouth Crisis (2001): 160, 161, 163, 192.
'Friends of Ilkley Moor': 134, 165, 166, 193, 194.
'Friends of the Manor House': 128.
Garlick Samuel: 32, 33, 174.
Gas (illumination of White Wells): 94, 95, 106, 184, 186.
Gas (supply to [Moorland] Tea Pavilion): 85, 88, 112, 113, 182, 187.
Gas (supply to White Wells): 85, 95, 154, 156, 157, 191.
Gas Works: 119, 124.
George, I King: 172.
George, II King: 172.

INDEX

George, III King: 5, 154, 172, 173.
George, IV King: 173, 174, 182.
George, V King: 77, 96, 180, 181, 184, 185.
George, VI King: 109, 185, 186.
Grand Hotel Scarborough: 36, 37, 40.
Granville, A B: 12, 19, 27, 28, 174.
Great Flood (of 1900): 63, 64, 116, 179.
Gregson, Mrs I: 85, 127, 128, 130, 131, 132, 133, 188, 189.
Grove Cinema: 126, 181, 183, 188.
Grove House ('Abbeyfield'): 43, 44, 175.
Grove Hydro: 41.
Gully, Dr: 35, 47, 174.
Hainsworth's Lodgings (see also Hillside Court, Hillside House, North View House, St Winifred's.): 42, 47.
Hainsworth, Marshall: 42, 47, 59.
Hainsworth's Pond (see also Paddling Pool): 47, 59, 62, 76, 89, 90, 181, 183.
Hangingstone Quarry: 45, 49, 102, 177, 178, 181, 185.
Harnett, Dr Peter: 159.
Harper, Anne: 7, 8, 173.
Harrison, Dr: 49, 176.
Haste Successors (developers): 145.
Hill, Mrs Marjorie: 103.
Hill, Councillor Rowland (of Ilkley Parish Council): 149.
Hillside Court (see also Hainsworth's Lodgings, Hillside House, North View House, St Winifred's.): 42, 47, 175.
Hillside House (see also Hainsworth's Lodgings, Hillside Court, North View House, St Winifred's.): 47, 159.
Heathcote (designed by Edwin Lutyens): 72, 124, 125, 180.
Henderson, Arthur (Home Secretary): 183.
Hendrix, Jimi: 41, 123, 188.
Howell, Mr C: 134.
Hudson, Mr Wallace: 57.
Hunnebell, Mark (& Everall, Joanne): 191, 192.
Hunter, Dr Adam: 11, 28, 70, 173.
'Hydropathy': 20-31, 33, 34, 43, 45, 46, 47, 64, 173, 178.
Ilkley Bath Charitable Institution (& list of subscribers): 20, 21, 25, 39, 43, 44, 61, 173, 175.
Ilkley Chamber of Commerce: 101, 104, 109, 185.
Ilkley Charity Hospital: 24, 43, 61, 90, 175.

Ilkley Civic Society: 42, 122, 128, 129.
Ilkley College of Housecraft (see also Bradford and Ilkley Community College): 40, 41, 42, 116, 117, 119, 122, 186.
Ilkley Couch: 45.
Ilkley Feast: 94, 95, 184.
'Ilkley Gazette' (newspaper): 14, 16, 25, 44, 65, 67, 71, 72, 73, 74, 75, 79, 80, 82, 84, 85, 86, 87, 88, 89, 90, 92, 96, 97, 98, 99, 100, 101, 102, 103, 104, 105, 106, 107, 108, 109, 110, 112, 113, 114, 115, 116, 121, 129, 130, 131, 132, 133, 134, 136, 137, 141, 142, 146, 147, 148, 149, 150, 151, 152, 153, 154, 155, 157, 161, 180, 181, 185, 186, 191, 193, 194.
Ilkley Illuminations: 94, 95, 106, 108, 184.
Ilkley Library: 56, 73, 98, 180.
Ilkley Lido: 96, 101, 111, 118, 119, 184, 186, 189.
Ilkley Local Board: 14, 39, 46, 49, 50, 51, 52, 57, 58, 59, 60, 62, 73, 116, 122, 147, 152, 175, 176, 177, 178.
Ilkley Moor Action Group: 152.
Ilkley Moor Golf Club: 40, 109, 178, 180, 185.
Ilkley Moor Hotel: see Middelton Hotel.
'Ilkley Moor Trust' (proposed): 165, 192, 193.
Ilkley Parish Council: 54, 143, 148, 149, 152, 161, 165, 190, 191, 193, 194.
Ilkley Urban District Council: 16, 18, 29, 58, 60, 64, 65, 66, 73, 76, 77, 79, 81, 82, 84, 85, 87, 88, 89, 90, 92, 93, 94, 96, 98, 109, 112, 113, 116, 126, 127, 128, 129, 130, 131, 132, 133, 134, 135, 136, 137, 143, 144, 145, 152, 180, 181, 182, 184, 185, 186, 187, 188, 189, 190.
'Illustrated' (magazine): 45.
Indoor swimming pool (adjacent to Ilkley Lido): 118, 189.
Irwin, Frazer: 159.
Jackson, Reverend Canon: 43, 175.
Jackson, John 'Donkey': 31, 72, 176, 180.
Joyce, William ('Lord Haw-Haw'): 103, 185.
Kellett, Arnold: 55.
Kerry, Mr Stephen (of Bradford Council Arts and Museums Department): 148.
King's Hall: 73, 77, 180, 181.
'King's Evil': 2, 172.
Kipling, Rudyard: 101, 102, 104.
Lancaster, Fred: 147.
Learoyd, Mr L T: 90, 183.
'Leeds Intelligencer' (newspaper): 5, 7, 24, 33, 34, 37.

INDEX

Leeds Town Hall: 36, 37, 38, 174.
Lido: see Ilkley Lido.
Lister, Mr Geoff & Mrs Barbara: 143, 145, 189.
Listers Arms Hotel: 43.
Lower tarn: see Tarn.
Lupton, Betty: 1.
Lutyens, Edwin (architect): 72, 124, 125, 180.
Macdonald, Ramsay (Prime Minister): 75, 184.
'Maclandsborough Plan' (waterworks on Ilkley Moor): 50.
Macleod, Dr William: 35, 36, 174, 175.
Major, Joshua (landscaper): 34, 36, 37, 175, 191.
Marlborough House Hydro: 43.
Marshall, James: 32, 33, 174.
Maude (poet): 3, 4.
Memorial Gardens: see Park.
Middelton, Adam de: 67, 71, 153.
Middelton, Charles (Squire 1885-1892): 49, 152, 177, 178.
Middelton, Marmaduke (Squire 1714-1757): 172.
Middelton, Peter (Squire at the time of the construction of White Wells circa 1700): 2, 152, 172.
Middelton, Peter (Squire 1847-1866): 36, 39, 44, 48, 152, 174, 175.
Middelton, William (Squire 1757-1763): 152, 172.
Middelton, William Constable (Squire 1781-1847): 5, 9, 44, 45, 135, 143, 144, 152, 172, 173, 174.
Middelton, William (Squire 1866-1885): 44, 45, 49, 52, 152, 175, 176, 177.
Middleton Hotel (Ilkley Moor Hotel): 43, 117, 119, 123.
Middleton Lodge (Middelton Lodge/ Myddleton Lodge): 36, 49, 67, 119, 120, 124, 178.
Mill Ghyll: 51, 53, 94.
Milligan, Mr C J: 31, 176.
Ministry of Labour and National Service: 41.
Monroe, Marilyn: 148, 190.
Moorland shelters ('Cuckoo Huts'): 58, 59, 62, 76, 94, 109, 112, 113, 152, 179, 181, 186, 191, 193, 194.
Moorland Tea Pavilion: see Tea Pavilion.
Moorlands Hydro: 43.
Mounting block (on Wells Road): 29, 30, 97, 98.

Mounting block (at White Wells): 29, 98.
'New Cinema' (see also 'Essoldo' Cinema): 105, 126, 183, 188.
North View House (see also Hainsworth's Lodgings, Hillside Court, Hillside House, St Winifred's.): 47, 48, 175.
Norwood Edge (TV transmitter): 124, 188.
'Old Pumphouse': see 'Old Reservoir'.
'Old Reservoir': 52, 53, 54, 97, 117, 128, 177, 193, 194.
'On Ilkla Moor Baht' 'At' (song): 54, 67, 102, 173, 176, 194.
Original bath at White Wells (and buried remains of): 2, 3, 4, 5, 6, 51, 52, 92, 94, 176, 183, 184.
Paddling Pool (see also Hainsworth's Pond): 47, 59, 89, 90, 95, 100, 111, 112, 113, 117, 126, 152, 183, 186.
Pankhurst, Mrs ('suffragette'): 61, 73, 75, 180.
Panorama Reservoir: 53, 72, 97, 179.
Park (Riverside Memorial Gardens): 73, 107.
Parlour, Captain: 40.
'Peter Jones China' (advertisement, 1990): 155.
Peterson, John Seymour: 112, 113, 187.
Petronius: 69.
'Pierrots' at the Tarn (Mr Cooper): 61, 72, 180.
Pink Tree (2005): 167, 192.
Ponting, Mr F W: 75.
Ponting, Herbert (Photographer on Scott's 'Terra Nova' expedition): 75, 77, 122, 181.
Pope, Alexander (poet): 69.
Prissnitz, Vinzenz: 20, 173.
Public Toilets (at White Wells): 24, 25, 68, 69, 74, 75, 76, 89, 138, 161, 163, 169, 181, 192.
Radick, Gregory (& Dixon, Mike): 48.
'Raikes': 45.
Railway (into Ilkley and development of): 35, 49, 175, 177, 178, 187.
Ramblers Association: 150.
Renton, Councillor Mrs Molly (of Ilkley Parish Council): 149.
Richardson, Dr: 2.
Rischanek, Dr Antoine: 32, 33, 35, 174.
Robinson, Mr (furniture maker): 45.
Rockwood Hydro: 42.
'Roman Baths': 5, 16, 17, 45, 65, 67, 71, 73, 78, 88, 94, 153, 154, 179.
Roman Fort (in Ilkley): 11, 46, 172, 182.

INDEX

Romans: 1, 11, 16, 46, 172, 173, 180, 182.
Rombalds Water Board: 126, 127, 128, 188.
'Royal, The' (TV hospital drama series set in the 1960's): 168-169.
Royal Geographical Society: 76.
Royal Hotel: 43, 126, 187.
Russell and Wilkes, Messrs (Contractors for construction of Ben Rhydding Hydropathic Establishment): 34.
St Winifred's (see also Hainsworth's Lodgings, Hillside Court, Hillside House, North View House): 42, 47, 189.
Sandy Dale (riverside bathing pavilion): 73, 178.
Scott, David: 16, 67, 68, 69, 70, 71, 77, 81, 154, 179.
Scott, Captain (Robert Falcon): 77, 122, 181.
Sculptures on moor: see Dalwood, Mr Hubert.
Semon Home: 116, 120, 122.
'Shepherd's Story': 1, 151, 172.
Shirwin, Frank (artist): 118, 187.
Short, Thomas: 2, 3, 172.
Signpost (direction marker) at White Wells: see 'Viewstation'.
Silverwell Cottage: 193.
Skinner, Mr A (surveyor): 96, 184.
Slingsby, William: 1, 172.
Smith, Dr Adam: 48.
Smith, Mr Raymond: 40, 185.
Snowden, Reverend: 43.
Spa Hydro (see also Grove Hydro): 41, 42, 184.
'Spadacrene Anglica': 1, 172.
'Spas of England, The': 27.
Spence, Dr John: 24, 28.
Spencer, Mr Jack: 135, 136, 137.
Stansfeld, Hamer: 21, 32, 33, 34, 35, 45, 174.
Stockham, George & Jean: 147.
Stony Lea Hydro: 42.
Storey, Mr H M: 108, 109, 186.
Strachan, Mr: 35.
'Suffragettes': 61, 73, 74, 75, 183.
Sunset View Hydro: 43.
Swastika Stone: 105, 192.
Sylvester's Peat Hole: 52.
Tarn (Craig Dam/Craig Tarn/Lower Tarn): 51, 53, 57, 58, 59, 60, 61, 62, 73, 85, 94, 101, 112, 113, 117, 119, 123, 152, 166, 176, 177, 179, 180, 193.

Tarn (lighting at): 59, 94, 184, 193, 194.
Tea pavilion (Moorland Tea Pavilion): 42, 82, 84, 85, 86, 87, 88, 92, 103, 106, 111, 112, 115, 126, 128, 129, 130, 131, 132, 133, 144, 182, 183, 184, 185, 186, 187, 188.
'Terra Nova' expedition: see Scott, Captain (Robert Falcon)
Tewit Well (Harrogate): 1, 172.
Thatcher, Margaret (Prime Minister): 75.
Thompson, John (Director of Art, Bradford, Keighley and Ilkley): 137.
'Titanic': 77, 181.
'Top Tarn' (near White Wells): see Upper Tarn.
'Totem Poles' at White Wells (2001): 134, 160, 161, 162, 163, 165, 167, 192.
Townend, Mr Bertram (Clerk of IUDC in 1970's): 137, 145.
Town Hall (Ilkley): 73, 180.
Tramway up Ilkley Moor (proposed): 59, 60, 178.
Troutbeck Hydro/Hotel: 41, 92, 119, 123, 182.
'Trust': see 'Ilkley Moor Trust.'
Turner, J H (& Collyer, Reverend Dr Robert): 56.
Underground reservoir tank (for Charity Bath): 26, 88, 141, 182, 189.
Upper Tarn: 52, 85, 88, 190.
Usher's Lodgings: 24, 174.
Vanhinsberg, Mr (& Alkister, Mr): 129, 134.
Victoria Hall (swimming bath): 73, 96, 178.
Victoria, Queen: 5, 32, 56, 62, 64, 174, 178, 179.
'Viewstation' at White Wells (see also Brumfitt, Mr George): 63, 66, 67, 96, 97, 115, 179.
Volume of bath at White Wells: 2, 5.
Vote to save White Wells by IUDC, 1973 (and names of Councillors involved): 137.
War Memorial Appeal: 107.
'War Weapons Week': 101, 102, 103, 104, 105, 107, 185, 186.
Waterworks on Moor: 49, 50, 51, 53, 64, 89.
Webster, Stanley (of Haste Successors, developers): 145.
Wells Court Flats: 43, 98, 123, 126, 187.
Wells House/Wells House Hydropathic Establishment/& Company: 14, 36, 37, 39, 40, 46, 47, 48, 49, 97, 114, 122, 154, 159, 174, 175, 176, 178, 182, 185, 186, 191.

West View House: 43.
West View Park (see also 'Darwin Gardens'[Millennium Green]): 51, 60, 61, 72, 95, 109, 110, 112, 159, 180, 186, 187, 192.
Westwood Lodge: 122, 160, 181.
Wharfedale Hydropathic Establishment: see Ben Rhydding Hydropathic Establishment.
Wharfedale Naturalists Society: 137, 146, 147.
Wharton, Nancy: 33.
Wheatley (village of): 32, 36, 119.
Wild, Mr T H: 82.
William III, King: 1, 172.
William IV, King: 174.
Williamson, Mr Arthur: 113, 114, 184, 187.
Williamson, Mrs Jesse: 42, 85, 103, 104, 105, 106, 111, 113, 114, 127, 184, 185, 187, 188.
Williamson, John: 106.
Willy Hall's Spout (waterfall): 50, 51, 64, 65, 176, 179.
Wilson, Dr: 35.
Wimpenny, Mr: 81.
Winter Gardens: 73, 77, 84, 87, 92, 181.
'Women's Social and Political Union' (see also 'Suffragettes'): 73.
Woodward, A M: 182.
'Wool Control Board': 36, 40, 114, 185, 187.
Wray, Mr A: 85, 87, 88, 182.
Wyvil, Marmaduke: 124.
'*Yorkshire Daily Observer*' (newspaper): 65.
'*Yorkshire Post*' (newspaper): 84.
Yorkshire Television: 168-169, 192.
Yorkshire Water: 54, 122, 193.
Youhill, Mr Chris: 106.